INSIDERS' GUIDE®

52 Great Weekend Escapes

in Northern California

Chris Becker

INSIDERS' GUIDE®

GUILFORD, CONNECTICUT

AN IMPRINT OF THE GLOBE PEQUOT PRESS

INSIDERS' GUIDE®

Text design and spot photography by Peter Friedrich
Map research by Danielle Becker, cartography by M.A. Dubé

ISSN 1554-7639
ISBN 0-7627-3087-0

Manufactured in the United States of America
First Edition/Second Printing

The prices and rates listed in this guidebook were confirmed at
press time. We recommend, however, that you call establishments to obtain current information before traveling.

*To my wife Danielle and our daughter Evie,
our biggest adventure yet.*

Contents

Spring

Easy

Medium

Difficult

Summer

Easy

Fall

Winter

Easy

Medium

Difficult

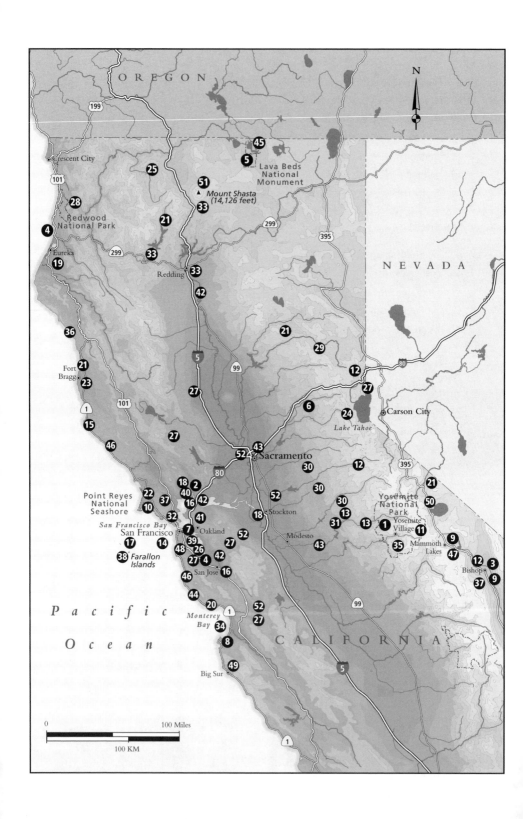

Introduction

Life gets busier all the time. Often this is the case simply because we grow older—like our parents and theirs before them, we tend to pick up additional responsibilities as we "grow up." Sure, finding time to play was easy as a kid, but soon education and the workforce world dictate our schedules to us. *That's the way it works,* our superiors say. *I'm coming in on Saturday, too.* But work, especially when we don't get much satisfaction out of it, leads to stress. Along come marriage and family life (both rewarding, but stressful nonetheless), attempts at a social life, etc.—the list can seem endless. It's often not until later in life, when things finally settle down a bit and retirement comes around, that we really get a good chunk of time for ourselves.

Most of us wait patiently for those lazy days to arrive. But doesn't it make more sense to enjoy life as you're living it today? Take some breaks when you really *need* them?

I know—"Are you nuts? I've got things to do!" And that's probably true—you do. Probably too much (go ahead, deny it). But when we take on seven more projects than we ought to, throw too many balls up into the air, stress shows its ugly face. Time off grows difficult to manage. The stress of being stressed causes more stress, and if left unchecked, the situation spirals out of control, and things get ugly. Why not escape, just for a great weekend at a time, to recharge your spirit and refresh your soul? Take a break to search out beauty and have some fun?

This book provides plenty of quick escape options to help you deal with that nasty thing known as the daily grind. And luckily, northern California is all about doing away with that grind, from fantastic San Fran to the depths of the Redwood Empire.

Before you folks in San Simeon wonder where *you* are, and you hikers start wondering how I could have forgotten King's Canyon and Sequoia National Parks, rest assured that I've covered them—in *52 Great Weekend Escapes in Southern California*. I wholeheartedly admit that portions of the previous book cover weekend destinations north of what most would consider southern California, but northern California is just so darn big that we had to inch the border up a little to include all the things we really, really wanted to write about. This book reaches from somewhere near Big Sur on the coast and Yosemite inland, all the way up to the top of the state. For the whole picture, pick both this book and *52 Great Weekend Escapes in Southern California*, which covers adventures near L.A., San Diego, and other points south.

A quick word about the word "weekend": Don't worry about missing out because your weekend doesn't happen to begin on a Friday. I've used the word to connote any two- or three-day stretch of time. In fact, most midweek "weekends" will save you money and help you avoid Saturday/Sunday crowds. Keep in mind, too, that while this book focuses on shorter trips, many of these weekends are easy to stretch into four or five days if you wish. Time's all relative here, and it's really up to you what to do with it once you decide to make it your own.

Above all, this book is designed to show you great escapes and help you grab some of your hours for yourself. While every weekend certainly doesn't need to be some elaborate adventure or ultra vacation, there are few better things than occasional short trips away to recharge and beat back some of that stress I've been talking about. The adventures in this book are easy to take on, as most of the homework has already been done for you—making it that much easier to drag yourself off the sofa and cut loose for a couple days. We all know excuses come a lot easier when vacation starts to resemble work in the planning, so this book tries to make that process as painless as possible.

With *52* in hand, you have that many prime opportunities to discover a new side to yourself, pick up a new hobby, find a little peace and quiet, enjoy a few days of R&R, or otherwise take control of your time away from the world at large, at least for a little while. Read through, skip around, and pick out a few choices; then dial some phone numbers, surf the 'Net, and start your weekend escapes. It doesn't get any easier than this.

How to Use This Guide

This book offers a year's worth of recreation options in northern California. I feel it's good practice to take weekend escapes as often as possible because you'll inevitably find yourself returning to your routine recharged and refreshed afterward. If you're feeling adventurous, try some activities you may have not tried before—go skydiving if it suits you, or take up scuba. There are incredible landscapes out there just waiting for you, beautiful forests and ocean vistas that are sure to inspire you just as they have inspired millions before you. This book also strives to get you involved with the organizations that protect so many of these valuable resources and phenomenal places. Read through the wealth of exciting options and pick out a couple to explore further. If you really want to get involved, make one of them a regular part of your life and explore it using my reading recommendations and additional resources. Have fun, and have a great weekend (or 52). Each escape is broken down into six sections:

Description

The chapters describe what each weekend entails—what to know before you go, what to expect, and how to prepare for the experience. I also provide inside info whenever possible or necessary—ideas, suggestions, even warnings to keep you informed on the aspects of the adventure that are hard to know about without some on-the-ground experience. Choose the adventures that sound appealing to you, make a few phone calls, prepare yourself, and follow my advice (and your outfitter's) about what to do once you are there.

Maps and Directions

The maps and directions lead you to the start of your adventure, whether it is a National Park entrance, trailhead, parking lot, or harbor. Some outfitters mentioned will meet you at your resort or hotel or arrange a meeting point. Others move around, depending on conditions. Use the maps in the book to get an idea of where your escape is located, and then follow the written directions to the start of the adventure. Detailed topographical or recreation maps make a good acquisition for certain types of adventures. For example, you may survive a climb up Mount Shasta without toting along a whole slew of wilderness topo maps, but I wouldn't recommend testing the theory. It's a good idea to do further research whenever you head off the beaten path or into backcountry areas. For this type of escape, detailed maps may be a necessity, and remember that if a map is required, do what it takes to get the map you need. It's also a good idea to have quality road maps in the car, especially when driving around bigger cities such as San Francisco. Of course, for many of these great weekend escape destinations, it's easy to find a map when you arrive. Finally, a map is not worth much if you can't read it—if you don't know how, take some time to learn.

Season

The activities and destinations are organized by their optimal seasons. (Keep in mind, though, that you may enjoy many of these adventures any time of the year.) Heed warnings about temperature extremes, especially in the summer and winter, and always remember to take plenty of water when you're exerting yourself. Be especially cautious when heading to mountainous regions, as temperature and weather can turn treacherous in an instant. For the sake of your wallet, also keep in mind that off-season or shoulder-season visits might save you a few bucks or keep the crowds at bay. Be sure to check with the respective management agencies and outfitters for weather updates, forecasts, and current conditions.

Difficulty

Please be advised that the levels of difficulty assigned to these escapes are based only on my opinions and those of the outfitters. I try to be fair and even conservative, but the difficulty levels should not be taken as an indication that everyone may be able to perform any activity. It is your responsibility, as the weekend warrior, to decide what kind of adventure you are physically and mentally able to undertake. Be aware that it's a good idea to prepare your body and mind for any of the adventures offered in this book, and that some activities clearly require more effort and training. Some even take months of preparation.

The ratings can vary greatly depending on how you choose to pursue the activity. For example, rock climbing in your local rock gym may be a moderate challenge, but taking a four-day big wall climb up El Capitan requires an entirely different level of fitness, dedication, and expertise. Likewise, white-water kayaking, hang gliding, and various other sports take fairly extensive training. I provide contact information for outfitters or guides that can help you learn the basics of each activity, but it is up to you to decide if you need more preparation for the challenge you choose. Just make sure your weekend of choice suits your skills and abilities, or practice and physically prepare yourself if it doesn't. Train up, then take on your Everest of choice.

As far as the ratings go, an easy adventure is one that most average people can do, with less regard to age or fitness level. Many are family-oriented activities and involve guided tours or seminars, tourist activities, or relaxing leisure destinations. Some require moderate amounts of easy hiking or walking but nothing that will bother most people with an average level of fitness. Minimal technical skills may be required. For example, houseboating the California Delta doesn't require much of any skill if you stay on the boat, but if you happen to find yourself overboard for some reason, you'll need to keep a clear head and at least doggie-paddle to stay afloat. Similarly, driving too big of an RV might not be appealing to some folks. While you should certainly not try anything you cannot handle, the simple fact is that because these are all active vacations, under the worst circumstances, things can go wrong. The easy rating indicates that the probability of things going wrong is at its lowest level, though it's always lurking no matter what.

A medium rating means there is either some prior skill required to perform the activity, a higher level of fitness required, or both. Renting a Harley is a medium-difficulty adventure because no one will rent you a $15,000-plus motorcycle if you've never ridden anything bigger than a ten-speed. On the other hand, mountain biking is a medium-level activity because it requires some fitness and endurance, as would hiking Mount Tamalpais. Some of these more difficult weekends are suitable as family activities, though there are fewer here than in the easy category. Of course, it depends on what your kids (and you) can handle. In general, expect to spend more time planning and preparing for medium-level weekend escapes, and expect that some physical training may be required. You may also need to purchase or rent the required equipment, and you'll often need some practice with the gear, or at least an outfitter to show you the ropes.

Difficult weekend escapes are tests of skill, endurance, and courage. This type of demanding weekend isn't suited to everyone, but the challenges will reward those who seek them out. These weekends require a top level of fitness, as well as previous active, outdoor experience. They are meant for those who feel proficient and at home in the wild outdoors and want to push themselves even further against more extreme conditions. Some are just plain tough, like big wall climbing or mountaineering, while others, such as windsurfing or paragliding, can be dangerous if you don't pay attention to what you're doing. Some of these difficult activities present "minor league" versions that allow you to whet your appetite and see if you want to push yourself any further; parachuting with an instructor, for example, precedes any solo jumping you might do. Remember: although you can take nearly every weekend escape here, across every difficulty rating, to the most extreme degree, you shouldn't attempt any activity that clearly exceeds your capabilities, especially without proper training and preparation. Most of the difficult weekend adventures take commitment, and the greater the challenge in getting there, the greater the reward when you've finally seen it through. In sum, as my mother always says: Please be careful.

I mentioned physical conditioning before, but it bears repeating. With any of these weekend escapes, your adventure will be more rewarding if you are physically prepared for it. It's no fun to be sore all week after a demanding weekend; you're less likely to look back at the experience with fond memories, and thus less likely to take a similar challenge in the future. Working with a health professional to prepare a proper regimen of aerobic exercise and strength training is a great way to both get in shape for your trip and generally improve the quality of your life. You can also simulate your adventure on a smaller scale by practicing near your home. Your local hiking trail may not be quite as rugged as the High Sierras, but it can certainly help train your legs. It comes down to this: The healthier your body is, the less of a factor physical work becomes in your escape, and the more you can enjoy your surroundings.

While you're preparing your body, don't neglect your mental plan, either, especially for the most challenging of the escapes. Although your goal is to relax and have fun, intense concentration is often necessary while white-water kayaking, rock climbing, paragliding, and during any other endeavor demanding close attention to detail. We all hope for the best situation, but the possibility of the worst is something you should be ready for, especially when the activity takes on an element of danger due to treacherous conditions; by being mentally alert and prepared when you go, you'll be better equipped to handle whatever your adventure might throw at you. First aid, CPR, and other medical training courses are not a bad idea, either.

Finally, don't be discouraged by any risks you might face. Just be ready for them. The better prepared you are to accept and deal with the inherent risks, often in an unfamiliar environment, the more you'll gain from your adventures. Fun trips are safe trips, and you are the one most responsible for ensuring both.

Price

Prices for many weekend escapes vary across a broad range, allowing for your individual preferences when it comes to lodging. From quaint seaside bungalows to redwood-ensconced B&Bs to luxury resorts, northern California has plenty of options. The local chambers of commerce or visitor bureaus listed in the additional information sources will help you find your dream digs. Remember some weekends are *al fresco* only, meaning you might be able to stay in an RV, or there may be cabins, but there's a good chance you'll be snoring in your tent. Within each chapter, I've also included an option for the cheapest way to sleep. This is often the best value in the area and usually involves pitching a tent.

The cost for your weekend will also depend on what level of adventure you're looking to take. Some of the weekend escapes offer a variety of options at different prices. Adding options such as the supplemental Ocean Experience at the Aquarium of the Pacific can increase the value of your experience. While this educational boat trip out into the harbor may cost more than just an entrance ticket, it's only a tiny additional price for an exceptional value. I offer suggestions, but the choices are up to you based on your budget. Finally, the price range does not include the cost of travel. With these destinations scattered all over the northern half of California, we've left it up to you to factor in the travel costs.

Outfitters and Contact Information, Recommended Reading

I know one of the hardest parts about getting away for the weekend is the planning, so I've listed tour operators, outfitters, and related contact information to make it easier on you. Everyone mentioned in this book is listed simply because they are considered among the best at what they do—no listing fees were charged, so no company bought their way in. These providers have proven themselves to hundreds, often thousands of active travelers, and each offers an enjoyable experience complete with excitement, education, relaxation, discovery, and fun. They have great safety records and excellent customer service skills, with guides and trip leaders who are pleasant, polite, technically skilled, and dedicated to ensuring a safe and stress-free outdoor experience. Your outfitter will inform you of any special equipment, training, or skills you'll need, as well as what it takes to be adequately prepared—both physically and mentally.

When I chose the outfitters and tour operators, cost was taken into account, but not as much as actual value. Other companies may be less expensive or less experienced than some of the ones included here; however, you may be sacrificing a fun vacation, a lifetime of memories, and maybe even your safety for the sake of saving a few dollars. Some advice: Don't do this. It's disappointing at best and literally deadly in a worst-case scenario.

Finally, just in case you want to read up on your chosen escape before you go, I've also included a list of good books to follow up with. It's quite understandable if your first skydive takes just a little extra convincing, so reading about some other folks who are already really good at it might just help you see that there's nothing to fear.

Make Your Adventure Memorable

So you've taken the plunge—you've scheduled a weekend of hiking, or skiing, or camping, and now you're anxiously waiting for the minute you can be on your way. As this will be something new and special, you'll want to make sure that your adventure stays fresh in your mind for a long time to come. Here are a few suggestions to make the memories last well into your future.

Take Lots of Pictures—I can't stress this enough. Photos are the best way to tote one-of-a-kind weekends back home with you. You might even want to invest in a 35mm or digital camera to record your adventures, rather than relying on junky throwaway cameras that take inconsistent photos. Digital cameras are better than ever and should improve even more as time goes on; for my money, they're the way to go for the amateur photographer. They eliminate the monetary and environmental costs of developing film, plus you can print out only the photos you want. In addition, with a digital camera you can shoot as many photos as you want and keep only the ones you like. Eventually, glancing back over all the great pictures becomes as much a part of your adventuring as the weekend itself, and gives you the added bonus of a photo album you can return to years after the escape is over. Best yet, showing your kids and even your grandkids that photo of you hang gliding or those shots of you at surf camp will likely, as they get older, help convince them to try on some fun for themselves. Photos help ensure you pass your adventurous, fun-loving spirit on to future generations.

Keep a Journal—Especially on hikes and drives, this method of capturing the moment is easy and intensely personal. Northern California offers many inspirational landscapes, from rugged and beautiful Big Sur to the Trinity River's winding, picturesque glory. Writing about the incredible sights, describing your feelings, and detailing your thoughts will allow you to appreciate the experience even more. Keep an ongoing travel journal, and you'll have interesting reading for the rest of your life.

Take Family and Friends Along—You can enjoy nearly all of these activities with groups of people; in most cases, they are *more* fun with family and friends. Learning to kayak or scuba dive alone is not nearly as enjoyable as learning with someone else, preferably one with whom you can share the activity after the initial training is completed. Moreover, if you find that you want to pursue the adventure further by becoming more proficient or turning it into a regular pastime, you'll have some partners who will enjoy traveling that road with you. The more, the merrier.

Join a Club—There are clubs and organizations for every kind of outdoor activity, from skydiving to skiing to spelunking. They're by no means limited to northern California, either—if you happen to take up rock climbing one weekend, you're likely to find an interested community back in Phoenix, or Saskatchewan, or just about anywhere. In our Internet-connected world, it's not hard to hook up with one of these clubs. Attend a meeting and check it out. There are always others just as interested in the same activities as you, and clubs are a great way to meet those people.

Buy Equipment—As you start your weekend adventures, you'll find that most outfitters are able to provide the major equipment needed for your escape. Nevertheless, if you find an activity that you plan to regularly pursue, a great way to improve your skills is to invest in your own set of gear, personalized for your specific body type, skill level, etc. Ask an expert you trust, so you know what you're looking for. Gearing up can get expensive, but if you talk to some folks already involved in the activity (try the clubs or the outfitters themselves), they should be able to direct you to the best stores and perhaps used equipment networks. Flea markets, yard sales, and Internet auction Web sites are great places to find inexpensive quality gear, too, once you know what you're looking for. Lastly, just making the commitment to purchase gear will probably make you more likely to pursue the activity in the future, as that great stuff plays around in the back of your mind (and closet).

Get to Know Your Outfitter—Any person who makes a living playing outdoors is worth keeping in touch with, especially if you're planning to stay involved. If you've had a great experience, tell them so and use them again the next time you're planning a similar escape. Many of California's outfitters even cross-specialize in multiple activities, and the company that took you kayaking may be the same one that can give you a screaming deal on a fantastic hiking adventure. At the very least, guides are likely to have good ideas for fun, whether inside their realm of expertise or elsewhere.

All in all, northern California boasts enough adventure to satisfy just about everyone. It's truly a shame to visit, or worse yet, to live here and not search out these great experiences. *52 Great Weekend Escapes in Northern California* is designed to set you well on your way to being that modern-day weekend explorer we all envy, that person who spends their time the way *they* want to. I also hope your adventures bring you toward a better appreciation of our amazing natural surroundings, and toward discovering exactly what role they can play in your fun and games. Use this guide as your starting point, and soon you'll be forging your own path, taking back your weekends, and sharing them with people who, like you, just want to get out and play.

Pick a great weekend escape and have some fun exploring northern California. Many safe adventures!

CAUTION

Outdoor recreation activities are by their very nature potentially hazardous. All participants in such activities must assume the responsibility for their own actions and safety. The information contained in this guidebook cannot replace sound judgment and good decision-making skills, which help reduce risk exposure, nor does the scope of this book allow for disclosure of all the potential hazards and risks involved in such activities.

Learn as much as possible about the outdoor recreation activities you participate in, prepare for the unexpected, and be safe and cautious. The reward will be a safer and more enjoyable experience.

Spring

CHRIS BECKER

Waterfall Hunting in Yosemite

California's Tumbling, Transitory Treasures

Think about California, and a flood of images will spill out: beach bums holding court out in the surf; herds of celebrities showing up for premieres or just taking the H2 out for groceries; too many landmarks to name, from the Golden Gate to Death Valley. California is so packed with activity and life that you might have trouble deciding where to start, particularly if you're looking for a little adventure. It's hard to figure out just what the right escape might be when you have a million choices that all sound mind-blowing.

Allow me a small suggestion: To connect with California, start with the great wide open, namely the state's staggering natural resources—its forests, mountains, beaches, and deserts. The most logical place to start this odyssey if you're covering the state's northern reaches is fabled Yosemite National Park, one of the National Park System's big two, along with Yellowstone over in Wyoming. At Yosemite you'll get a big dose of California's outdoors no matter what you do, but a tour of the park's waterfall system—one of America's greatest natural treasures—makes a nice focus for your intro trip.

The truth is that the falls, or rather the water that flows through them, have built much of the Yosemite we know. About ten million years ago, a lift underneath the Sierra Nevadas tilted the mountains,

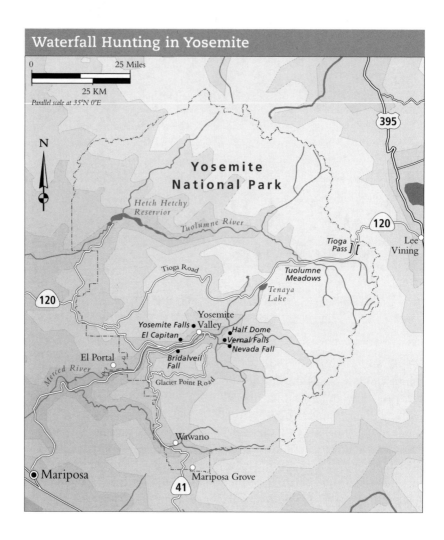

0   25 Miles

25 KM

Parallel scale at 35°N 0°E

N

Yosemite National Park

395

Hetch Hetchy Reservoir

Tuolumne River

120

Tioga Pass

Lee Vining

Tioga Road

Tuolumne Meadows

120

Tenaya Lake

Yosemite Valley

Yosemite Falls

El Capitan

Half Dome

Vernal Falls

Nevada Fall

El Portal

Bridalveil Fall

Merced River

Glacier Point Road

Wawano

Mariposa

Mariposa Grove

41

increasing the steepness of streams and riverbeds and allowing that relentless water to carve canyons reaching 4,000 feet in depth. The shifts and flows also exposed walls of ancient granite, for which millions of rock climbers are eternally grateful, and created towering mountain vistas that top out at more than 13,000 feet. Rolling glaciers helped things along and sliced out the U-shaped Yosemite Valley, where most visitors end up. Water is still shaping the landscape, too, as 1,600 miles of stream flow through the park, along with two massive, federally protected rivers (the Merced and Tuolumne).

Today Yosemite, designated a World Heritage Site in 1984, enjoys an international reputation. Yet within these borders, brimming as they are with natural wonder, the rolling waters continue to draw a huge share of first-time visitors, who time their vacations with the waterfalls' high season. Later in the spring, melting snow from upper elevations feeds the falls system—as a result, the flows are powerful, high, and awesome to behold. You still won't see as many people as you will in the summertime, though, which makes for a nice merging of lighter crowds and maximum spectacle. In addition, if you come out at the end of the summer or in the fall, when most everyone else does, you may be disappointed in the amount of water flowing; some of the waterfalls, even major ones like Yosemite Falls itself, dry up to little more than a trickle after the snow's all spent.

Keep in mind, though, that spring in Yosemite still feels like winter in a lot of other places. Temperatures in May will still drop into the low 40s, while certain areas (the Tioga and Glacier Point Roads, in particular) may be snowed over until late in the month. Yosemite Valley and Wawona stay accessible by car all year, but you might want to bring tire chains just in case you get into a bind. Also, if you do happen to come later in the year, swimming in areas leading to the waterfalls may look like a good idea. No matter how pretty and inviting, this is not wise, as you may find yourself getting caught in the current and heading for a dive--from a couple hundred feet. The fences and signs are barriers, not tests for you to pass, so let them do their job.

Once you're prepared to hunt the falls, you'll want to start with some easy targets. Luckily, the big finds don't hide themselves— you'll find awe-inspiring falls all over the place, so take your pick. Towering Yosemite Falls, the fifth-tallest waterfall in the world at 2,425 feet, is truly behemoth; every spring, sweeping snowmelt creates a roaring ode to gravity that you can feel and hear throughout the Yosemite Valley. Bridalveil, one of the world's most famous falls and the first waterfall you'll see upon coming through the south entrance, isn't quite as large as Yosemite, but it's no less powerful to behold when the melt is flowing. In May and June you can see falls from just about everywhere in the park, and some areas, like Sierra Point, afford multiple falls from the same vantage point.

Before you start to feel the "seen one, seen them all" syndrome coming on, consider the incredible variety I'm talking about when I say "falls." Some of these water formations, thunderous in their

Yosemite Falls powers its way down into the Yosemite Valley. CHRIS BECKER

power, elicit awe; others, like the ephemeral El Capitan Falls, seem to marry with the air on their way down. Though visitors can access many of them without much trouble, others remain hidden treasures, rewards redeemable only after strenuous seeking. It goes without saying that bringing your camera is a must here; anyone who's seen a fair amount of outdoor photography knows that waterfalls make incredible subjects, thanks to their constant movement and grace. If you're so inclined, make sure to play with your shutter speed at each waterfall you photograph—this way, you'll get both naturalistic, frozen-in-time shots and the more fleeting, impressionistic blur of the water in motion.

Because there are so many falls in so many places, this adventure works for just about anyone. Satisfied with checking out the big guys with the majority of the other visitors? Have at it. Looking to reach more obscure, out-of-the-way locations like Snow Creek? Feel free to do that, too. However, when you're ticking off your falls that have been named, don't forget to keep an eye open for the ones that aren't. With the 1,600 miles of running water around you, all of it fat with snowmelt, you're bound to catch sight of minor falls that, with all the big boys around, haven't even warranted a title. They may be too fleeting to name; after all, the high waterfall season is relatively short, roughly April or May through June, and there's a big chance that the impressive, unmarked falls you see will fade completely into memory within a couple weeks.

Whether you're just tooling around California for a few days or living here without getting out of the house much, the call of the Yosemite waterfalls is well worth heeding. Nowhere else will you find a natural phenomena more majestic, yet strangely fragile thanks to its transitory nature. Be sure to get there at the right time, capture the evidence on film, and continue exploring California's outdoors in the weeks and months afterward (with my help, of course).

Price: $40–$100 (park admission, camping, food)
(Spring, Easy)

DRIVING DIRECTIONS

From the San Francisco Bay, take Interstate 580 east to Interstate 205 east to Highway 120 east into Yosemite (Big Oak Flat entrance). From L.A., take Interstate 5 north to Highway 99 to Fresno. From Fresno, take Highway 41 north into the park (south entrance).

OUTFITTERS

Yosemite National Park
www.nps.gov/yose

FOR MORE INFORMATION

THE YOSEMITE ASSOCIATION
El Portal, CA
(209) 379–2646
www.yosemite.org

YOSEMITE AREA TRAVELER
INFORMATION
www.yosemite.com

RECOMMENDED READING

Brown, Ann Marie. *Foghorn Outdoors: California Waterfalls.* Emeryville, Calif.: Avalon Travel Publishing, 2000.

Frank, Susan and Phil Frank. *The Yosemite Handbook: An Insider's Guide to the Park.* Petaluma, Calif.: Pomegranate, 1998.

Medley, Steven P. *The Complete Guidebook to Yosemite National Park,* 4th ed. El Portal, Calif.: Yosemite Association, 2002.

Misuraca, Karen. *Insider's Guide to Yosemite,* 2nd ed. Guilford, Conn.: Globe Pequot Press, 2004.

SLEEP CHEAP

Though Yosemite is full of camping options, the Yosemite Bug, located just 23 miles from the park in Midpines, offers an alternative to these often packed tent-pitching places. It's primarily a hostel, but you'll also find a wide range of other options—private cabins with baths, bed-and-breakfast-style private rooms with shared bath in the main lodge, wood frame tent cabins, and campsites of every kind. Prices run from $17 for campsites all the way up to $115 for private cabins, so you can pick your level of style and price to within a few bucks. Call (209) 966-6666 for info, or visit www.yosemitebug.com.

Napa Valley Hot-air Ballooning

Grapes on the Ground, Romance in the Sky

You won't have much trouble finding things to do in the Napa Valley. You're probably drawn there for the same reason I am—*it's the wines, stupid,* as my wife would say—though the countryside is a huge plus, too. Driving through those rolling, vine-covered hills, however, does not compare in any way to soaring above them.

Since the late eighteenth century, human beings have taken to the sky via one of the business world's primary resources: pure air. Hot-air balloons represent a great way to take to the heavens without a ton of preparation and/or physical training—attributes airplanes, hang gliders, and paragliders all require. You'll reach heights approaching a whole mile, floating slowly and silently on the wind and loving every minute of it.

The 26-mile Napa Valley is uniquely suited to balloon flight—the cool morning temperatures allow air to flow down the valley, carrying balloons "downstream" and letting balloon pilots navigate their way using subtle temperature differences at different altitudes. Add that to the incredible scenery of the vineries, and you've got a weekend escape that combines new experiences, delicious wine, and beautiful rolling hills in a ripe-for-romance recipe.

In a state full of romantic escapes, Napa stands head and shoulders above most. Bed-and-breakfasts seem to sprout from the fertile

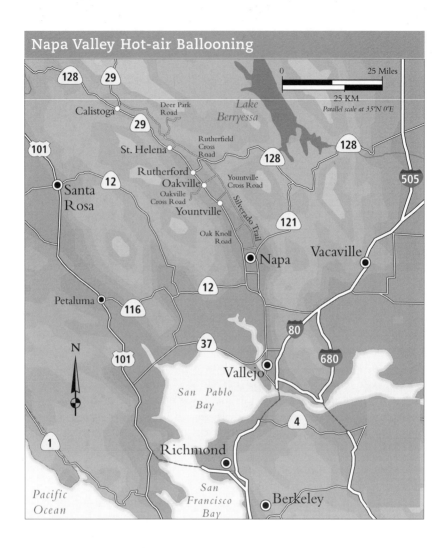

Napa Valley Hot-air Ballooning

ground like so many grapevines, along with the high-end restaurants and the fantastic wineries you would expect from the seat of America's domestic wine production. In all, the region represents a perfect opportunity to spend some quiet quality time with your hubby or honey away from kids, jobs, and all the other things that get in the way of everyday love. Taking the balloon ride while you're there builds on this promise—a literal escape from all the things that keep you tied up when you're on the ground.

When you go a-ballooning, there are a few things you don't want to forget. The camera first and foremost: The view begs for recording up there, so make sure you stop for a disposable shutter-snapper if you don't have a rig of your own. If, like me, you've got a Bruce Willis-esque shaved head going, bring a hat—the burners that fire hot air up into the envelope (fancy speak for balloon) run pretty hot, and they radiate a lot of heat when you're first gaining your altitude. You'll be more comfortable, though you will want to take care you don't lose your pate cover when the wind blows. Don't let the flaming engines of hot air deter you, either—they aren't on while in the midst of soaring, which is the better part of your ride. It's a small price to pay, for sure.

Now that you've got a reason to head up to Napa, and hopefully someone to head up there with, you have to find the right chariot to the sky. Luckily, this is a snap—you'll find plenty of companies willing to take you up and over the Napa Valley, all of which offer a multitude of flights and packages. Make sure to call around, and you'll end up with the best company for your budget and desires. For example, if you're looking for more personalized, romantic flights, go with Above the West Ballooning, which costs a bit more but ensures no more than six people on any flight, or four if you're willing to pay extra.

For the most part, you'll want to bring your appetite on your ballooning excursion; recreational balloon rides traditionally end with some kind of meal or at least a snack. Napa Valley Balloons offers a delicious postflight brunch, complimented by terrific sparkling wine and champagne, some of which is bottled right down in the countryside you just flew over. Napa Valley Aloft—which operates three different ballooning services in the Valley—also offers a well-appointed breakfast. Balloons Above the Valley even offers wedding catering services, which tells you just how good they are at putting together a postflight feast. Bonaventura Balloon Company gives you a host of choices among some fine Napa dining establishments, so you can pick and choose what delicacies you wish to nosh on after you soar.

Keep in mind that every one of these companies starts their flights early in the morning, when the weather is most friendly to balloons. As the day wears on, the sun heats the ground, creating hot air "bubbles" that render steering a balloon impossible. As such, you're going to want to stay in the area the night before to make sure you're on time for your ride. The early departure time lets you turn your four-hour balloon adventure into a weekend Napa getaway, complete with equal doses of skyborne escapade, tasty wine, and

The Napa Valley's Carneros district. Napa has produced some of the world's best wine over the last century—only in the last few decades, however, has the region attracted the respect it deserves among wine connoisseurs. ROBERT HOLMES/CALTOUR

picturesque landscape. Lodging options in the Napa Valley are many, so you would be well served by talking to the company you choose about the lodging options they recommend—a few even have deals worked out for reduced rates at select establishments for preflight (or postflight) guests. In this case, a little additional communication with your outfitter might save you a couple bucks on your room, freeing up some cash and letting you take that extra wine-tasting tour.

A lovely little word about romance: Napa just might be the best place outside of the Italian countryside to snuggle up with your significant other over wine and candlelight. The Napa balloon companies all know it and hold this idea in high regard; each one offers its own great way to show him or her that the fires are still burning bright. Take Bonaventura Balloon Company, for example—the company's owner, Joyce Bowen, is a licensed minister, and she can help you tie the knot as you soar on waves of wind and love. Bonaventura can even help you take care of flowers, photography, catering, lodging for out-of-town guests, and the other vagaries of wedding planning.

Silently floating over the grapes of Napa makes for relaxing, scenic fun, and it goes down even better with a loved one by your side. After a night of wine and roses, you and your partner couldn't find a better way to start the morning after than a slow ride down the air stream, enjoying the sunrise view in the endless quiet that miles of open skies brings. What better way to spend true quality time with the one you adore?

Price: $150–$500-plus (for some package deals that include lodging, special extras, etc.)

(Spring, Easy)

DRIVING DIRECTIONS

From San Francisco: Take Highway 101 North to Interstate 80 east toward Oakland. Then continue on I–80 to Vallejo, and exit on Highway 37 West (Marine World Parkway). Take Highway 37 and turn right at Highway 29 North (Sonoma Boulevard). Follow the exits on Highway 29 to enter Napa. To go to Yountville, Oakville, Rutherford, St. Helena, or Calistoga stay on Highway 29.

From Sacramento: Take Interstate 5 South and connect with the I–80 West bypass, and follow the signs to San Francisco. Then take Highway 12 toward Napa and turn right on Highway 29 North. Follow the exits on Highway 29 to enter Napa, or stay on for the other Valley towns.

OUTFITTERS/PROVIDERS

ABOVE THE WEST BALLOONING
(PART OF NAPA VALLEY ALOFT)
Yountville, CA
(707) 944–8638
(800) 627–2759
www.napavalleyaloft.com

ADVENTURES ALOFT
(PART OF NAPA VALLEY ALOFT)
Yountville, CA
(800) 944–4408
www.napavalleyaloft.com

BALLOON AVIATION
(PART OF NAPA VALLEY ALOFT)
Yountville, CA
(800) 367–6272
www.napavalleyaloft.com

BALLOONS ABOVE THE VALLEY
Napa, CA
(800) 464–6824
(707) 253–2222
www.balloonrides.com

BONAVENTURA BALLOON COMPANY
Oakville, CA
(707) 944–2822
(800) 359–6272
www.bonaventuraballoons.com

FOR MORE INFORMATION

NAPA CHAMBER OF COMMERCE
Napa, CA
(707) 226–7455
ww.napachamber.org

RECOMMENDED READING

Feil, Charles and Ernest Rose. *Napa Valley: A View From Above.* Scarborough, Maine: VFA Publishing, 2002.

Kalakuka, Christine and Brent Stockwell. *Hot Air Balloons.* New York: Metro Books, 1998.

O'Rear, Charles. *Napa Valley: The Land, the Wine, the People.* Berkeley, Calif.: Ten Speed Press, 2001.

SLEEP CHEAP

If curling up in a sleeping bag with your honey is your pinnacle of romance, Napa's a tough nut to crack—most of the land is privately owned. However, there are some places that provide respite and a place to pitch a tent. Skyline Wilderness Park provides tent camping sites for $15 per night, as well as RV sites and some great hiking. There are only twenty tent campsites, so make sure to call ahead of time. Rest rooms and showers are located on-site. Call (707) 252–0481 for more information or for reservations.

Tracking Mustangs in the Pizona Wilderness

The Last Wild Herds

Think about America's wildlife heritage, and you'll come up with a ton of awe-inspiring animals that symbolize it—the bald eagle, an obvious choice; the grizzly bear, powerful denizen of the forests; the stately but tragic buffalo of the plains, with all its troubled history. All of these creatures greeted European settlers when they reached the New World, and all of them play a part in this country's folklore and the heritage of America's frontier and wild lands. They and their kin stand for untamed wilderness and undomesticated nature, and as much as we might relate to them, animals like these belong to a completely different world than the animals we deal with on a daily basis, the ones that populate our barns and living rooms.

Other wildlife icons, however, demonstrate just how thin the line is between these wild creatures and the furry friends who keep us company. In the New World, for example, the horse died out about 8,000 years ago, ending its legacy in the place where the first single-toed mammals evolved. When the Spanish came to the New World in the fifteenth and sixteenth centuries, however, they brought more horses with them—mostly hardy Spanish mustangs bred for endurance and agility. As more Spaniards came with their steeds in tow, some of those horses inevitably escaped and met other escapees of the opposite sex. Before long, the descendants of these horses formed herds that migrated all over what is now the

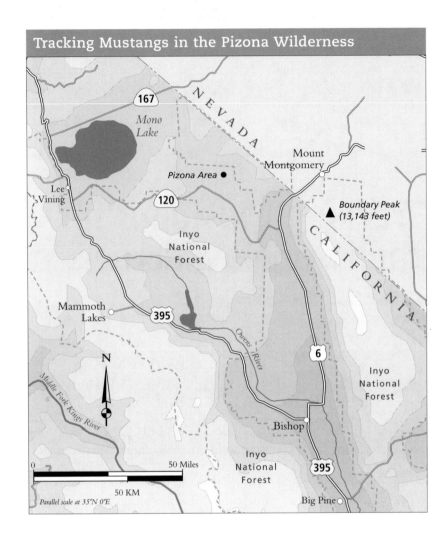

167

NEVADA

Mono
Lake

Pizona Area ●

Mount
Montgomery

Lee
Vining

120

Boundary Peak
(13,143 feet)

CALIFORNIA

Inyo
National
Forest

Mammoth
Lakes

395

Owens River

N

6

Inyo
National
Forest

Middle Fork Kings River

Bishop

0   50 Miles

Inyo
National
Forest

395

50 KM

Parallel scale at 35°N 0″E

Big Pine

western United States, and set the stage for a revival in America's
equine population. By the late nineteenth century, for example,
more than one million mustangs roamed Texas alone. Even as
recently as the early 1900s, more than two million wild mustangs
populated America's grasslands.

Today, unfortunately, development has all but wiped out a large
part of our wild horse habitats, replacing the wide-open spaces with
towns, cities, farms, and the like. Luckily, the mustangs have not
succumbed—instead, they have taken to more and more remote
locations, places where the human population is still about zero,

and the number of people who do pass through is limited by a complete lack of civilization. In fact, many of those who do see wild horses these days make the trip for that sole reason, taking to the most secluded wilderness areas in order to look upon these last herds, some of the nation's most treasured wild resources.

Just north of Nevada's Boundary Peak, you'll find Pizona, a big chunk of barren high desert within Inyo National Forest that fits the remoteness bill to a T. As a result, the area plays host to North America's wildest bands of mustangs and presents a perfect opportunity to observe these spectacular animals in their natural habitat. It takes some time and effort to get back there, but the spectacular creatures and landscape you'll see when you reach your destination make it all worthwhile.

The irony is, of course, that these descendants of domesticated Spanish horses now populate one of the continent's wildest remaining stretches of backcountry. To get there, you'll need to enlist some help—namely Rock Creek Pack Station, the premier guide company running horseback expeditions into Pizona. They don't do a whole lot of trips each year, but if you plan ahead and get yourself on one, you'll be party to one of California's most rare and special wilderness treks. And don't be intimidated if you haven't done a lot of riding before, either—this is an adventure for just about any age and skill level. Of course, a certain level of physical activity is required, but you need not be afraid that you'll be a greenhorn in a pack of cowhands.

The trips generally last three or four days, making them slightly longer than the average weekend escape, but it's worth the extra day for the unique trip you're taking. The rides happen in May and June, when there are plenty of little foals prancing around and large groups are more easily seen among the highland meadows. What's more, the swingin' single stallions are aiming to bring together their own bands about this time of year, and thus start mating. (A mustang band consists of the male, along with two to eight females.) However, the competing 'stangs don't tolerate competition too well, so "stud fights" between them often break out as they form their groups. All of these factors make late spring a truly amazing time to be among wild horses, all the more so if you've got great guides like the folks at Rock Creek to show you where to be and when.

You won't just be looking at the horses, either—you'll be learning about them, thanks to seminars that take place on each day of your trip. Map orientation, wild horse history and behavior, ecology,

A mustang braces itself against the wind. "Mustang" comes from the Spanish *mesteño*, meaning wild or stray. IVAR TEUNISSEN/ISTOCKPHOTO.COM

and current mustang issues are all covered topics, and you'll be returning home with much more than a few nice horse pictures if you pay attention. That being said, let's not downplay nice pictures: Remember to bring a camera to get those too, and make your memories a multimedia presentation.

Rock Creek provides an extensive list of things to bring, though they're mostly clothes and miscellaneous accessories (e.g., sunglasses, tissues, fishing gear if you feel the urge). However, the max you're allowed to tote along is 30 pounds, so leave anything you won't need or use behind. Rock Creek provides tents over your head and food for the trail, and though your guides will prepare your meals, any help is much appreciated. If you're interested in learning the skills associated with backcountry horse/mule packing, go ahead and help out when it's time to roll up camp, and you'll get a hands-on lesson in how to fit all your gear into saddlebags and onto mule backs.

You don't need your own stable to make that experience pay off, either. Rock Creek offers a number of other horseback trips, from horse drives twice a year to excursions up to twelve days long into other High Sierra heavens. If you can't make it out to see the mustangs, the folks at Rock Creek can still show you a great time on horseback any time the weather's nice (spring through early fall). Just give them a call or visit their Web site, and see what works for you. (Check Escape 9 in this book, too, for more information on horsepacking.)

Untouched country stretching for miles in every direction; smart, capable guides with which to share the trail; and wild horses galloping across meadows and fields to top it off. Memories of your trip to mustang country will never leave your mind, no matter how long you cherish them—animals that majestic refuse to be forgotten. Like the California countryside, they will inspire you with their presence and nearly break your heart when you have to part ways. Luckily, they will still be there when you leave, protected and always awaiting the few who choose to cross their uncultivated paths.

Price: $500-plus
(Spring, Easy)

DRIVING DIRECTIONS

Rock Creek Pack Station is located 24 miles north of Bishop. Take the Rock Creek Lake exit from Highway 395, and then go 10 miles up the paved road. If you're arriving by plane (via Bishop or Mammoth Lakes airports) or bus, the folks at Rock Creek are happy to make pickup arrangements for you.

OUTFITTERS/PROVIDERS

ROCK CREEK PACK STATION
Bishop, CA
(760) 872–8331
www.rockcreekpackstation.com

FOR MORE INFORMATION

INYO NATIONAL FOREST
Bishop, CA
(760) 873–2400
www.fs.fed.us/r5/inyo

RECOMMENDED READING

Dines, Lisa. *The American Mustang Guidebook: History, Behavior, and State-By-State Directions on Where to Best View America's Wild Horses.* Minocqua, Wisc.: Willow Creek Press, 2001.

Ryden, Hope. *America's Last Wild Horses.* Guilford, Conn.: Lyons Press, 1999.

Spragg, Mark. *Thunder of the Mustangs: Legend and Lore of the Wild Horses.* San Francisco, Calif.: Sierra Club Books, 1997.

SLEEP CHEAP

Camping is included in your Rock Creek excursion, but if you need to camp before or after your trip, check with Inyo National Forest— you'll find plenty of campsites available for group, tent, and trailer camping throughout the forest.

Learning to Sail in Northern California

Drinking in the Lapping Pacific

A word of advice when you're traversing the stunning northern California countryside: Make sure you look west every once in a while. I don't mean immediately west; I mean *west,* as far out as you can look, until the only thing you see is the broadest expanse of blue water on the planet—the gorgeous, immense Pacific. That ocean, all by itself, counts as a destination, too. Sure, you've got fishing, surfing, and a ton of other shoreline activities, but there's a whole lot of water to see out there, and you won't get a true sense of its scale until you're surrounded by it on all sides. Why not head away from that beautiful coast for a few days and venture into the legendary blue via one of the world's most venerable methods of locomotion, the lofted sail?

To sail is to negotiate, partner, and labor with the sea. The world's largest body of water—even in its smaller capillaries—can be capricious, even seem like it's out to get you, but you can learn how to read it, and take advantage of that information to ply the waves safely and serenely. Taking a few days and learning to sail with one of northern California's sailing instruction outfits brings you into concordance with the act of sailing, the skills it requires, and the Pacific itself. Afterward, you may find yourself seeking additional contact with the waves, perhaps even wonder what it would take to pick up a vessel of your very own.

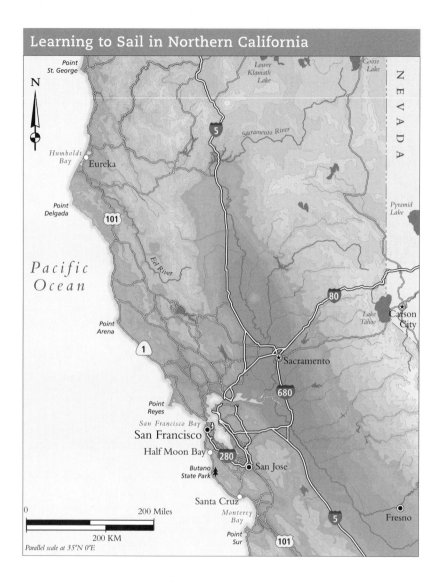

Two factors will govern the kind of sailing adventure you have: the water itself and the teacher you decide to go with. Though you may have no control over the oceans and bays, you can play Scouts and be prepared; know what weather you're getting into before you set out. Peaceful seas and clear skies will treat you novices better than rolling swells, and if you don't get seasick, you'll stand a better chance of wanting to try your hand at the rudder again sometime. And no matter what the forecast, bring rain gear—the weather can change out there fairly quickly, for one thing, and the waters off northern California are typically chilly for another. Pretty much any spray is cold spray.

"Wait a tick—seasickness, you say?" I hear the doubt washing over you. Let's be honest: Yes, it's out there, and yes, you may find yourself succumbing to it *if* you're not careful. Seasickness is by no means unavoidable or even inevitable; just get yourself ready before you head out. For a nice initial test, try reading a newspaper in a moving car. If you feel okay doing that, seasickness shouldn't be an issue on a fairly calm voyage. If the seas swell on you, though, and you start feeling nauseous, take the proper steps—get plenty of fresh air, stay to the stern (the rear of the boat, which moves less), and stay away from alcohol, cigarettes, and greasy foods. In addition, take the medication you picked up before your trip. Bonine, Dramamine, or scopolamine patches (need a prescription for this one—ask your doctor) will all help you maintain should you get the spins. Finally, keep in mind that if you get caught in high, rough seas, chances are the professional sailors on board aren't feeling too well, either; they just have their mental game down and don't let the motion of the ocean bother them. It won't be easy, but try not to think about the pitching and rolling, and you'll go a long way toward defeating your rebellious stomach.

Now let's talk about who you're going to go sailing with. Location will probably narrow your search right off; if you're in Eureka, for example, your sailing adventure will probably begin on beautiful Humboldt Bay. Head to the docks in San Fran, and you'll be tooling around that Bay while you get your sea legs. After deciding where to search, start doing your homework on the charter companies nearby. Do you want your lessons to stretch out over a few weeks or take place within the space of a weekend? And what skills do you want to learn—the bare essentials, or how to race like a true yachtsman? Or maybe you don't even want to learn the craft right off—maybe you want to see how being on a sailboat sits with you first, then go all in for the lessons. Decide exactly what you want first, and the outfitters listed here will be able to fit the bill you come up with.

Spinnaker Sailing in San Francisco is an especially good outfitter to start with if you want to learn just how it's done. The company offers sailing lessons on the San Francisco Bay, as well as charters and boat rentals for those of us who already know our way around the sails. Humboats up in Eureka has similar offerings, along with

Catching wind on the San Francisco Bay. CHRIS BECKER

kayak and canoe rentals. Ocean Voyages in Sausalito offers longer chartered voyages on the *Martin Eden,* a four-sail ketch, and Bay excursions on the 72-foot *Gas Light,* a working replica of the famous San Francisco hay scows that populated the Bay way back when.

Most of the charters listed here have similar offerings—they'll take you out, many will feed you, and a few will let you experience nights sleeping on the sea. The ones that offer longer trips do so on a custom basis, and you will have a strong hand in determining how your trip plays out and what you'll do out there. If you're taking lessons, chances are you won't get out into the deep blue water right away, but you will learn what it takes to get there eventually. Who knows—you might even get yourself trained up enough to take on charters of your own somewhere down the line; many companies offer "bare boat" charters to experienced sailors who have the skills but no ship of their own. Of course, this takes some serious certification, but it's worth it to know you can go anywhere in the world, rent a boat, and disappear out into the blue for a while.

Another word on sailing lessons, or lessons of any kind for that matter: participate. At some point, someone will ask you to do something, whether it's just moving out of the way or pulling on a particular line. Just do what you're asked unless you don't feel comfortable doing so, and everyone should get along famously. But do what you can, and listen to what you're told—there's no better way to learn than with your hands on. Above all, be respectful of your captain and crew, as they are the ones who know what they're doing; even if you've been sailing before, let them run the show without your input and take away what they're offering you in the form of internalized knowledge.

Sailing is one of the most relaxing things you can do—it lets you take in amazing natural beauty while teaching a new outdoor skill that you can use forever and pass on to kids, friends, and everyone else you know. After a few voyages, you'll have the skills to partner up with that water all by yourself, without any help, and trust me when I say it's one of the most satisfying feelings around to cut through the ocean with no other assistance than what the wind provides. Just your know-how, the water, and the air—now *that's* locomotion.

Price: Depends on what you're looking for; if you just want a sailing sample, you can get on the water for a half day for as little as $100. For a battery of lessons, prices approach $1,500 at some places. Obviously, know what you're getting before you fork over the cash, and rest assured that four days' worth of lessons in a new skill you'll have for life is certainly worth it.

(Spring, Easy)

DRIVING DIRECTIONS

The outfitter you go with will give you specific directions to their marina. Driving west is a good start, however.

OUTFITTERS

CLUB NAUTIQUE (THREE LOCATIONS)
Alameda, CA
(800) 343–7245

Sausalito, CA
(800) 559–2582

San Mateo, CA
(888) 693–7245
www.clubnautique.net

HUMBOATS
Arcata, CA
(707) 444–3048
www.humboats.com

OCEAN VOYAGES
Sausalito, CA
(800) 299–4444
(415) 332–4681
www.oceanvoyages.com

SPINNAKER SAILING
Redwood City, CA
(650) 363–1390
www.spinnakersailing.com

FOR MORE INFORMATION

AMERICAN SAILING ASSOCIATION
(310) 822–7171
www.american-sailing.com

RECOMMENDED READING

Jobson, Gary. *Sailing Fundamentals: The Official Learn-to-Sail Manual of the American Sailing Association and the U.S. Coast Guard Auxiliary.* New York: Simon & Schuster, 1998.

A member of the Arcata fishing fleet heads out to sea. While you're out for a sail, don't forget to bring along the fishing gear if you can. CHRIS BECKER

Patterson, Kevin. *The Water In Between: A Journey at Sea*. New York: Alfred A. Knopf, 2001.

Seidman, David. *The Complete Sailor: Learning the Art of Sailing*. New York: McGraw-Hill Professional, 1995.

SLEEP CHEAP

San Francisco has a multitude of nearby camping options; no other city has so many protected wilderness areas so close. Butano State Park, located between Half Moon Bay and Santa Cruz, plays host to 39 campsites, secluded in a redwood-thick canyon. You'll find running water and public rest rooms here to boot, and in the summer rangers give guided nature walks and weekend kids' campfire programs. No showers, though. Call (650) 879–2040 for information; reserve a site by calling (800) 444–7275.

Exploring Captain Jack's Stronghold

Lava Beds National Monument

Life has flourished in the Klamath Basin for thousands of years. Though it stands remote and nearly forgotten in today's coast-centric California, it contains some of the most beautiful country in the West, as well as one-of-a-kind habitats like Tule Lake, winter home to hundreds of bald eagles. Known as a kind of "Western Everglades," the Basin plays host to nearly 80 percent of the birds moving through the Pacific flyway during their migrations up or down the coast. People have also enjoyed a long, fruitful history in this area; from the ancient Native Americans who settled there thousands of years ago to the 10,000 lucky Modoc County residents of today, people have migrated to the area and taken advantage of its excellent growing conditions and plentiful waterfowl hunting. Truly, Klamath is a hidden gem, a place where you'll find solitude among the birds and the spirits of history.

One group in particular is still well remembered, though not without tragic implications. The Modoc Indians settled in the Basin sometime in the 1840s, and by the 1860s they were raising domesticated animals, building ranches, and otherwise acting a lot like you'd expect people to act in their homes. By the 1870s, however, white settlers were laying claim to that very same homeland, and, as it was wont to do in those days, the government eventually decided that the Modocs had to go. Government negotiators tried to get them to move north and merge with the Klamaths, another tribe that lived a similar lifestyle but didn't get along very well with their Modoc neighbors. The Modocs wanted their own reservation on the Lost River, but the government wouldn't budge. As the negotiations dragged on, the Modoc's leader Kientpoos (otherwise known as Captain Jack) tried to keep his people out of trouble and moved frequently to accommodate the encroaching white settlers.

As you can imagine, the story gets worse before it gets better. In November 1872, after a confrontation with cavalry troops that left one soldier dead and seven wounded, Captain Jack and his followers fled into the lava formations that now make up Lava Beds National Monument, a remote tribute to both nature's raw power and man's inability to get along with his fellow man.

Captain Jack's Stronghold, the area where the leader and his followers sought refuge and defense, lies just outside Lava Bed's gates and a short distance from Tule Lake. The Stronghold Trail will take you around the various natural features and man-made structures that still mark the battle site. The area is heartbreakingly lonely if you're starved for human contact; if you enjoy communing with nature and history one-on-one, however, you will not be disappointed.

Captain Jack met up with another band of Modocs later that November morning, one led by a subchief called Hooker Jim. Hooker Jim's band was into a lot more trouble than Jack's was—they had recently finished a vengeful killing spree, in which they killed twelve male settlers in response to having a number of their own tribe killed during a fight with Army volunteers. Jack took in this other band, despite his disapproval of their actions, and proceeded to hole up in the stronghold, fewer than sixty men versus a growing contingent of U.S. cavalry. The cavalrymen struck a few months later and saw thirty-seven soldiers fall without a single Modoc death, a testament both to Captain Jack's prowess and the solidity of his natural fortress. More attacks followed, but the Modocs held out, buoyed by their successes and secure position.

The Stronghold Trail isn't terribly difficult, so feel free to bring the kids up. Though there are some tight squeezes and wooden bridge strolls over crevasses and trenches where warriors on both sides once hid, there's nothing that would cause real problems for anyone with a healthy ability to walk. You have two trails to choose from: the long trail, which marks the perimeter the Modocs had to defend, and the short trail, which marks the boundary of the defenders' main camp. Both of these paths demonstrate the tactics

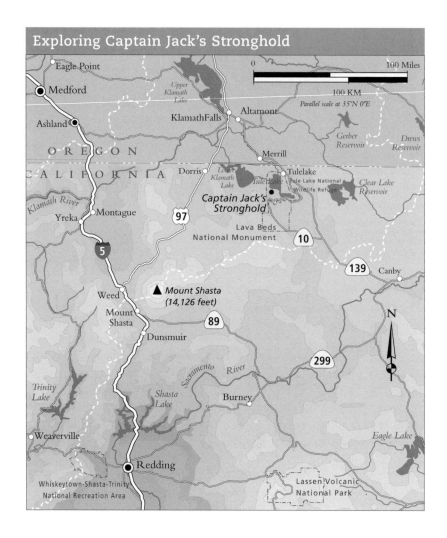

and fortifications the Modocs used, as well as how the cavalry dealt with the challenge.

The natural landscape is just as remarkable as that created by the combatants. Lava formations run throughout the area—rock-filled sinkholes pock the space between trenches; hills of porous stone push up through the ground; and rolling hills trail off into the brush-covered landscape. The area looked a lot different back when Captain Jack had his run of the place, of course; for one thing, the irrigated fields around Tule Lake were nonexistent. For another, grazing animals—the main reason the white settlers felt they needed the Modocs' land—destroyed all of the native bunchgrasses and sagebrush, leaving the land to be overrun by an annual grass from Europe. The general layout is the same in the stronghold as it was then, though, so you get a pretty good idea of what went on from both the well-preserved volcanic landscape and the excellent reading material you can pick up at the trailhead. (It's well worth the quarter, believe me.)

Sadly, and perhaps obviously, the cavalry eventually defeated Captain Jack. The army force continued to grow, while Captain Jack slowly ran out of options. Half-starved, tired, and demoralized, the Modocs succumbed to their attackers and surrendered in small groups. They did not get their reservation, but they did manage to hold off a much larger, better armed force for almost five months—with only sixty fighting men.

The ultimate irony of the Modoc War, as Captain Jack's struggle came to be known, may be that while the Indians were forced to leave in order to give the settlers their "due," those very same settlers were pushed off the land fewer than fifty years later thanks to conservation concerns. Lava Beds National Monument was established in 1925 to preserve the unique terrain, home to more than 380 lava tube caves and a moonscape of volcanic rock. (Apparently, preserving the natural state of the area was more important than preserving the culture that preceded the settlers'—but I digress.) Anyway, the war marks the only Native American confrontation on California's soil, something of a surprise given the state's formerly heavy native population.

For history and natural beauty with a strong added dose of solitude, make your way up, way up, to Lava Beds and Captain Jack's Stronghold. In that pure, clean isolation, the spirits are more palpable, more present, than they are in better-trod locations. Only a few footfalls separate you from the Modocs themselves and from their struggle. Walk on their paths, remember them, and learn from their sad tale that irony is no substitute for losing your home and everything you hold dear.

Price: $20–$40

(Spring, Easy)

DRIVING DIRECTIONS

If you're traveling north on Highway 139 from Alturas, you'll see signs 27 miles north of Canby directing you into Lava Beds.

Spectacular scenery outside of Lava Beds National Monument. Make sure to pull over often as you drive across northern California to take pictures, relax, and otherwise breathe in the amazing landscapes. CHRIS BECKER

You can also hit Highway 139 coming northeast from Redding on Highway 299.

OUTFITTERS

LAVA BEDS NATIONAL MONUMENT
Tukelake, CA
(530) 667–2282 (headquarters)
(530) 667–2282, ext. 232 (visitor information)
www.nps.gov/labe

FOR MORE INFORMATION

LAVA BEDS NATURAL HISTORY
ASSOCIATION (FOR SPECIAL EVENTS,
EDUCATIONAL MERCHANDISE, ETC.)
(530) 667–2282

RECOMMENDED READING

Brown, Ann Marie. *Foghorn Outdoors: Day-Hiking California's National Parks*. Emeryville, Calif.: Avalon Travel Publishing, 1999.

Reed, Mabel and Mary Ellicott Arnold. *In the Land of the Grasshopper Song*. Lincoln, Neb.: University of Nebraska Press, 1980.

Wallace, David Rains. *The Klamath Knot: Explorations of Myth and Evolution, Twentieth Anniversary Edition*. Berkeley, Calif.: University of California Press, 2003.

SLEEP CHEAP

As there is no lodging in the Lava Beds, sleeping cheap is really the only option close by. Indian Well Campground in the south end of the park has forty campsites suitable for tents and small- to medium-size RVs. Fees are $10 per night, per site, and though there aren't a lot of amenities, water and flush toilets are available. Sites are available on a first-come, first-served basis, and while you can't collect firewood at the campground, you can go a quarter mile from the developed area and at least 100 feet from any road or trail to grab some.

White-water Rafting on the American River

Three Routes through the Rapids

You hear the white water long before you see it, a taunting echo coming across the relatively calm water you've seen so far. Once-mild river transforms around you, accelerating and beating itself against the banks and itself until it no longer flows, but jumps and bucks under your raft, which seems less and less adequate. Through all the water pounding outside and the blood pounding in your skull, your guide's instructions slice like water skis in a gale, bringing you back to your oar and to the rapid realization that you're in good hands; the thought lets you take anxiety down a few notches and put your energy into doing what you're told, doing what needs to be done. Paddling furiously, you hit the first wave of white water—or rather, it hits you—and the adrenaline you've been accumulating since hearing the first echoes of that roaring water starts flowing into your muscles, finally put to good use.

This is white-water rafting, one of those legendary outdoor activities that hooks just about everyone who tries it. From novices to hard-core backcountry wanderers, young to old, nothing gets the blood pumping quite like a rough-and-tumble trip down cascading, foamy water, shooting through some of the prettiest untouched country you're likely to see. Rafting in northern California is particularly fantastic, as the region boasts some of the nation's least-accessed waterways, wet backcountry passages that take you over hill and dale into awe-inspiring forests you won't see otherwise.

The American River, located up near Sacramento, is an all-purpose rafting paradise, a perfect place either to start your adventures on the high white water or to continue them. Three forks make up the American system: the South, the Middle, and the North. The South works great as an introductory adventure; the rapids are easy Class III, no sweat for beginners with a professional team of guides in tow to—well, guide. Class III rapids entail plenty of waves, high rocks, and narrow cannonlike chutes to blow through, so you'll certainly get your adventure dollar's worth no matter what your skill level. But on the American, the South Fork is the place to be for newbies, as the Middle and North Forks can get a little too hairy for those with scant experience. The South is especially suited for multiday adventures, too; all the companies listed below offer overnight trips on that part of the river.

The Middle Fork, by contrast, is a bit tougher and shorter, and it requires some additional experience you can get away with not having on the South. Here the big draw is incredibly pristine wilderness, cut only by 18 miles of river running through a deep, isolated canyon. Wait a minute—let's face it: The *big* draws are the Class III and Class IV rapids that dash through all that gorgeous wild country, testing boaters' strength and stamina all the way. Class IV rapids are long, powerful, and occasionally punishing, with large, dangerous rocks and boiling eddies jumping out at you from all sides. This is not to say that there aren't stretches of the Middle Fork that let you kick back and relax; particularly on two-day trips, the middle passage presents opportunities to fish, take some pictures, or just lie on the bank and take in the big wild world out there.

Rafting stands as a great way to spend time with the whole family outdoors, as the minimum age on most rafting trips is in the mid-teens. One company, however, W.E.T. River Trips, offers a trip specially suited for even younger adventurers: a three- to five-hour jaunt on the lower Middle Fork, where calm Class I and II waters help to break in little river rats. This trip obviously sticks to the mellower sections of that Middle Fork; it's more a playtime than a river run, so don't worry about the kids drifting into places they won't be able to handle. You can even bring the littlest little ones on this trip—minimum age is a year and a half—and you grown-ups can try kayaking while the kids paddle around in their rafts. It's a great way to get the whole family out on the river, and perfect for

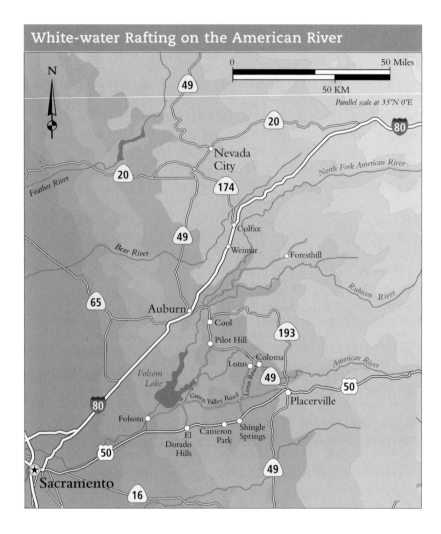

White-water Rafting on the American River

new parents who want to break their kids into the outdoor lifestyle they themselves already love.

The North Fork stands as the most difficult adventure on the American, and thus requires previous experience and a willingness to get awful darn wet. It starts out mild enough, but right about the time you might be feeling a little too relaxed, the acceleration begins until it hits full speed at the Class IV Chamberlin Falls Gorge. This fork only runs in the spring and early summer, when snowmelt from the Sierras fuels its roiling rage. You'll drop through some steep gorges between condo-size boulders and over massive waterfalls that will leave you breathing a whole lot heavier, all the while paddling like mad to keep yourself on target. The rapids here can seem endless, so it goes without saying that you shouldn't hit the North Fork without a good set of muscles on you, nor should you set out without prior rafting experience. If you bring these things to the table, though, this fork presents the most bang for your buck, though usually in a smaller dose. (North Fork trips are typically only one day, though many companies offer two-day trips that pair a warm-up run on the Middle or South Forks with a blast down the North.)

Selecting your white-water outfitter comes down to what kind of trip you're looking for and, to a lesser extent, price. Most outfitters listed here will provide everything you need for your trip, down to the wet suits to keep you warm. They all offer first-rate camping facilities on multiple-day trips, and terrific backcountry menus to boot. Price-wise, rafting for a few days is pretty cost-efficient, as your company will feed you quite nicely and provide great outdoor accommodations, along with the river run. For $200 to $300, you'll be taken care of in between splashy drives down the river. You may want to bring a bunch of friends on your rafting trip, too, as rafting with a few buddies is a great way to spend some quality time (as well as garner sweet group discounts); however, rafting is one of those activities that draws both men and women in fairly even numbers, so you single folks will have a fine time signing up all by yourself and making new friends as you shoot the rapids.

The American River, more than most white-water meccas, offers something for every kind of rafter, from first-timers to hardened river rats. No matter who you are, the American's tumultuous waterscape will draw you in, while the backcountry scenery will fill your downtime with calm—the eye of your white-water hurricane, so to speak. Set yourself up with one of the companies listed below, and head out to experience this sweet storm for yourself.

Price: $75–$150 for a one-day trip; $300–$450 for two- or three-day excursions.

(Spring, Medium)

DRIVING DIRECTIONS

The American River put-ins are located in different areas—you'll be going in at different places depending on the length of your trip,

You'll get wet, but the soak is well worth it. CHRIS BECKER

the fork you'll be taking, and which company you choose. Get detailed directions from your outfitter.

OUTFITTERS

ALL-OUTDOORS CALIFORNIA
WHITEWATER RAFTING
(800) 247–2387
www.aorafting.com

AMERICAN RIVER RECREATION
Lotus, CA
(530) 622–6802
www.arrafting.com

AMERICAN WHITEWATER
EXPEDITIONS
Sunland, CA
(800) 825–3205
www.americanwhitewater.com

RIVER RUNNERS
Calabasas, CA
(800) 818–7238
www.riverrunners.org

W.E.T. RIVER TRIPS
Sacramento, CA
(888) 723–8938
www.raftwet.com

WHITEWATER VOYAGES
El Sobrante, CA
(800) 400–7238
www.whitewatervoyages.com

ZEPHYR WHITEWATER EXPEDITIONS
Columbia, CA
(800) 431–3636
www.zrafting.com

FOR MORE INFORMATION

AMERICAN WHITEWATER
www.americanwhitewater.org

RECOMMENDED READING

Bennett, Jeff. *The Complete Whitewater Rafter.* Columbus, Ohio:
McGraw-Hill Companies, 1996.

Kuhne, Cecil. *Whitewater Rafting: An Introductory Guide.* Guilford,
Conn.: Lyons Press, 1995.

Long, John. *Liquid Locomotive: Legendary Whitewater River Stories.*
Guilford, Conn.: Globe Pequot Press, 1999.

SLEEP CHEAP

Obviously, you won't have to worry about accommodations if you
take a multiple-day trip. If you aren't, but you still want to stay in
the area for a few days, check out Folsom Lake State Recreation
Area, where you'll find good camping as well as 32 miles of bike
path connecting Folsom Lake with several Sacramento County parks
and Old Sacramento. Call (916) 988–0205 for information, or (800)
444–7275 for camping reservations.

Tiburon
and Angel Island

*Ellis Island and New England
Way Out West*

Marin County, located north of San Francisco, has a lot going for it.
First off, it's right next door to one of the best-known, hippest cities
in the world. Second, it enjoys one of the highest standards of living
in the country, along with dozens of outdoor adventuring options—
Mount Talampais is just a short hop away, and Point Reyes National
Seashore makes up its western border. Muir Woods National Park
lies along the Pacific, too, while the Mission San Rafael Arcangel,
one of California's venerated Spanish missions, decorates the heart
of San Rafael.

However, into all this sunshine some rain must fall. Marin suffers from some first-class traffic headaches, particularly during rush
hour; unfortunately, the Golden Gate Bridge looks a whole lot better
from afar than it does when you're stuck on it. Making one's way
over the bridge and up Highway 101 beyond Santa Rosa takes nothing less than Herculean effort, coupled with the kind of patience the
airport requires during a snowstorm. Yes, you'll find a whole lot of
good stuff in Marin—the problem is getting to it without ripping
your hair out and going loony.

Fixing for a break from these lines, these *herds,* of unruly auto-
mobiles? Never fear: Simply try to imagine the quaintest, tidiest,

sweetest little town you're liable to find anywhere. Then, come up with the place where the people who live in that perfect little town go for fun. Try to imagine ditching your car and pedaling yourself around for the next few days, free of traffic travails. Do this day-dreaming, and then make those mellow imaginings come true with a trip out to Tiburon and Angel Island State Park, where folks get off on pedaling, rather than rubbernecking.

The Tiburon peninsula and Angel Island are two chunks of East Coast charm dropped into a distinctly West Coast slot. I say "slot" because both sit sandwiched between the San Francisco Bay's many geographic forces—the Golden Gate, the Marin County towns farther up Highway 101, and the Bay itself. Yet, Tiburon, Spanish for "shark," somehow manages to feel like a village off the Connecticut coast, a place where anglers still mosey through the streets and sail-boats charge around just offshore. You'll find excellent shopping and waterfront restaurants, as well as terrific museums, historical sites, and a Bay view that absolutely begs for gawking. You'll catch yachters, windsurfers, and water rec enthusiasts of all kinds cavorting on the water, further demonstrating the powerful lure of the San Francisco area.

But you didn't come for the water sports, did you? (Rent that Jet Ski next time.) Once you mount up on your two-wheeler of choice, start tooling up and down Tiburon's pretty streets; if you're feeling adventurous and fit, take a ride up Paradise Drive, along the rural north side of the peninsula. Here you'll find brutal uphills, along with some nice speedy coasts back down. Just make sure you know what you're doing here—there are cars on this road, and though most of the drivers you'll see are biker-friendly, you still don't have the benefit of a dedicated lane. Keep your eyes open.

When you've finished exploring Tiburon, catch the ferry out to Angel Island and experience the odd feeling animals must get when they look out of their windows at the zoo. The island is isolated, its own habitat, yet it presents spectacular views of the surrounding city, especially at night when San Fran is blazing. You won't be dis-appointed in the natural surroundings, either, as Angel offers great native flora and fauna (seals, sea lions, hawks, wildflowers) accessi-ble through a 13-mile network of trails and fire roads. You can bike the fire roads and the scenic perimeter road that circles the island, taking in the city across the bay and the natural world around you while you pedal.

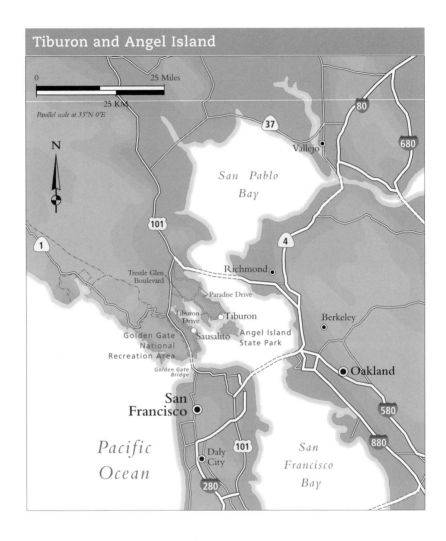

0   25 Miles

25 KM

Parallel scale at 35°N 0°E

N

80

680

37

Vallejo

San Pablo Bay

101

1

4

Trestle Glen Boulevard

Richmond

Paradise Drive

Tiburon Drive

Tiburon

Berkeley

Golden Gate National Recreation Area

Sausalito

Angel Island State Park

Golden Gate Bridge

Oakland

San Francisco

580

Pacific Ocean

Daly City

101

San Francisco Bay

880

280

There's a local human component, too—the island has a storied history, one steeped in the very essence of San Francisco's growth and identity. Once known as the "Ellis Island of the West," the immigration station on Angel saw countless immigrants pass through its gates. It was also a military garrison as far back as the Civil War and served as a departure area for GIs returning from the Pacific Theater in WWII. More recently, the island played host to a Nike missile base, though it is no longer operational (or so the feds tell us). You can choose to take in these sites yourself, via bike or hike, or you can take the island's tram and see them all with minimal fuss; with a bike, however, you have maximum mobility, the freedom to linger if you want to, and the added bonus of a great workout. None of the riding on the island is that terribly hard, either—there are 8 total miles of bikeable trails on the island, a short jaunt even for beginners.

Hitting Angel Island does require some planning on your part, though. The various ferry services don't run all night; in fact, the ferry from Tiburon stops in the mid-afternoon on weekdays. Make sure you time your exploration to end up at the drop spot when you're supposed to, or you may find yourself camping a little more primitively than you might like. This isn't to say that you can't miss the ferry on purpose; camping is available on the island, and there aren't too many places in the world you can camp smack in the middle of a city and still not have a single car drive within miles of your site. It's a strange sensation, and one worth looking into.

To enjoy your escape to the hilt, follow this recipe: Take a Blue & Gold Fleet ferry from San Fran to Tiburon with camping gear and bicycles in tow; enjoy. Then, after a healthy dose of small-town magic (and maybe some shopping—just nothing too big!), go for a challenging ride up Tiburon's north side. Take the last ferry out to Angel when you're done, and make camp for the evening. In the morning savor a couple hours riding around the island, taking in its many pleasures; then catch the afternoon ferry, another Blue & Golder, back to your starting point. Repeat as necessary, and be sure to change things up for variety. For example—ride out over the Golden Gate in the bike lane, where things aren't so ridiculous.

Feeling lucky? Then try driving out to Tiburon instead. There's certainly no harm in it. However, I would recommend leaving *very* early, before the waves of traffic hit the Bay, as sitting in the car while a place like Tiburon waits for you is akin to Chinese water torture. But if you insist on heading out after work or a day downtown, go ahead—just don't say I didn't warn you.

Price: $40–$200 (depending on shopping, bike rental, etc.)
(Spring, Medium)

DRIVING DIRECTIONS

Access to the island is by public ferry or private boat. You'll find ferry services running from Tiburon itself, as well as from points around the Bay. Call the ferry providers listed below for locations.

More than most American cities, San Francisco lets you experience country and city in close proximity. BRAD RALPH/ISTOCKPHOTO.COM

To drive out to Tiburon, simply hop on Highway 101 heading north out of San Francisco; then take the Tiburon Boulevard exit and drive out to the tip of the peninsula.

OUTFITTERS

ANGEL ISLAND STATE PARK
(415) 435–1915
www.parks.ca.gov/default.asp?
page_id=468

ANGEL ISLAND COMPANY
(TRAM TOURS, BIKE RENTALS,
GROUP EVENTS)
Pleasanton, CA
(415) 897–0715 or (925) 426–3058
www.angelisland.com

FERRY SERVICES:
Blue & Gold Fleet, San
Francisco, (415) 705–5555

Vallejo Baylink Ferry,
(707) 643–3779

Oakland/Alameda Ferry,
(510) 522–3300

Angel Island/Tiburon Ferry,
(415) 435–2131

FOR MORE INFORMATION

Angel Island Association
Tiburon, CA
(415) 435–3522
www.angelisland.org

RECOMMENDED READING

Feldmeth, Robert and Allan A. Schoenherr. *Natural History of the Islands of California*. Berkeley, Calif.: University of California Press, 2003.

McGehee, Roger. *Mountain Biking Northern California*. Guilford, Conn.: Falcon, 2001.

Soennichsen, John. *Miwoks to Missiles: A History of Angel Island*. Tiburon, Calif.: Angel Island Association, 2001.

SLEEP CHEAP

There are primitive campsites on Angel Island—just make sure you call ahead to reserve one, as there aren't many, and they go fast. Costs are $10.00 per night between May 15 and September 15 and $7.00 per night the rest of the year (though it is far more difficult to reach the island in the winter, as fewer ferries run). There is also a kayak-accessible site ($20.00 per night, holds up to twenty people). For reservations call Reserve America at (800) 444–7275 or visit www.reserveamerica.com.

Golfing and Sightseeing at Pebble Beach

The Mecca of the Links Congregation

Ask anybody what the most famous golf course in the world is. Go ahead—pick ten people or so, for some variety. I'll wait.

Now that you're back, what answer did you get the most? If your poll went the way my informal studies did, the overwhelming answer was Pebble Beach Golf Links, home of multiple U.S. Opens (among other tournaments) and the course that Jack Nicklaus chose as the one he'd hit if only given the chance to play one more round for the rest of his life. Most any golfer, no matter how big the handicap, would readily donate an arm for just a few holes on this storied stretch of green, as beautiful as it is famous, and even anti-golf traveling companions can enjoy the Pebble Beach/Carmel area for its other merits.

If you're looking for a golf vacation to end all others, make the pilgrimage and enter the gates with reverence—you're on sacred ground now.

If golf in America has a capital, it's Pebble Beach, from the links to the venerable Lodge, built in 1919 after a fire destroyed the log cabin original. The course also opened that year and since then has grown into its current state of adoration. In the 1970s Pebble Beach really started to take off in terms of professional use—the U.S. Open first came in 1972, and the course saw its first PGA Championship five years later. The 2000 U.S. Open, its centennial edition, played out at Pebble Beach, with Tiger Woods smacking back the competition by fifteen strokes and tying the lowest 72-hole total in the tournament's history. In 2001 *Golf Digest* ranked Pebble Beach the number-one golf course in the nation, the first time ever a public course has taken the honor.

With a history and background like this, it's no wonder greens fees are a little steep. The price of admission pushes $400 and soars even higher if you're not staying at a Pebble Beach-area resort (Spanish Bay or Pebble Beach itself). Only resort guests can book a tee time more than twenty-four hours in advance, too, so you might have a hard time getting on from the outside, particularly from March through November. Your best bet, though it's a little pricey, is to book yourself a weekend at one of the resorts and make a high-end escape out of the whole experience. This way, you guarantee yourself a place on the course, as well as a few days to tool around and explore what is one of northern California's ritziest little enclaves.

If you've decided to take the plunge and play the big PB, you might as well go ahead and splurge on a caddy, too—walking the course with one of these seasoned pros simply adds a bigger, cooler dimension to the whole experience. These guys are a whole lot more than bag toters; a Pebble Beach caddy can tell you all about the course's storied heritage, as well as let you know you want a lot more club on 14. These guys are legendary for their knowledge and skill, but be careful—you may find yourself wanting their job before too long. (Who *wouldn't* want that view every day of the week?) It goes without saying that you'll be walking if you take a caddy, but even if you don't, think about doing so—you're just spending more time out there if you do, and that's never a bad thing in a place like this one.

The other local courses are pretty expensive, too, but they aren't quite as steep as Pebble Beach itself. If you're looking to save a few dollars for a romantic dinner or two, they might be the way to go. The Links at Spanish Bay simulate Scottish golf courses in all their rough, cragged majesty, complete with gusting wind and a bagpipe to mark the end of the day's play. Spyglass Hill is a brutally tough course—actually the toughest in northern California and one of the toughest in the world (as measured from the championship tees). This course opened in 1966 and immediately earned its bad-man reputation; it now hosts the annual AT&T Pebble Beach National Pro-Am, as well as qualifying rounds for the California State

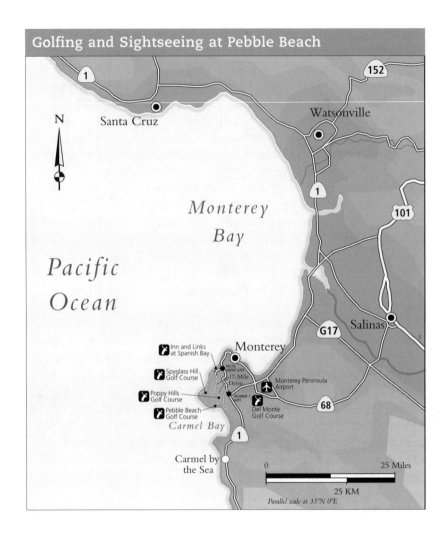

Amateur tournament. The Del Monte Golf Course is located up the Pacific Coast Highway a little ways, but the drive is worth it—this is the oldest continuously operating course west of the Mississippi, and its narrow inland fairways present a different kind of challenge than you'll find along the ocean blue.

Pebble Beach plays host to some other courses as well, some of which are private and off-limits. Others, however, are not nearly as expensive to play as the Pebble Beach-affiliated courses but still offer some great golf in beautiful country. Poppy Hills Golf Course, for example, is home to the Northern California Golf Association and is the first course in the United States to be owned by an amateur golf outfit. The play is challenging, and though you don't get the breathtaking ocean vistas you would at Pebble Beach, the course is well worth your time for its playability.

Looking to improve your game? Take advantage of the world-famous golf academy at Pebble Beach, and you'll definitely come away with a few strokes lopped off your score. You can take individual lessons or go with a group, and work on skills from the intro level all the way up. You can even play a whole round with your pro, providing you with the opportunity to work out kinks in your game on some of the prettiest holes in the world. Be advised, though: You have to stay at the resort to take advantage of the lessons. Yet another reason to turn the whole trip into a couple days of getaway rather than a couple rounds of golf.

Those of you who aren't interested in the "golf thing" should not be discouraged, either. Pebble Beach has diversions galore, from terrific scenic motoring on the fabled 17-Mile Drive to high-end shopping in the stores at both the Lodge and the Inn at Spanish Bay. The Del Monte Forest surrounds Pebble Beach, providing cool shade for your inland pursuits and great sightseeing to boot. And if you feel like getting away from all the swinging clubs for a day, head into beautiful Carmel—Clint Eastwood's no longer the mayor, but they've still managed to keep the place in beautiful shape.

Granted, these swinging and shopping adventures can get awful expensive, particularly if you want to play more than one round while you're out here. But how many times in your life do you get to play courses like these—places infused with this much history, beauty, and pure challenge? Not many. So save up for a few months, make your reservations, and indulge.

Price: $500–plus

(Spring, Medium)

DRIVING DIRECTIONS

San Jose International Airport is about an hour and a half north, and San Francisco International Airport is about two hours north. However, Monterey Peninsula Airport is right down the street, and a few major carriers have routes there from nearby Western cities (Los Angeles, San Francisco, Phoenix). From San Jose and San Francisco: Take Highway 101 south approximately 50 miles to Highway 156 West (Monterey exit). Follow 156 West for about 6.5

The long view at Pebble Beach. Despite the course's sterling reputation, you won't find a lot of snobbishness among the staff—folks are friendly, and willing to help the most amateur of amateurs. CHRIS BECKER

miles until it becomes Highway 1 South; stay on Highway 1 for about 15 miles, to the exit for Highway 68 West (Pacific Grove/ Pebble Beach). From Monterey Peninsula Airport: Turn right at the stoplight outside the airport onto Highway 68 West (to Monterey). Follow the signs to Highway 1 South, and then take the exit for 68 West (Pacific Grove/Pebble Beach).

OUTFITTERS

PEBBLE BEACH GOLF LINKS (AND OTHER AFFILIATED COURSES)
www.pebblebeach.com

THE LODGE AT PEBBLE BEACH
Pebble Beach, CA
(800) 654–9300 (reservations)
www.pebblebeach.com

THE INN AT SPANISH BAY
Pebble Beach, CA
(800) 654–9300 (reservations)
www.pebblebeach.com

POPPY HILLS GOLF COURSE
Pebble Beach, CA
(831) 625–2035
www.poppyhillsgolf.com

FOR MORE INFORMATION

THE PEBBLE BEACH GOLF ACADEMY
(831) 622–8650
www.pebblebeach.com/4.html

CARMEL AREA RESERVATIONS, INFORMATION
www.carmel-california.com

RECOMMENDED READING

Hogan, Ben. *Five Lessons: The Modern Fundamentals of Golf.* New York: Fireside, 1985.

Hotelling, Neal. *Pebble Beach Golf Links: The Official History.* Chelsea, Mich.: Sleeping Bear Press, 1999.

Penick, Harvey. *Harvey Penick's Little Red Book: Lessons and Teachings from a Lifetime in Golf.* New York: Simon & Schuster, 1992.

"The rough" at Pebble Beach. CHRIS BECKER

SLEEP CHEAP

There are two California State Parks within 30 miles of Pebble Beach. Both offer camping among the beautiful forests and beaches of Big Sur and are well worth the stay even if you're not planning to play the links. Pfeiffer Big Sur State Park offers beautiful forest sites and is a mere 25 miles south of Carmel; call (831) 667–2315 for information. Andrew Molera State Park Trail Camp is even closer—only 20 miles south—and offers first-come, first-served camping at twenty-four sites. Call the number above for more information, or visit www.parks.ca.gov for the lowdown on either park.

Horsepacking the High Sierras

Trotting to Paradise

You're lost, but in a good way. There are others on the trail who
know what's going on—your guide, the couple who rode this route
last spring. They know just where they are. Some of the other folks
riding with you have been hiking nearby (i.e., within 200 miles or
so), but they are in new territory now, too. You, yourself, don't have
the foggiest idea where you'd show up on a map, nor do you want
one. You pat your steed's neck, scratch him right underneath his
mane, and whistle softly as you take in an immense green and gold
vista opening up to your left. All you know now is that within a
very short period, you've ridden from end of the day, uncasual
Friday beyond the boundary between nature and the human world—
into the territory otherwise known as the High Sierra.

The Sierra Nevadas are almost too big to conceive of, in terms of
adventures to be had. The region encompasses some of the best-
known backcountry in the world: Lake Tahoe, Mammoth Lakes,
Yosemite, Kings Canyon, Sequoia. These are just a few of the more
famous sites in this miraculously beautiful, and generally unspoiled,
area. It goes without saying that you'll find activities aplenty here,
no matter what time of year you visit; winter brings downhill and
cross-country skiing, while boating, fishing, backpacking, and biking
(among other things) fill the rest of the year. You'll find all the stuff
you'd expect to find, as well as some things that you may not have.

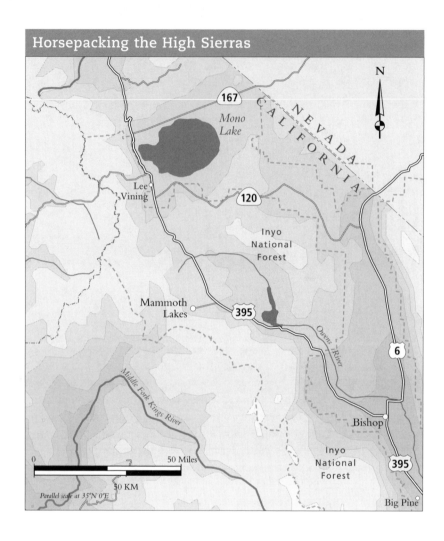

Horsepacking the High Sierras

But don't we take to the wilderness in order to find new things? To expand our library of experiences? Don't we light out for the territories so we can bring back new memories?

If you answered "yes" to these questions, wind into the High Sierras not on foot, nor astride your mountain bike. Chances are you've done these things before somewhere. For a truly original experience, try horsepacking—an activity that not only gets you into some beautiful country but also does so while letting you bond with the best backcountry trail companions in the animal kingdom.

Ever spent hours or days hiking under a heavy gear load? If so, you know that it gets old pretty quick. Hitting the trail on horseback saves you a ton of exertion and doesn't tax the horses too heavily, either—the rides are pretty low-impact for them, as the country is fairly gentle, and they're trained to do their jobs admirably. In fact, these horses live cooler lives than most of us. Think about it: How would you like to ply the High Sierra Trails for a living, for the price of carrying a light gear load around?

Horsepacking outfitters offer a number of different adventure options, depending on where you'd like to go, how long you'd like to be on the trail, and what you expect from your backcountry diversion. Most offer short (two-hour to half-day) rides, perfect for beginners looking to get their first horse-borne experience. Shorter rides also make a perfect family activity, a nice way to give the kids their first taste of the High Sierra. For these excursions, no riding experience is necessary—your guides will get you all set up and make sure everybody has a great time.

The guide services also offer a ton of camping options at some of the prettiest mountain sites you've ever seen. Packing overnight works like this: Your guides will stow all the camp gear on mules, which will follow behind as you trot down the trail. Your steed will know exactly what it's doing out there—these animals are probably better hikers than most people, and you needn't fear for their abilities. Sit back and enjoy the scenery, along with the pleasant sensation of a backpack-free back. You'll cover a lot of ground in a pretty short time, thanks to all the hooves, thus seeing more of the countryside than you would if you were humping it yourself. If you want to hike, however, feel free—just lead your new walking buddy until you feel like hopping back up. Trips can run from two days all the way up to twelve or more, depending on how much you want to see and how much time away from the daily grind you've earned.

Rock Creek Pack Station offers some of the coolest trips among the High Sierra outfitters, to destinations all over the place. They also illustrate a fundamental point when it comes to horsepacking, or hiking, or any other outdoor pursuit that is simply glorified locomotion: There's more to do out there than just get out there. Fishing plays a part in nearly every excursion; many fall trips take advantage of the High Sierras' excellent Indian summer fishing, while others set out to teach beginners how to hook up. Just talk to them and they'll set you up with the right ride.

Moseying on down the trail. ROBERT HOLMES/CALTOUR

For more experienced riders, several outfitters offer livestock drives a couple times a year, when they need to bring their stables from winter pastures to summer haunts and back again. Riding experience is essential during these drives—generally, riders have to participate in the action and do some work to keep the whole thing going. Bob Tanner's Pack Station, for example, offers multiday drives that evoke an Old West vibe, and require guests to participate in driving more than 100 horses and mules. You'll sleep under the stars, hear the intense, awe-inspiring echo of 400 hooves off the walls of mountain passes, and otherwise take part in a nearly forgotten practice. Mammoth Lakes Pack Outfit conducts a similar drive, as does Rock Creek. All three of these drives take place twice a year at the same times (June and September) and have limited enrollments, so call early if you want to get a spot in one.

Obviously, all these trips are going to take you through places that, relatively speaking, very few people have ever seen. Don't forget your camera, and snap as many shots as you can—capture those out-of-the-way places. Also, be sure to practice all your best low-impact camping techniques. The territory you'll be moving through is true backcountry, and anything you leave there will be there for a long, long time. Camp, ride, and pack smart.

Whatever ride you select, you'll enjoy one excellent side benefit: trail companionship with folks who obviously share some interests with you. Hiking or biking with your typical trail buddies is fun and everything, but a horsepacking expedition will give you the chance to interact with a whole new group of adventurers and let you speak pretty much the whole time without gasping for breath. Enjoy the changes, revel in them, and make some new friends among the High Sierras' paradisiacal territories.

Price: $500-plus for longer trail rides, much less ($30 and up) for short rides

(Spring, Medium)

DRIVING DIRECTIONS

The location of your trip will vary with the trip itself and the outfitter you choose. Contact the outfitter you want to go with, and they will give you relevant directions.

OUTFITTERS

ROCK CREEK PACK STATION
Bishop, CA
(760) 872-8331
www.rockcreekpackstation.com

MAMMOTH LAKES PACK OUTFIT
Mammoth Lakes, CA
(888) 475-8747, (760) 934-2434
www.mammothpack.com

BOB TANNERS PACK STATION/RED'S MEADOW PACK STATION
Mammoth Lakes, CA
(760) 934-2345, (800) 292-7758
www.reds-meadow.com

FOR MORE INFORMATION

HIGH SIERRA HIKERS ASSOCIATION
South Lake Tahoe, CA
www.highsierrahikers.org

USDA FOREST SERVICE (FOR ALL THE HIGH SIERRA NATIONAL FORESTS)
(202) 205-8333
www.fs.fed.us

RECOMMENDED READING

Secor, R. J. *The High Sierra: Peaks, Passes, and Trails.* Seattle, Wash.: Mountaineers Books, 1999.

Elser, Smoke, Bill Brown. *Packin' in on Mules and Horses.* Missoula, Mont.: Mountain Press Publishing Company, 2003.

Farquhar, Francis P. *History of the Sierra Nevada.* Berkeley, Calif.: University of California Press, 1989.

SLEEP CHEAP

If you're not going for an overnight horsepack, a whole bunch of camping choices await you in the High Sierra after your day of riding. In the Mammoth Lakes area, however, Sherwin Creek Campsite offers the most in the way of amenities and facilities. There's fishing and hiking right on-site, as well as shopping and restaurants nearby if you want them. Plus, it's cheap—only $15 per night. Call (760) 924-8233 for details, or save a spot at www.reserveamerica.com.

Romantic Relaxation at Point Reyes National Seashore

Sand, Surf, and Your Sweetheart

We outdoor types view the natural world as inherently romantic, with enough intense activity, spectacular viewing, and beautiful weather to fill a million days. We love being outside and revel in sharing our favorite outdoor places with people we love. After all, how much more beautiful is that impressionistic sunset when you gaze on it with the sun to your solar system by your side?

If that special someone doesn't happen to be as into the experience as you are, a special sort of challenge arises: how to make them feel the same longing, the same awe, that you do when faced with nature's majesty and grace. Maybe you've found true love in the arms of a city slicker, someone who doesn't know a tent stake from an ice axe. If that's the case, go ahead and feel free to check out chapters in the "Easy" sections of this book, and break them in softly (maybe with some intro camping—see Escape 15 on Manchester State Beach). However, if you and your partner enjoy lighting out together, taking in the outdoors as a team rather than individually, this escape is tailor-made for you.

Point Reyes National Seashore lies just an hour away from downtown San Francisco. John F. Kennedy designated the area a National Seashore in 1962 (funny that we owe this romantic

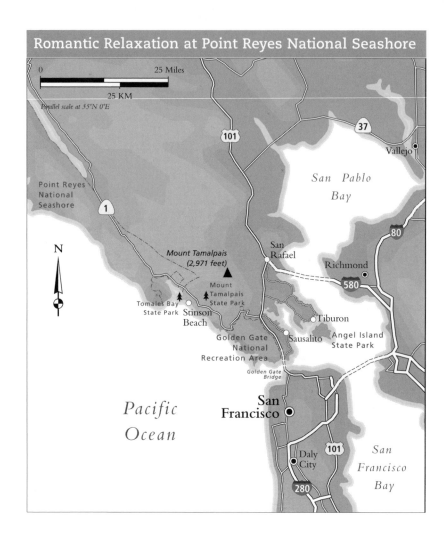

0   25 Miles

25 KM

Parallel scale at 55°N 0°E

101

37

Vallejo

Point Reyes
National
Seashore

1

San Pablo
Bay

80

N

*Mount Tamalpais
(2,971 feet)*

San
Rafael

Richmond

580

Mount
Tamalpais
State Park

Tomales Bay
State Park

Stinson
Beach

Tiburon

Golden Gate
National
Recreation Area

Sausalito

Angel Island
State Park

*Golden Gate
Bridge*

*Pacific
Ocean*

**San
Francisco**

Daly
City

101

280

*San
Francisco
Bay*

resource to that particular Casanova), and today the area trades on
the beauty and recreation residents of northern California are so
lucky to have right in their backyard. Point Reyes might not be the
best place to head for your first outdoor experience, but folks who
already know their way around a campsite will get a huge kick out
of the Point Reyes backcountry experience. You'll enjoy things three
times more in the company of an experienced outdoor companion,
preferably one with whom you can share your sleeping bag.

Of course, you have to keep in mind that the park is right next
door to San Francisco, and making reservations well ahead of time

is a foregone conclusion; the park takes reservations as long as three months in advance, so find some days that far out in your calendar, mark them, and start salivating at the prospect. Weekend-length escaping is particularly suited to Point Reyes camping, too; the max number of nights you can stay is four, or thirty in any given year. Also know that camping in Point Reyes is a tad more difficult than in most national parks—there are no car camping sites in the whole park, which means you have to hike, bike, or ride via horseback to backcountry areas.

Once you've got your campsite, take some time to get acquainted with Point Reyes's denizens. Wildlife viewing is exceptional here, particularly among the feathered set—about 45 percent of the bird species sighted in the entire country have made an appearance at Point Reyes at one time or the other. Let's mention that again: not 45 percent of the species in California, but in the *entire country*. If you show up in the spring, make sure you keep your eyes glued to the Pacific, as you might catch sight of migrating gray whales engaging in the longest animal pilgrimage on Earth: 10,000 miles, between chilly Alaskan waters and sun-drenched Baja California. Point Reyes stands as one of the best places to observe these wandering giants, and the best time to take them in is during the northern migration in mid-March, when the weather is nice. However, if you have to wait until later in the year, don't worry—late April and early May see mothers and their calves drifting close to shore, providing the rare opportunity to glimpse these mysterious visitors for a brief moment before they return to the dark, mysterious depths.

These aren't the only animals you'll have a chance to visit with, either. Elephant seals began moving back into the park in 1981, and their numbers continue to grow dramatically every year. Coho salmon and steelhead spawn every January and show themselves in rainstorms' wakes. It goes without saying: bring your camera, and carry it ready to shoot—you never know what's going to cross your path. If you can, you might want to show up on a weekend and take advantage of the ranger-led geology or wildlife tours, and learn a little about the animals you'll see. You truly hard-core outdoor couples might even want to take in a course from the Miwok Archaeological Preserve of Marin, which conducts classes in Native American survival skills, from the traditional uses of native plants and fire making to bow and arrow construction.

Let's not get too far off topic, though—romance is the name of the game here, and there's little more romantic to a lover of the

One of the many spectacular seaside views at Point Reyes. COURTESY OF THE NATIONAL PARK SERVICE

outdoors than just losing track of civilization within nature's embrace. For this, Point Reyes is particularly suited—the park is big, boasting 80 miles of untouched, virginal coast, along with 147 miles of hiking trails and a couple thousand tons of beach sand for sunset strolling. Horseback riding courtesy of Five Brook Ranch, located within the park, presents another great option for taking in the countryside. The stable provides guided group tours, private tours, even riding lessons if you feel so inclined.

For the pinnacle of romance, however, you might want to think about a particularly private kind of camping, available on the west-side National Park beaches north of Tomales Bay State Park: the boat-in variety, thanks to a rental kayak or your very own vessel. This adventure requires a different level of commitment and attention to detail than even the backcountry camping described above; for one thing, you'll have to pack out all of your waste, and I mean all of it—human waste, too. Fires are okay with a permit, but only with the free wood provided at the national park visitor centers. You also need to carry fresh water with you, as there's a pretty good chance your beachside campsite will not have any. But you have to figure that the benefits outweigh these minor inconveniences—after all, have you ever awakened next to your sweetheart with nothing to keep you both company except for the broad expanse of the Pacific?

It's true that tents, campfires, kayaks, and binoculars aren't everyone's idea of a romantic weekend escape. However, you folks who dig the outdoors will find romance in the air at Point Reyes, along with plenty of fragrant sea spray and flocking birds. Just lace up your boots, take his or her hand, and head out the door fully equipped and ready to gaze into each other's eyes over a weekend's worth of lovin' among some of the most picturesque oceanfront real estate you can conceive of.

Price: $50–$200; count on the upper end if you'll be renting kayaks, or taking a horseback ride.

(Spring, Medium)

DRIVING DIRECTIONS

The Pacific Coast Highway runs right by Point Reyes, just north of San Francisco. Just follow the signs once you cross the Golden Gate and leave the city.

OUTFITTERS

BAY WATER KAYAKING
(415) 663–1743
www.bwkayak.com

FIVE BROOKS STABLE (FOR HORSEBACK RIDES)
Olema, CA
(415) 663–1570
www.fivebrooks.com

MIWOK ARCHAEOLOGICAL PRESERVE OF MARIN
San Rafael, CA
(415) 479–3281
www.mapom.org

POINT REYES NATIONAL SEASHORE
Point Reyes, CA
(415) 464–5100 (visitor information)
www.nps.gov/pore

SEA TREK OCEAN KAYAKING CENTER
Sausalito, CA
(415) 488–1000
www.seatrekkayak.com

You'll find plenty of wildflowers coming up during the spring in Point Reyes.

FOR MORE INFORMATION

POINTREYES.NET (RESOURCE FOR VISITORS)
www.pointreyes.net

TOMALES BAY STATE PARK
Inverness, CA
(415) 669–1140
www.parks.ca.gov/?page_id=470

RECOMMENDED READING

Evens, Jules G. *The Natural History of the Point Reyes Peninsula*. Point Reyes National Seashore Association, 1993.

Goodwin, Kathleen and Richard Blair (photographer). *Point Reyes Visions*. Berkeley, Calif.: Wilderness Press, 2001.

Lage, Jessica. *Point Reyes: The Complete Guide to the National Seashore & Surrounding Area*. Berkeley, Calif.: Wilderness Press, 2004.

SLEEP CHEAP

Since the whole point here is to camp out at Point Reyes, you'll probably be sleeping cheap right there. Just keep in mind that every site at the seashore is a backcountry site, and you'll have to pack in most of what you'll need. Call (415) 663-8054 up to three months ahead of time to reserve a site; you can also visit the Point Reyes Web site, download a reservation form, and fax it to (415) 464-5149. There aren't a lot of campsites in the park, so calling ahead is essential.

Climbing Yosemite's Big Walls

The Absolute Pinnacle

You'll find some challenging activities in these pages, adventures that will test your mind, your body, and your resolve. They involve difficult tests—from flying, to strenuous physical work, all the way up to real danger for the careless; some of the most difficult involve all three. However, my nominee for the toughest escape of this fifty-two, the summit of the challenges you'll find here, puts even the other rough ones to shame by a big fat long shot.

Compared to big-wall rock climbing, mountaineering is a snap. At least you've got ground to stand on.

Compared to big-wall climbing, paragliding is no trouble. At least you don't have to sleep up there.

Compared to big-wall climbing, off-roading is an absolute breeze. At least the truck's doing the scaling.

Big-wall rock climbing stands, in my mind, as the most strenuous, difficult, and rewarding escape northern California has to offer—which is a great reason to try it out. After taking on an adventure like this, you'll know yourself and your abilities better than just about anyone out there knows theirs; you'll feel secure in the knowledge that you've pushed your boundaries as far as they can go, reached the summit, and came back to tell the tale. It's livin' large, and not just talking about it.

Big-wall climbing is, in essence, camping on sheer cliff faces. You climb with all your gear in tow—shelter (otherwise known as a portaledge), sleeping bags, water, food—and take on multiple-day routes that require overnighting on the way up. If this sounds punishing, that's because it is; big-wall climbers reach the summit with bruised, swollen fingers, exhausted limbs, and the kind of mental duress that only comes when extreme exertion meets unwavering concentration. After all, rock climbing in and of itself is no picnic, and doing it for days at a time while you're humping a bunch of gear raises the difficulty level a few hasty notches.

To get the job done, you'll make use of various pins and hooks hammered (by you) into the climbing surface, in order to create holding points for all your gear and yourself. Since few cracks run all the way to the top of any rock, you'll have to employ various techniques to get between them. One of the more prevalent of these maneuvers is the pendulum, which sounds exactly like what it is—a swing from one crack across the rock face to the next one. You swing out across the rock, gaining momentum and speed until you can manage to clutch whatever outhanger or flake presents itself to you. It's time-consuming, brutal business, resulting in those bumps and bruises we talked about earlier; it also requires dedication and focus, as placing those little metal babies determines whether you'll stick to the wall or not. At 1,000 feet of elevation up a sheer rock face, issues like these are just a little beyond important, as you can probably imagine.

And then there are the walls themselves—towering monstrosities, shooting thousands of feet in the air, giant stones that will not give you an inch you don't earn. Take Yosemite's Half Dome, for instance: at 2,000 feet, it's more than a third of a mile's worth of punishment, even for good rock scramblers. El Capitan (El Cap to the initiated) is even more daunting, and until 1958, when the very first climbers made their way up its face in a mere thirteen days, it was considered impossible. Today, of course, El Cap is certainly possible, and some experienced climbers take it on in a single twenty-four-hour stretch of continuous climbing; its familiarity does not detract from its sheer difficulty, however. Even experienced climbers still say that their knees literally quaked the first time they stood at the base of this inanimate, unforgiving creature—thinking that somehow, over the next few days, they had to get up the thing.

It's safe to say that wall climbing is not everybody's cup of tea. Climb failure rates can surpass 65 percent up there, usually because

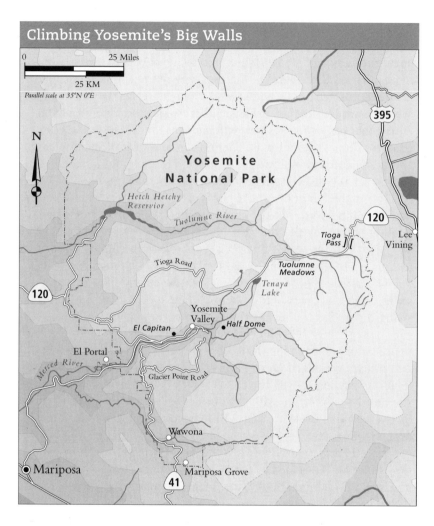

climbers crap out mentally before they hit the summit, letting fear grow and crossing the invisible, wavering psyche-out line. With dozens of pitches looming up in the distance, it isn't hard to figure out how this happens; as many climbers will tell you, conquering big walls will kick the stuffing out of you, and the amount of work you'll do hammering in pitons, dragging up your gear, and simply hanging on will take everything you've got. The secret is perseverance, along with a huge dose of focus and a few healthy ounces of training and preparation. Take things one step at a time, conquer the small challenge in front of you, and then move on to the next one.

As you might already know, regular rock climbing (without the camping) is a fair-size challenge. Luckily, even if you've never scaled a pile of stones, the good folks at Yosemite Mountaineering School will be glad to help you along. They will even take you up El Capitan—a good way to reach that summit, especially if you've never done a big wall before. They can show you the ropes and make sure that you're doing everything right. As you might imagine, big walls are logistical nightmares; you have to figure out a way to get all that gear, and yourself, up the wall as efficiently as you can. By scaling with tried-and-true experts, you won't forget anything that will make you regret the whole trip a few hundred feet up the rock. Instead, you'll have all your i's dotted, which leaves you better able to concentrate on the climb and the scenery.

Yosemite is world-famous for its big walls; in fact, almost every hard-core big-wall climber out there has cut their chops on El Capitan, the most famous stone monolith in the world and the largest in America. In joining their ranks, you'll be challenging nature's toughest denizens—massive stone leviathans that will beat you down, surely, but not put you out, provided you've got the tools to fight back. Then, once you're at the summit, in that rarified air, nursing your aching fingers and glad it's over, you'll know that you've conquered the impossible, gone up against a million tons of pure stone and come out on top. For my money, there's no more worthwhile challenge.

Price: $500-plus (guided trips can get fairly expensive)
(Spring, Difficult)

DRIVING DIRECTIONS

There are four entrances to the park: the south entrance on Highway 41 north from Fresno; the Arch Rock entrance on Highway 140 west from Merced; the Big Oak Flat entrance on Highway 120 west from Modesto and Manteca; and the Tioga Pass entrance on Highway 120 east, from Lee Vining and Highway 395. The Tioga Pass entrance is closed from the first major snowstorm in November until late May to June due to snow. All other park entrances are open all year but may require tire chains because of snow anytime between November and April.

Getting started on one of Yosemite's massive granite monoliths. CHRIS BECKER

OUTFITTERS

YOSEMITE MOUNTAINEERING SCHOOL
(209) 372–8344
www.yosemitepark.com/activity
list.cfm?SectionID=80&PageID
=237

FOR MORE INFORMATION

YOSEMITE NATIONAL PARK
www.nps.gov/yose

YOSEMITE AREA TRAVELER
INFORMATION
www.yosemite.com

RECOMMENDED READING

Falkenstein, Chris and Don Reid. *Rock Climbing Tuolumne Meadows,*
4th ed. Guilford, Conn.; Falcon, 2005.

Long, John. *How to Climb: Big Walls.* Guilford, Conn.: Falcon, 1998.

McNamara, Chris. *Yosemite Big Walls.* Mill Valley, Calif.: SuperTopos,
2000.

Reid, Don. *Yosemite Climbs: Big Walls.* Guilford, Conn.: Falcon, 1998.

SLEEP CHEAP

Though you'll probably be sleeping on the wall, Yosemite provides
plenty of cheap camping options for the way in before your climb
and for recuperating when you're done. (Make sure you give yourself a few recovery days for taking in the wilderness—you'll be glad
you did.) Just check out the Yosemite Web site above to scout out
the sites, then call (800) 436–7275 or visit http://reservations.nps
.gov to make reservations.

Skiing the Tahoe Backcountry

Feel the White Powder Rush

Let's say you're already a skier—maybe a darn good one. You've conquered black diamond trails from Mammoth to Killington, so many that you're searching for a new challenge. You need a new patch of mountain and snow to show who's boss; you need to pull out the stops even further.

Or maybe you need a new way to look at skiing—a view outside of the chairlifts, base lodges, and crowded mountains you've taken on so far. Maybe you need to head out where the snow is deep, the trails (if you want to call them that) are tough, and the humanity is thin. Maybe the backcountry is the place for you, and there's no better area to find out than the Tahoe Sierra.

People who know about such things are nearly unanimous in their agreement: Few places in the world treat backcountry skiers more kindly than the Tahoe area. The snow is fairly reliable (in that you probably won't fall into a massive sinkhole), avalanches are fairly easy to see coming, and the deep, powdery snow presents a pliant, spectacular canvas for your snow carvings. You won't want to get out here if you've just started taking on blue squares at your local ski mountain, though; this adventure is for people who have big confidence in their skills and the credentials to back it up. Backcountry skiing can be unpredictable, tiring, and very difficult. You have to be prepared, both skill- and fitness-wise, to get it done.

You also need to find some friends—never ski the backcountry solo, no matter what kind of snow-time guru you think you are. If you get yourself into a situation out there, it's imperative that you have somebody along to dig you out, take care of bumps and bruises, or provide whatever other assistance you might need. Recruit a like-minded buddy to hit the hills with you, or contact one of the outfitters below to get in on one of their trips.

There are a couple different ways to ski the backcountry. Of course, you're probably going to be hiking a bit; getting to the top of the mountain is the only way to get back down. If you haven't done a bunch of climbing, you might want to brush up a little beforehand—Alpine Skills International, for example, offers courses in ski mountaineering, as well as three-day seminars in telemarking and backcountry skiing. (Telemarking is that combination of cross-country and downhill skiing that you've probably seen at the local ski hill but never quite understood.) This climbing necessitates a degree of physical fitness beyond what regular skiing—even difficult skiing—entails. It also requires a bit more equipment; avalanche gear, for example, isn't something you'll need down at the ski lift, but you will need to carry it into the backcountry, where avalanches are a legitimate possibility.

You can reduce your chances of getting stuck in an unfortunate situation by taking an avalanche preparation course at any of the outfitters below. In fact, you really ought to think about doing so whether you've had any backcountry experience before or not. The Tahoe backcountry can be pretty dangerous if you don't know how to handle it or if you're not prepared. That preparedness carries over into the gear you bring along, too, as you'll need all the tools at your disposal out there, from your skills on the skis to good maps, research, and a whole bunch of common sense. Take those things with you, and you'll have a much better, safer time.

In addition to avalanche prep training, the outfitters below can show you the best places in the Tahoe region to get your deep-snow backcountry ski on. The best time to hit the area is in the spring, when the snow is best and the stable weather lessens the chances of avalanche and storm. During that period, companies like Cosley & Houston Alpine Guides, Mountain Adventure Seminars, and the aforementioned Alpine Skills International all offer trips of varying length and cost into the fun stuff; you can go for a day or two, or pack off for a whole week in the bush if your schedule and wallet allow it. If you're just getting started in the backcountry, visit with

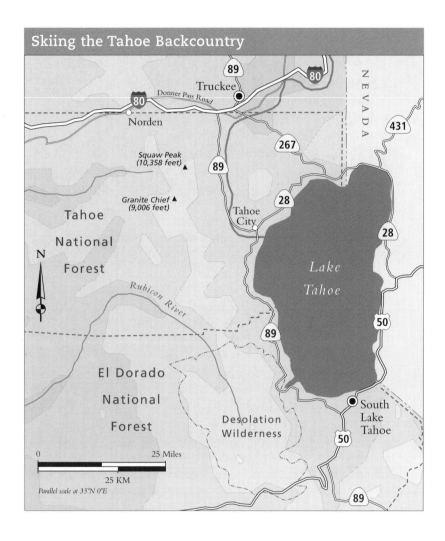

the North American Ski Training Center (NASTC), which offers classes in backcountry skiing as well as trip packages that will take you to some of the Sierra's finest slopes. They'll supply some of your meals for you, too, since the instructional experience takes place a little closer to civilization—namely at Tahoe's finest ski resorts—than the backcountry excursions generally do.

But going out into the backcountry doesn't have to cost you the price of an outfitter or a guide to show you where to go. Those of you who already know what you're doing will love just getting out there and investigating the possibilities on your own, provided you do your homework ahead of time. You'll find a mountain of resources out there for your perusal, from great independent Web sites (tahoebackountry.net) to relevant books (see the recommended reading below). Above all, make sure you get your research in before you get out there, and learn as much as you can; you'll get tips on where to go, what to see, and how to ski from people intimately familiar with the area, people who love the region and want you to love it, too.

The Tahoe backcountry presents a great opportunity to strut the ski skills you've picked up on those black diamonds. Sure it's tough, but it's worth the challenge to see places that very few people get to see even when there's no snow on the ground. The peace you'll find out there, in beautiful white country nearly devoid of tourists, will put you in a pure state of mind that few people ever get to experience.

If you need to get your skills up to par, do it. If your legs need a bit more muscle, get it. Tahoe's hidden snows are well worth the toil.

Price: If you hit the backcountry on your own, this is a very cost-effective adventure—you're basically using gear you've already got. Go take a class or a guided tour, though, and the cost will rise to $200–$400.

(Spring, Difficult)

DRIVING DIRECTIONS

The Tahoe backcountry comprises five rough areas, three of which are in California. The Granite Chief/Northwest Shore area is right off the lake near Tahoe City and Tahoe Vista. The Donner Pass/ Castle Peak area lies just off Interstate 80, and the Desolation Wilderness reaches down into the southern portion of the western Tahoe region. Check the resources listed below for detailed directions to the trail you decide on, or talk to your outfitter—they'll let you know where to go.

OUTFITTERS

ALPINE SKILLS INTERNATIONAL
Truckee, CA
(530) 582–9170
www.alpineskills.com

COSLEY & HOUSTON ALPINE GUIDES
Bishop, CA
(760) 872–3811
www.cosleyhouston.com

Shredding up the backcountry. COURTESY OF MAMMOTH MOUNTAIN SKI RESORT

MOUNTAIN ADVENTURE SEMINARS
Bear Valley, CA
(209) 753–6556, ext. 1
www.mtadventure.com

SIERRA MOUNTAIN CENTER LLC
Bishop, CA
(760) 873–8526
www.sierramountaincenter.com

FOR MORE INFORMATION

TAHOE BACKCOUNTRY
www.tahoebackcountry.net

LAKE TAHOE SKIING AND
SNOWBOARDING GUIDE
www.snoweb.com

RECOMMENDED READING

Felser, Doug and Jill A. Fredston. *Snow Sense*. Anchorage, Alaska: Alaska Mountain Safety Center, 2001.

O'Bannon, Allen. *Allen & Mike's Really Cool Backcountry Ski Book*. Guilford, Conn.: Falcon, 1996.

Sprout, Janine and Jerry Sprout. *Alpine Sierra Trailblazer*. Berkeley, Calif.: Diamond Valley Company, 2004.

Tremper, Bruce. *Staying Alive in Avalanche Terrain*. Seattle: Mountaineers Books, 2001.

SLEEP CHEAP

The Clair Tappaan Lodge, located in Norden, makes a terrific, inexpensive wintertime lodging option. Here you'll find affordable rates that include nightly family-style meals, along with the highest average snowfall of the entire Sierra Nevada range. The lodge will serve as a wonderful home base for your ski adventure, and when you don't feel like a downhill ride, cross-country and snowshoe paths await nearby. For more info, call (530) 426–3632, or visit the lodge online (www.sierraclub.org/outings/lodges/ctl).

White-water Kayaking Tuolumne Canyon

Foamy Road, Take Me Home

Located just outside Yosemite National Park, the Tuolumne River is the greatest that most Americans have never heard of. You won't find a more raw, untouched artery of water anywhere in California; while nearby Yosemite can get overwhelming at times, with its press of tourists and traffic, the Tuolumne (too-ALL-o-me) provides out-of-the-way escape, secluded and unscathed wilderness. It's a place for people who know how to treat the outdoors and how to enjoy it on its own terms, without developed campgrounds, outdoor super-stores, or pamphlet-packed visitor centers. For dyed-in-the-wool outdoor folk, Tuolumne feels a whole lot like home.

The river has a fascinating background—Congress gave it National Wild and Scenic protection in 1984 after a protracted leg-islative battle, and as a result wilderness lovers everywhere are free to enjoy it, undeveloped, forever. Thanks to this regulation, only two commercial trips can take to the river each day, limiting its human exposure during the dam-controlled running season, March or April through October.

Yosemite births the Tuolumne River's headwaters at around 13,000 feet, high in the Sierra Nevada. From there, the river picks up steam, carving out canyons and providing 18 miles of hard-core white water that puts it at the top of any self-respecting kayaker's wish list. The water corridor remains the quickest, most breathtaking way to see the Tuolumne, though it requires a high level of skill and fitness, particularly when you're shooting the rapids with a kayak. If you're close to graduating into Class IV rapids, the Tuolumne is a great place to do so, provided that you're ready for it—a two-day trip to the next level in natural splendor and your skills.

For those of you who aren't white-water savvy yet, rapids rate on a set scale from Class I to Class VI. Class I runs consist of fast moving water, with a few easy-to-negotiate hazards and only a low chance of injury if you have to bail. On the extreme, far opposite hand, you've got Class VI—unrunnable by most standards, except for a few half-crazy adrenaline junkies. These expert paddlers attempt Class VI runs once in a while, but only when water levels are favorable, after serious scouting, and with all safety bases covered. Those of you who already paddle know that increasing your skills will let you increase the rating you're comfortable with; the better you get, the less risk you face, thanks to the skills you develop climbing up the ladder.

Here's a hitch: Lots of outfitters offer white-water rafting trips on the Tuolumne, but none offer kayaking trips, as fewer people are capable of taking on the river in a kayak (insurance concerns also play a part). For this reason, kayakers should expect to do their own planning and packing, unlike the rafters you'll see out there. This is not to say the guided white-water services can't help you out—two guided trips launch nearly every day from the drop-in at Meral's Pool, and running parallel with a group will give you some folks to talk to and share the experience with, always a bonus. You may even persuade them to share their four-star backcountry cuisine—a lot of raft guides spend the equivalent of months on the river each year, and as a result they know what they're doing in their makeshift, riverside "kitchens." Ask nicely, and maybe you'll be mingling with the other boaters over plastic cups of boxed wine, rather than chowing on your own meager (but conveniently packed) provisions.

Set out for the Tuolumne with other kayakers, even if you're rowing with an outfitter-led expedition. If you don't already know fellow boaters who can make the trip, you probably won't have much of a problem finding them—the river is a true mecca, and as a result it draws a ton of very good kayakers who usually rub elbows at the La Casa Loma River Store, alongside Highway 120 east of Groveland. The store is a traditional meeting spot for trips on the main Tuolumne, along with the lesser-known Cherry Creek run, a tough bit of world-class water that serves as the standard by which all Class V runs are measured. From April through September, boaters of all kinds meet at La Casa Loma, arranging for rides into

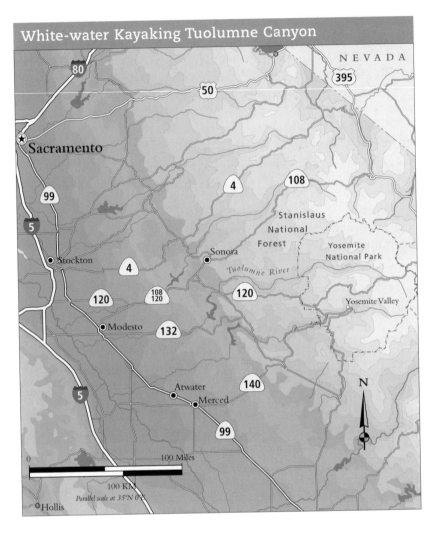

the canyon and setting up groups. The store also has a limited selection of supplies, so if you forget anything you should be okay after passing through.

Tuolumne's Class III and IV rapids start right off, soon after you put in at Meral's Pool. Rock Garden and Nemesis, two class IVs, greet you as soon as you set out, followed in quick succession by another five Class IV challenges. The early action goes to show that this adventure is not for those just getting their oars in the water—you need to know what you're doing, and you'll find out very quickly if you do. Make sure you're up to the task. As for trip duration: You can get down the whole 18-mile stretch in a long day, but why would you want to? Take your time, and you'll get to enjoy the multitude of activities the Tuolumne offers. Take a backcountry hike to the area's secluded swimming holes, or relax your paddle-weary muscles on white sand beaches near incredible campsites far removed from the overused, trampled campgrounds we've all seen in more populous sites. Make the trip in a weekend, or stretch it into a three-day float if you *really* want to enjoy your time back there.

You'll also be impressed with the wildlife viewing possibilities—golden eagles, river otters, and ring-tailed cats all make their homes here—as well as the historical context. The Tuolumne Canyon was a favorite destination during the California Gold Rush, and home to the Miwok Indians for more than 1,500 years. When you jump out of your kayak, you'll have no shortage of sights to consider, both wild and human in nature, along with those natural features I've already mentioned.

The U.S. Forest Service manages access to the Tuolumne, in efforts to protect the river from overuse and promote safety among boaters. Obtain your permit to float the river at the Stanislaus National Forest's Groveland Ranger District Office, a short hop from the put-in point. The permits are cheap, and you should call ahead to reserve yours in advance of your trip. The rangers can also give you accurate information on water flow and other important factors, so take advantage of their knowledge before you set out.

Phenomenal scenery, mouthwatering rapids, great dry land diversions—all these things await you on the mighty, magnificent Tuolumne. Eighteen miles of pristine canyon, complete with white beaches and the Sierra wildlife to keep you company, all of it without the interruption of development, without modern baggage to get in the way. If you're looking to improve your kayaking skills, looking for a spectacular Class IV to conquer, then throw the ol' boat on your roof and get to it. By the time you're done, you'll feel as if you're home again.

Price: $40–$100 (provided you have access to a kayak)
(Spring, Difficult)

DRIVING DIRECTIONS

Directions to La Casa Loma River Store and Deli: from Groveland, take Highway 120 east toward Yosemite. Seven miles out of town,

Kayaking isn't for the faint of heart—conditions can get pretty rough in a hurry. Make sure you bring a couple buddies in case of trouble. CHRIS BECKER

Ferretti Road intersects Highway 120. La Casa Loma is located on the northern side of the highway, on an access spur just west of the intersection. (Ferretti Road first crosses Highway 120 in the town of Groveland; La Casa Loma, however, is located at the second crossing, which is well east of Groveland.)

OUTFITTERS

SIERRA MAC RIVER RAFTING TRIPS
(RAFTING OUTFITTER)
Sonora, CA
(800) 457–2580
www.sierramac.com

WHITEWATER VOYAGES (RAFTING
OUTFITTER)
El Sobrante, CA
(800) 400–RAFT
www.whitewatervoyages.com

O.A.R.S. (RAFTING OUTFITTER)
Angels Camp, CA
(209) 736–4677, (800) 346-6277
www.oars.com

ECHO, THE WILDERNESS COMPANY
(RAFTING OUTFITTER)
Oakland, CA
(800) 652–3246
www.echotrips.com

FOR MORE INFORMATION

For kayaking skills and safety classes:
OUTBACK ADVENTURES
San Jose, CA
(408) 551–0588, (888) 441–PEAK

STANISLAUS NATIONAL FOREST, GROVELAND RANGER DISTRICT
Groveland, CA
(209) 962–7825
www.fs.fed.us/r5/stanislaus

RECOMMENDED READING

Bennett, Jeff. *The Essential Whitewater Kayaker: A Complete Course.* Camden, Maine: International Marine/Ragged Mountain Press, 1999.

Dutkey, Paul. *The Bombproof Roll and Beyond.* Birmingham, Ala.: Menasha Ridge Press, 1993.

Pike, Charlie. *Paddling Northern California.* Guilford, Conn.: Falcon, 2001.

SLEEP CHEAP

If you're spending a few days on the river, there are a bunch of campsites available on a first-come, first-served basis as you float. Just take to the first unoccupied one that strikes your fancy. Four sites are reserved for commercial outfitters—Clavey, Grapevine, Wheelbarrow, and North Fork—though even these are okay provided there are no commercial outfitters using them. If you're running the river in a day and need something nearby but not on the water, contact Stanislaus National Forest and get area information. Call (877) 444–6777 for reservations, or visit the forest Web site (www.fs.fed.us/r5/stanislaus).

Summer

FRANCINE GARRIGUS

Deep-sea Fishing off San Francisco

On the Hook

Your muscles are relaxing more and more by the second, and that's not a good thing. The sky and surf, the sun playing off the water, all of it puts you into a state of comfort that makes the fishing rod in your hand seem heavier and heavier, more and more unnecessary... until the hit comes.

When it does, your hands awaken a split second before the rest of you does. They tense and squeeze, responding to the pressure at the other end of the line. Your mind snaps into focus just after that, remembering to set the hook as your hands follow through without any prompting. A quick jerk, and you know the hook's hit home and that if you play your cards right, you'll be hauling up a few dozen pounds of swimming fillets and steaks, hopefully the salmon you've been hankering for ever since you booked your charter. "Reel 'em in!" the deckhand shouts, his knife inserted into someone else's catch, and you start reeling away, hoping your catch hits his blade next....

Deep-sea fishing is a great way to fulfill a whole list of adventure priorities. Beautiful scenery? Check—I'm talking about open ocean off one of the prettiest coastlines in the country. Physical challenges? Double check—ever try hauling a 30-pound fish out of the water? (It ain't knitting, that's for sure.) Pure fun? Well, if you've ever popped a beer as you sit on a deck chair and feel the ocean wind streaming by, mist and all, then you know you'll be getting plenty of that. Yup, deep-sea fishing has it all, and San

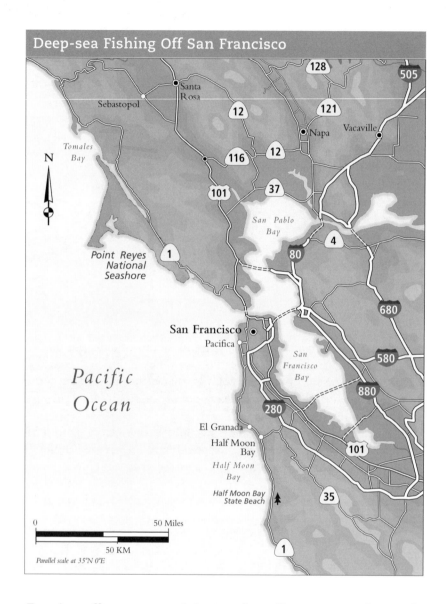

Francisco offers an array of charters that will get you out there and put a couple big ones on your hook.

You have to know that any city featuring a Fisherman's Wharf will offer some great fishing. In fact, the fishing's even better than you think—the richest fishing region on the Pacific coast of North America is the strip that lies right off the San Francisco Bay, thanks to the relatively shallow water and the related upwelling in the spring, which brings cold, mineral-rich water to the surface where sunlight causes tiny aquatic organisms to blossom in huge numbers. With these little guys serving as the base of the food chain, you've got a ton of bigger fish congregating, until you reach the apex of the food chain with the great white sharks that prowl here in the fall.

The fish and other sea creatures you'll find look great on a plate—shrimp, anchovies, and herring come to eat the aforementioned plankton, which in turn draws hordes of king salmon, the real stars of the fishery. You won't find these salmon anywhere else on the Pacific Coast; what's more, the salmon swim here year-round, making for a permanent, catchable population that never fails to disappoint.

Those salmon can get downright beastly, ranging up to 50 pounds—more than enough for a barbecue of ridiculous proportions. The fishing season starts in March and usually runs into October; in the summertime, though, immense schools of anchovies migrate inshore off Half Moon Bay, Pacifica, and Marin County, causing the salmon to band together and follow the little fish toward the shore. The result: incredible fishing, with glassy seas and large packs of hungry salmon willing to bite on the bait you throw into the water. You've got other fish in the sea, too—and in the Bay—to choose from. Striped bass, leopard sharks, and a ton of other sport fish await your line in the summer time, and during those pretty months you're liable to feel bites from any of these species.

You can fish these waters in a couple different ways, though two general methods dominate: trolling and "mooching," or simply throwing in your line and waiting. While trolling results in bigger catches, mooching gets you the big fish, since you can feel every bite that hits the line. Of course, mooching is a bit more fun, too, since you get to actually catch the fish, rather than simply look at the catch once it flops into the boat.

A number of charter boats run out of San Francisco and the surrounding cities. Day tripping is probably your best bet for getting out into the water, though some companies offer multiple-day trips if you're interested. The coolest thing about the San Fran–area fishing, though, is that the best of it takes place not more than 30 miles offshore, so you can get yourself some fantastic fish without having to sign on for a weeklong excursion. This is a weekend escape, but one you can do in conjunction with a few nice days in San Francisco and the surrounding area. If you haven't done a lot of boating before, you'll want to be sure and bring along some seasickness medication; bouts with a queasy stomach can ruin your good

The fleet at Fisherman's Wharf. ROBERT HOLMES/CALTOUR

time quick as a wink, rendering you incapable of fishing or doing much of anything else. The good news is that with proper preparation and the right over-the-counter pills, you'll be just fine out there, even if you've never tossed a line into the ocean before.

So don't be afraid of the water if you're a beginner—this is a great escape for anybody, even the landlubbers among us. If you want the chance to take in the Pacific while taking aboard some fish to bring home, deep-sea fishing off the San Francisco coast is a perfect getaway. Whether you go out for the day or take a longer jaunt into the deep blue, you're sure to come away with some serious salmon in your cooler. Just make sure you don't relax *too* much out there—those fish will gladly pull that rod right out of your hand to save their hides. Wouldn't you?

Price: $60–$100, more for multiple-day trips
(Summer, Easy)

OUTFITTERS

San Francisco has a ton of charter boats; most of these operate independently, rather than as part of larger companies. For a list of the charter fleets at Fisherman's Wharf and the surrounding areas, visit www.sfsportfishing.com, a guide to both the fleets and fishing conditions in the area. You'll find charter boats here, too, so check out their information, then call around to see which one appeals to you most. There are other Web sites that list SF–area charters, too; check out the World Wide Fishing Guide (www.worldwidefishing .com) for one of these.

Other options:

HUCK FINN SPORTFISHING
El Granada, CA
(650) 726–7133
www.huckfinnsportfishing.com

RIPTIDE SPORTFISHING
(888) 747–8433
www.riptide.net

FOR MORE INFORMATION

Check the San Francisco Sport Fishing Web site (www.sfsport fishing.com) for information on conditions, fish, weather, or anything else concerning fishing in and around the Bay.

RECOMMENDED READING

Hemingway, Ernest. *Hemingway On Fishing.* New York: Lyons Press, 2000.

Kovach, Ron. *Saltwater Fishing in California: Secrets of the Pacific Experts.* Aptos, Calif.: Marketscope Hourglass Books, 2002.

Ries, Ed. *Tales Of The Golden Years Of California Ocean Fishing 1900–1950.* Laguna Hills, Calif.: Monterey Publications, 1998.

Rychnovsky, Ray. *San Francisco Bay Areas Fishing Guide.* Portland, Ore.: Frank Amato Publications, 1999.

SLEEP CHEAP

If you're doing your fishing in Half Moon Bay, stop by the Half Moon Bay State Beach and get in on the camping lottery, conducted at 12:30 in the afternoon. Otherwise, you'll get stuck with first-come, first-served accommodations. The lottery system ensures that the fifty-four sites at Francis Beach are parceled out fairly, as demand is pretty high. Although you won't find RV hookups here, you do have outside showers and flush toilets—perfect for roughing it within full view of beautiful seaside scenery. Call (650) 726–8819 for more information, and remember: You need to enter the lottery by noon, so step lively!

Coastal Camping at Manchester State Park

Beginner's Luck

Let's face it: You're not the outdoorsy type. You never measured your walking distances in miles, but in mall lengths or city blocks. You haven't ever worn a backpack, much less toted one over hill and dale, and you are amazed at the fact that people would willingly walk for two days just to get away from the world and see some pretty scenery.

But aren't you the least bit *curious* about all that? Sure, you don't get it yet, but maybe you're wondering what the fuss is about. Maybe you're considering the outdoors, but you're not sure where to begin or what to do. After all, there's a whole roster of choices— hiking or biking? Kayaking or backpacking? Glider soaring or horseback touring? If you haven't been active in the outdoors before, the choices can get the best of you, no matter how long you spend thinking about them.

Have no fear—I'm here to help. There's no reason you can't go forward with any of the aforementioned activities; my suggestion, however, is to first perfect a skill that applies to each and every one, the foundation for outdoor adventure if ever there was one: camping.

Not backpack hauling, backcountry camping—we're talking about good-time camping, camping with all the essentials, camping meant to save you a bunch of scratch and add another dimension to your vacations. This is lodging that keeps you closer to the adventurer's

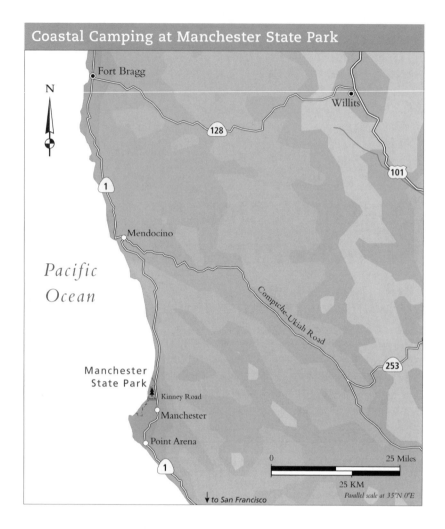

Coastal Camping at Manchester State Park

N

Fort Bragg

Willits

128

101

1

Mendocino

Pacific
Ocean

Compiche-Ukiah Road

253

Manchester
State Park

Kinney Road

Manchester

Point Arena

1

0   25 Miles

25 KM

Parallel scale at 35°N 0°E

↓ to San Francisco

life, even when you're not actually doing much besides packing up the car, heading to the site, and pitching camp like a champion. It's a skill every aspiring outdoor denizen must learn, and one that will pay off big time once you've got it all down.

Even though it's your first time, there's no reason you can't head somewhere great—no need to subject yourself to a run-down campground with dusty dirt tent plots, smelly clogged-up bathrooms, and hundreds of noisy neighbors who don't know the meaning of lights out. In fact, a terrific first time is sure to get you closer to your second, so I want you to have a great time. With that idea in mind, head up to Manchester State Park, right off the Pacific

Coast Highway just south of Fort Bragg, and you'll find yourself already planning your next trip as you learn the camper's ropes, spikes, and posts bellied right up to the Pacific.

First thing: There is some investment involved, unless you know some outdoor types who can hook you up with first-timer's gear. If you do finance yourself, however, don't get crazy and start buying the top-of-the-line stuff for top dollar. Particularly in coastal California, the conditions are hardly ever bad enough to warrant sleeping bags tested to 40 below, or single-walled tents capable of weathering Everest's storms. To start out, just pick up a simple tent (Coleman makes some very basic, very affordable yet sturdy models) and a sleeping bag with a nylon shell and a liner that zips out to accommodate warmer weather. Don't forget to pick up a sleeping mat when you grab your bag; even a foam bed liner will work, and you can get one for a few bucks at a discount store. Even if the sleeping bag is comfy as an old sock, you'll be glad you picked up the extra padding. After all, a tent floor is nothing more than a tarp, and a floor that thin still counts as the ground.

Next, figure out how you're going to cook. Since you'll have the car for toting things around, don't be afraid to use it—throw in the cooler for sure, and maybe pick up a nice gas cookstove. These run the gamut in price and complexity, from a single burner with a tank for a few bucks, to deluxe grill-style beasts with triple-digit price tags. If you want to avoid these trappings of luxury all together, simply pick up some firewood, kindling, and waterproof matches, then grill up the doggies over your very own campfire. Whatever you decide, the cooler is the essential—visit the grocery store before your trip and load up so you don't run low on provisions once you're sitting in a comfy seat by the fire.

There's other gear you can pick up, too, all of which will help you have a nicer time while you rough it. Of course, there's no need to grab everything right off the bat—you're just starting out, after all, and after buying what you've had to already, you may not be keen to shell out more dough. The bells and whistles break down in terms of importance; for example, flashlights or lanterns are essential, no doubt. Fire-starter sticks are not, but they make lighting your fire painless, even in a stiff breeze. Folding camp chairs are certainly not a requirement, but they sure are cool to have around and can make the difference between sitting on the rocky ground for a few days and lounging by the fire the way you were meant to. Camp chairs with footrests are just icing on the cake. (Hint: The fire pits at Manchester don't all have seating nearby. Camp chairs looking even better....) Above all, realize that you will forget things—you'll wish you had this or that, and curse yourself for not grabbing it. Just start up a list, and pick up that stuff the next time.

Manchester State Park is great for first-time campers for two major reasons. It's beautiful, first off; the beach is audible in the distance no matter where you camp, and the dunes make for great, easy hiking. It's also right down the street from a KOA campground—one of the best in their system, actually—so if you forget anything, these folks are in a great position to help out. They also provide respite for those of you not quite ready for isolated camping—Manchester is not terribly busy, particularly during the week or cooler times of year, so you can feel pretty alone out there. You don't have the lights of civilization polluting the sky, either, so while the stars can be breathtaking, they can also be pretty darn dim when the sun goes down. If you'd rather have some lights guiding you on the way to the john (other than your own), spend the first night at the KOA, then move out to a beachside, secluded spot the next. Just remember that help is always down the road if you need it, and enjoy the solitude when you're ready.

The goal here, of course, is to prep you for camping adventures yet to come. Soon, you'll be ready to hit more isolated spots without fear of forgetting everything but the tent. But whatever you eventually decide to take on, a few nights at Manchester will set you up for future nights spent under the stars and for outdoor escapes you haven't even thought of yet.

Price: $15–$50

(Summer, Easy)

DRIVING DIRECTIONS

Manchester State Park is located in Mendocino County on the Pacific Coast Highway, about 7 miles north of Point Arena. The park surrounds the town of Manchester; the entrance is ½ mile north of town on Highway 1. Turn off on Kinney Road toward the ocean to get to the park; you'll see the KOA on your right before the entrance.

The cliffs at Manchester State Beach. CHRIS BECKER

OUTFITTERS

MANCHESTER KOA
Manchester, CA
(800) 562–4188 (reservations)
(707) 882–2375 (information)
www.koakampgrounds.com/
where/ca/05182.htm

MANCHESTER STATE PARK
Manchester, CA
(707) 882–2463
www.parks.ca.gov/default.asp?
page_id=437

FOR MORE INFORMATION

MENDOCINO COAST BOTANICAL
GARDENS
Fort Bragg, CA
(707) 964–4352
www.gardenbythesea.org

MENDOCINO COUNTY
www.mendocino.org

RECOMMENDED READING

Harmon, Will. *Leave No Trace*. Guilford, Conn.: Falcon Press, 1997.

Jacobson, Cliff. *Basic Essentials® Camping*, 3rd ed. Guilford, Conn.: Globe Pequot Press, 2005.

Mai, Bill. *The Best in Tent Camping: Northern California: A Guide for Campers Who Hate RVs, Concrete Slabs, and Loud Portable Stereos*. Birmingham, Ala.: Menasha Ridge Press, 2001.

SLEEP CHEAP

Campsites at Manchester State Beach are given on a first-come, first-served basis. Contact the park directly for information at the number above. You have a number of campsites to choose from, including environmental, family, group, and bike campsites, and the price is nice—only $8.00 for a traditional tent camping site. The KOA is a bit more expensive but still reasonable.

Great America and Six Flags Marine World

Wild 'n' Wooly Cali

So you love the outdoors—I mean *loooove* it out there. You've got a closet full of backpacks, kayaks, and carabiners, and you don't need too much help on the weekend escape front. "I've got plenty of my own ideas for weekend escapes, thanks," you say to yourself as you read on, convinced that the only fun-time authority you need is yourself.

But all of a sudden, there you are, sitting on the couch, that equipment just burning its way through the closet door, almost mocking you. Yeah, you've got calluses on your rock-steady hands and strong legs to take you up mountains and down canyons, but you've hit on that rarest of occasions: the one weekend out of a hundred that you just don't *feel* like getting your feet muddy. You don't *feel* like hiking all day with the promise of setting up a campsite at the far end of the walk. No, this weekend, you just don't *feel* like the backcountry thing, and you're feeling terrible about it.

Don't. Very few of us are gung-ho for the unbeaten path all the time. You don't have to feel like you're letting down the gods of nature if you happen upon a couple days where you'd rather have fun in more domesticated settings. Of course, just because you don't feel like hitting the outdoors doesn't mean you have to give up on your sense of adventure; California offers a ton of cool fun that

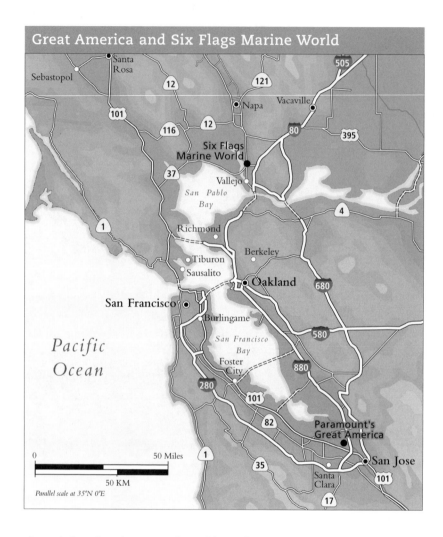

Great America and Six Flags Marine World

doesn't involve the natural world at all. For a big, heaping sample, head to the Bay area, where two of the state's biggest adventure attractions sit almost side by side: Paramount's Great America and Six Flags Marine World.

Marine World, located in Vallejo in the East Bay, is a Six Flags park, which gives you adventure options from wild animal interactions to breath-stealing roller coaster gyrations. The wildlife here is of both the landlubbing and seafaring varieties; the 2,800-seat Dolphin Harbor Stadium and the Sea Lion Stadium play host to the park's complement of aquatic performers, while tigers, giraffes, and elephants populate its landed walkways. In fact, the wild population is still growing by leaps and bounds; in April 2004, the park welcomed Shouka, a two-ton killer whale, along with about 400 other animals from anteaters to tarantulas.

You don't have to sit content just watching the animals play, either. Marine World offers plenty of close-up interactive programs, designed to put you in contact with your favorite beastie. Dolphin Discovery and Sea Lion Celebration are just two of these programs, and they enable parkgoers to mingle with the cuddliest creatures this side of the sea: bottlenose dolphins, Pacific harbor seals, even the huge and majestic California sea lion. Of course, the programs are conducted with the highest standards of training and safety—classroom instruction precedes the hands-on interaction, as the park's staff teaches you how to properly approach the animals. This program costs a bit more in addition to admission, but the experience, it goes without saying, is well worth the bucks. Just make sure you make your reservations ahead of time—as you can imagine, face-to-face meetings like this sell out pretty quickly.

If you can't get a spot, though, don't worry, because there are lots of opportunities to feed, watch, and otherwise take in the other animals throughout the park. Take a look at Marine World's Web site for other cool activities like sleepovers for the kids and safari summer camp—and above all, call with any questions you might have.

The animals at Marine World give reason enough to make a beeline there. But let's not forget about the rides—gaggles of them, from Zonga, the park's newest roller coaster, to the supercool rides for little sailors in the Looney Tunes Seaport. You might want to set aside two days for Marine World, just so you can take in all the shows, ride all the rides, and visit all the critters on the itinerary without having to rush by anything.

South of the Bay in Santa Clara, Paramount's Great America leaves out the animals but tosses in major doses of movie magic to complement its slate of death-defying rides. You also get a ton of splashable fun: The new Crocodile Dundee's Boomerang Bay is a water park inside the park, boasting eleven waterslides, as well as play areas just for little blokes and sheilas. What's more, you don't pay any extra for the privilege of getting soaked; admission to Boomerang Bay is included with your admission to the park, so feel free to take the plunge after taking on some of the West Coast's screamier rides.

Like the Xtreme Skyflyer, for instance. This wild experience

Taming the tigers at Marine World. ROBERT HOLMES/CALTOUR

simulates hang gliding, with riders donning harnesses and shooting 153 feet up into the air, then diving at speeds up to 60 miles per hour as they drop 17 stories back to the ground. Or check out Delirium, the first ride of its kind in North America—think of a pendulum spinning and swinging through the air at nutty speed, and you've got some idea. Then there are the coasters, a whole bunch of them, each with its own special allure. The all-wooden Grizzly, for example, is a classic straight from the get-go, while Top Gun, California's longest inverted coaster, provides buckets of adrenaline for the junkies among us.

The movie magic comes in when you seek out the shows playing throughout the park. Paramount's Magic of the Movies puts you in the middle of spectacular effects from Hollywood blockbusters like *Sleepy Hollow* and *Titanic*. Younger theatergoers will get a kick out of meeting their favorite characters from Nickelodeon, as well as classic clowns like Scooby Doo. Throw these shows into a day otherwise filled with thrill rides both dry and soaking, and you've got yourself one heck of an escape that you didn't even have to break out your helmet for.

Great America and Marine World sit close to San Francisco, so if you'll be spending any time in the area, or you live there full time already, there's no good reason not to hit one or both for a little domesticated thrill. Don't worry—I won't tell your hiking, biking, and climbing buddies. Who knows? You might even see them in line at one of the bigger, badder coasters you decide to take on. After all, you aren't the only one who needs the occasional breather from the backcountry!

Price: About $100 for admission to both parks; less for two-day passes to just one, or more if you want to go in for more days. (Plus food, souvenirs, etc.)

(Summer, Easy)

DRIVING DIRECTIONS

Great America: located 50 miles south of San Francisco and 6 miles north of San Jose on Great America Parkway, between Highways 101 and 237 in Santa Clara.

Marine World: From Interstate 80, take the Marine World Parkway (Highway 37) exit. From 101 North, take Highway 37 east to Marine World Parkway.

FOR MORE INFORMATION

SIX FLAGS MARINE WORLD
Vallejo, CA
(707) 643–6722
www.sixflags.com/parks/
marine world

PARAMOUNT'S GREAT AMERICA
Santa Clara, CA
(408) 988–1776
www.pgathrills.com

RECOMMENDED READING

Rutherford, Scott. *The American Roller Coaster.* St. Paul, Minn.: MBI Publishing, 2000.

Samuelson, Dale and Wendy Yegoiants. *The American Amusement Park.* St. Paul, Minn.: MBI Publishing, 2001.

SLEEP CHEAP

If the idea of spending a whole weekend away from the wilderness is just too abhorrent for you to contemplate, never fear—primitive camping conditions are just down the road from Santa Clara, where Great America makes its home. Castle Rock State Park doesn't have drive-in camping, but it does have primitive backpacking sites, along with 32 miles of hiking trails to tool around on. It's only $10 per night, too, which makes the price right. Call (831) 338–8861 for reservations.

Offshore Birding in the Farallon Islands

Making Feathered Friends

Wildlife watching can take you into the deepest backcountry searching for specimens. Particularly if you're looking for the bigger beasts—wildcats, bear, deer—you've got to journey far from man's strongholds and become a part of the wilderness they call home; to really get to know them, you've got to get back there for an extended period of time. They aren't the kind of hosts that join the party easily. You might be in the bush for a week before you so much as catch a glimpse of a black bear or bull elk, or you might never see one at all. Either way, you're spending a lot of time looking for creatures that may not even show up.

If you're looking for birds of the feather, though, you're likely to meet with a lot more success. Birds are less shy than their furry mammalian cousins, at least from a distance, and they tend to congregate around human settlement, where scraps of food and garbage make their way from our dinner tables and trash cans out into the world, where they become meals for avians. Yes, bird-watching makes great entertainment for those of us who want our wildlife fix without the backcountry journey, and the object of the game—to record as many species as you can in your birding journal—lends an aspect of competition and skill to the proceedings.

Even if you've never done any bird-watching, you can pick it up in a snap just about anywhere—simply get yourself a birder's

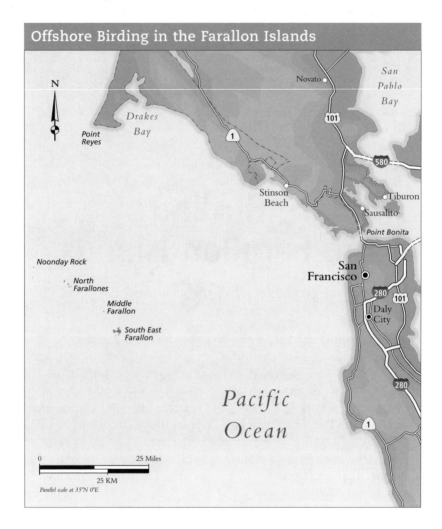

N

San
Pablo
Bay

Novato

Drakes
Point   Bay
Reyes

101

Stinson
Beach

Tiburon

Sausalito

Point Bonita

Noonday Rock

North
Farallones

Middle
Farallon

South East
Farallon

San
Francisco

280   101

Daly
City

Pacific

Ocean

280

0   25 Miles

25 KM
Parallel scale at 35°N 0°E

1

journal, and start recording your finds. Don't think that bird-watching is simply setting up a lawn chair and looking through your binoculars, though; to catch really good specimens, you will have to beat the bush just a bit and seek out the habitats those rarer fliers call home. The good part is that these habitats aren't isolated areas of the backwoods, but bodies of water and wetlands that often lie quite close to California's coastal population centers, both for better and worse: For worse because development can damage the delicate systems at work in those habitats, and better for you, as a bird-watcher, since you'll see a whole lot of feathers without journeying terribly far.

The Farallon Islands fit this bill perfectly. Located in the Gulf of the Farallones, which was designated a marine sanctuary in 1981, the islands are full of natural wonder for your perusal. They lie close to San Francisco, making them extremely accessible; they boast an incredible diversity of wildlife, from humpback and blue whales to California sea lions and the rarer, larger Steller's sea lions; and for birds, the place is unmatched—more than 300,000 seabirds congregate here every summer to breed and raise their chicks, making it the largest seabird rookery in the contiguous forty-eight states. A trip out to the islands will bring you into close contact with breeding petrels, cormorants, auklets, and gulls of all kinds. In addition, rarer avians like the Arctic tern, albatross, and even tropical specimens on their way north or south occasionally make an appearance. In all, it makes for exciting viewing and presents a perfect opportunity to start your birding journal with some first-rate entries.

The islands' location accounts for much of their value as a sanctuary; they lie close to the edge of the continental shelf, right where the upwelling of water from deeper sections of the Pacific brings nutrients and nutrient-packed water up to the surface, fueling an active and inclusive food chain. Unfortunately, you can't just head out to the islands and camp out for a few days, waiting to see what flies by; largely because it is such a great natural asset, access to the islands is extremely limited. You can, however, get a great view of the proceedings from any of the charter boats that run out to the Farallones.

Call the charter companies below to see who's offering the best trip for you. If you really, really want to get into your birding, Bay Adventures offers bird-focused cruises along with their more frequent whale-watching offerings. The Oceanic Society in San Francisco has been offering cruises into the Farallon Islands since 1972 and now runs excursions leaving from both Tiburon and San Francisco. Whale watching is the ostensible purpose of the Oceanic Society expeditions, but they do head to the Farallones, so you birders won't have any shortage of sightings. What's more, these charters both feature on-board naturalists who are more than happy to tell you all about every creature you'll see on your journey. And remember: The water off San Fran is pretty cool, particularly in the morning when your expedition will leave, so come prepared with heavier clothing in tow.

Of course, birds aren't the only animals you'll see on a jaunt out to the islands, which lie 27 miles off the San Francisco coast.

Birding isn't just for adults—kids love taking a closer look at their feathered friends as much as the grownups do. CHRIS BECKER

Whales of all kinds roll through the deeper waters west of the islands, as do lots of porpoises and dolphins. You might even catch a glimpse of that legendary predator, the great white shark; in October and November you stand a pretty good chance of seeing one of those telltale fins splitting the water as you cruise the islands. If you're feeling especially adventurous after seeing this rare sight, you might want to get even closer to those massive teeth via a great white shark diving expedition (see Escape 38).

If you can't make your way out to the boats for some reason, never fear—you'll be able to catch up with a lot of your feathered friends on shore, right down the street from the Golden Gate. The Point Reyes Bird Observatory works to understand and preserve the bird habitats of northern California; to get a better feel for the organization, you can tag along for birding trips throughout Marin County on the first weekend of every month. You can also take in the observatory's visitor center and learn more about birds through interactive displays along with where else you can go to see the most feathers in the Marin/Point Reyes area.

Birding is a hobby you can take with you on every weekend escape, no matter where you're headed. It's fun, relaxing, and even a little competitive—a perfect compliment to whatever else brings you outdoors. Be warned, however: after your trip to the Farallon Islands, you'll be hard-pressed to find better birding anywhere. Just don't let that fact stop you from trying!

Price: $75–$100

(Summer, Easy)

DRIVING DIRECTIONS

San Francisco Bay Whale Watching departs from Sausalito, while the Oceanic Society has boats leaving from both Tiburon and San Francisco. Get in touch with the company you choose for exact directions to the departure point (or visit them online). The Point Reyes Bird Observatory's visitor center is located at its Palomarin Field Station, at the southern end of the Point Reyes National Seashore. From San Francisco, just take Highway 101 north to the exit marked STINSON BEACH RT. 1. Then exit bearing right, and head to the light at Tam Junction and turn left onto Shoreline Highway. Just after Bolinas Lagoon ends, you'll see an unmarked turnoff to the left; take it, then go 1 block and turn left again, following this road

Bird on a log. I leave it to the birders among you to identify him! DANIELLE BECKER

around to the other side of the lagoon. Turn left at the first stop sign, then right at the second stop—Mesa Road. The observatory is 4 miles down this road.

OUTFITTERS

POINT REYES BIRD OBSERVATORY
Stinson Beach, CA
(headquarters)
(415) 868–1221
www.prbo.org

SAN FRANCISCO WHALE WATCHING
Sausalito, CA
(415) 331–3804 (reservations)
(415) 331–0444
www.sfbaywhalewatching.com

OCEANIC SOCIETY
San Francisco, CA
(800) 326–7491
(415) 474–3385 (reservations)

FOR MORE INFORMATION

FARALLON NATIONAL WILDLIFE
REFUGE
(510) 792–0222
http://pacific.fws.gov/refuges/
field/ca_farallen.htm

GULF OF THE FARALLONES NATIONAL
MARINE SANCTUARY
http://farallones.noaa.gov

RECOMMENDED READING

Fisher, Chris and Joseph Morlan. *Birds of San Francisco and the Bay Area*. Auburn, Wash.: Lone Pine Publishing, 1996.

Kemper, John. *Birding Northern California*. Guilford, Conn.: Falcon, 1999.

National Audubon Society. *National Audubon Society Field Guide to California*. New York: Alfred A. Knopf, 1998.

SLEEP CHEAP

Camping in Point Reyes is a little tougher than it is in most other national park areas—all the sites are backcountry and thus require you to walk to them. However, the Petaluma KOA, located about 30 miles north of San Francisco just off Highway 101, presents a more "civilized" alternative, though you will have to drive just a bit farther to get to your cruise operators and Point Reyes, and pay a tad more to put up your tent. Just visit online (www.koa.com/where/ca/05330) or call (800) 562–1233 for reservations.

Houseboating the California Delta

1,000 Miles of Freedom to Keep under Your Hat

If you're looking for one heck of a way to escape routine's crush, try renting a houseboat. Few activities let you own your downtime in quite the same way and give you such a prime opportunity to be ruler of your vacation realm, if only for a little while. For the duration of your stay, you get to go where you want and take your home away from home with you, *sans* all the things that make hotel living, at times, a major drag: loud, stomping neighbors with 5:00 A.M. wake-up calls; stonefisted cleaning ladies banging at your door long before you're ready to venture from between the sheets; views that range from the Denny's next door to the brick walls of nearby Econolodges.

Yes, hitching a ride on the nearest houseboat presents a bunch of leisure options that you may have never considered before–motoring around all day, exploring new waters while you cook burgers with your onboard grill, or renting a ski boat and cutting your own wakes in between swims. On the other hand, those of you who revel in the Zen idea of relaxing while doing nothing might wish to enjoy your time away from the mainland prone and smiling in a deck chair. Whatever you decide, only you control the tone and direction of your leisure time, and no one–I mean *no one*–is going to deprive you of that wonderful right.

Another huge plus you'll soon figure out: the instant gratification of it all. No need to search out the ol' fishin' hole when you're already floating on it—just drop your line and get angling. The same goes for just about any waterborne activity you can think of. Just motor for a while and you'll get there, or leap off the deck and get wet. Thanks to all these options, houseboating is perfect for family reunions and similar events; while adventurous souls are taking to water skis and wakeboards, tamer folk can enjoy themselves under more relaxed circumstances. Bringing along the toddlers is okay, too, as long as you take proper precautions (e.g., life vests, alert supervision).

If you want to try a dose of this indulgent brand of vacationing, look no further than northern California's not-entirely-famous California Delta, located a short hop from Sacramento and only two hours east of San Francisco. Five major rivers, including the Sacramento and San Joaquin, feed the freshwater delta, which lies just below sea level and boasts an under-the-radar status that makes it largely free of the crowds that occasionally sully more popular attractions. Many Californians, let alone out-of-state visitors, are unaware of the Delta's existence, as evidenced by the area's rural charm; many of the river villages that dot the area have changed little from their Gold Rush days, when the waterways were a tool of commerce rather than recreation. Their ignorance is a little strange, given the 1,000-plus miles of waterway you'll find to explore here, but why ask why—just come out and see what they're missing.

Not to say that recreation hasn't been an important part of the Delta's past. Many Delta-area recreation outfits began operating before World War II and started to take off when the GIs came back and made their way to Cali. Fishing craft made up the bulk of this early pleasure traffic, with some companies boasting fleets of more than one hundred fishing boats. About the same time, people started cruising the Delta in rented houseboats, often using the occasion as their first experience behind the wheel of a watercraft. Today, you still don't need a lot of boating experience to sample the pleasures of the houseboat; in fact, most rental companies will let you out on your own with a little on-the-helm training and instruction.

Once you're out and about, the sheer number of activities the Delta offers will make you wonder how the place manages to stay so incognito. Birding, windsurfing, hunting, swimming, "gunkholing"—the practice of just dropping anchor and hanging out where you stop—are just a few of the pursuits available during your stay here.

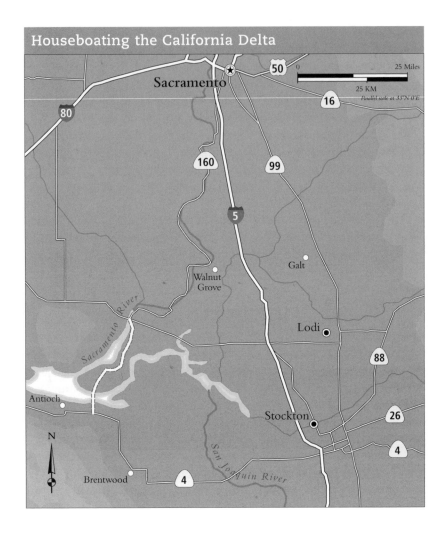

Fishing in particular gives visitors the opportunity to sample the Delta's natural resources; from tiny crawdads, to tasty catfish, to 6-foot catch-and-release sturgeons, the area offers something for experienced anglers and eager novices alike. Even fly fishers will enjoy their time here, as striped and largemouth bass present terrific and plentiful targets. And as if the fishing alone weren't cool enough, there's an added bonus: the cooking setup you'll use to grill up the catch. Nothing tastes better than fresh fish, and you'll be able to throw those fishies on the fire within minutes if you're so inclined. Just bring along your favorite recipes for bass, catfish, shad, and even salmon (along with somebody who can do the gutting!).

Waterskiing is another big-time activity here and has taken on something of a cultural air. Folks do it year-round—using a wet suit or dry suit in the winter—motoring all over the Delta's tributaries. Though there are waterskiing clubs dotting the Delta, some areas are more involved than others; Discovery Bay, for example, features some truly great skiers, as well as frequent exhibitions and competitions. If you're new to the sport, check out one of the area's waterskiing schools to get a leg up and advance quickly through the ranks of surface skimmers. Wakeboarding and barefoot skiing are two more options, depending on just how extreme you've gotten in the past or how extreme you're looking to get. Talk to your houseboat rental company about renting yourself a ski boat during your stay and about where you'll want to ski yourself—based on your skill level and desires, they will point you in the right direction.

The best way to houseboat is to bring along as many buddies as you can. Most boats available for rent in the Delta sleep at least six; more expensive and glitzy boats can accommodate ten or twelve guests but also cost a good deal more. However, think of it this way: If you round up a group of friends or family to come along, you'll end up getting a pretty good deal, even on the more pricey boats. Bringing six to go in on a $1,500 three-day rental works out to be more expensive per person than bringing twelve to go in on a $2,500 rental. (You'll get better amenities on a big boat, too!) Bring more folks, and you'll have more to spend on fun stuff, too—it's easier to get a bunch of people to contribute a couple bucks for a ski boat rental than it is to convince a few to put up real money for one.

If you're the type who feels pushed around, a little too governed by your everyday rituals, rent yourself a houseboat and take charge. Feel like a swim? Then abandon ship. If the grill calls for fish, drop a line and catch dinner for everyone. And if it's calm, floating rest that beckons you, do nothing at all. Whatever you decide, you're the master of the castle and head of your floating household. Just don't tell *too* many people where you're going for that spell of freedom—no reason to crowd the waterways, is there?

Price: $150–$1,000-plus (if you don't get enough friends to tag along!)

(Summer, Easy)

Your houseboat may not look like this behemoth, but it will feature most of the same amenities. CHRIS BECKER

DRIVING DIRECTIONS

The California Delta is located between Stockton and Sacramento and covers over 1,000 waterway miles. Ask your houseboat outfitter exactly where they are located before you head out.

OUTFITTERS

Houseboat Rental Companies

HERMAN & HELEN'S MARINA (ALSO RENTS SKIBOATS AND WAKEBOARDS)
Stockton, CA
(209) 951–4634, (800) 676–4841
www.houseboats.com/herman andhelens

DELTA HOUSEBOAT RENTALS
Walnut Grove, CA
(800) 255–5561 (houseboats)
(916) 776–4270 (marina)
www.deltahouseboats.com

PARADISE POINT MARINA
Irvine, CA
(800) 752–9669
www.sevencrown.com/water
ways/delta.html

Waterski Schools

DISCOVERY BAY
Wakeboard and Ski Center
Byron, CA
(800) 266–7789
www.h2oskiya.com

FOX SAFE BOATING INSTRUCTION
Discovery Bay, CA
(925) 393–9127

FOR MORE INFORMATION

CALIFORNIA DELTA CHAMBERS &
VISITOR'S BUREAU
Lodi, CA
(209) 367–9840
www.californiadelta.org

RECOMMENDED READING

Griffes, Peter L. (ed.). *Pacific Boating Almanac 2003: Northern California
& the Delta.* Ventura, Calif.: Western Marine Enterprises, 2003.

Wing, Charlie. *The Liveaboard Report: A Boat Dweller's Guide to What
Works and What Doesn't.* New York: McGraw-Hill, 1997.

SLEEP CHEAP

The cost of your lodging is included in the adventure.

Road Biking Eureka, Taking in the Six Rivers

On Top of Ol' Cali

Eureka, located *aaaallll* the way up Interstate 101, probably won't make too many day trip itineraries. It takes a long time to get there from just about anywhere, as the immense, largely undeveloped mass of far northern California protects it from the encroachment that has swallowed so many neat little towns farther south. Eureka holds on to its unique character with ease, as there's little reason for large retailers, restaurant companies, and other harbingers of urban sprawl to set up shop here. You won't find a discount store within miles, nor will you see fast-food joints putting their neon to the sky all over town. Instead, you'll find a whole bunch of quaint boulevards, especially in the historic parts of town, where the region's disparate and fascinating history remains vibrant and alive.

Like I said, a day trip this ain't. However, if you venture into the area, you won't want to leave after twenty-four hours anyway. Take your time while you take in all this great history and scenery, and get some exercise while you're at it—bring along the ol' two-wheeler. Biking a town like Eureka gives you ample opportunity to see everything you want to see, along with a little extra time to enjoy the surrounding countryside for a while.

Great thing about Eureka: It's smack in the middle of the Redwood Empire, one of California's most scenic regions, and right outside the Six Rivers National Forest, which stretches from the

Eureka's Victorian architecture comes courtesy of its deep pockets—fish, lumber, and gold made the town a frontier Beverly Hills back in the day. CHRIS BECKER

Oregon border 140 miles down into northern California's remote forest lands. Since you've already got a bike in tow, you might as well use it out here, too—there are miles of great trails throughout the wilderness, though my money says the Smith River region packs the most backcountry punch for bikers. As a use of the time you saved by biking Eureka rather than strolling it, a daylong bike excursion into the forests up here is about as good as it gets.

Eureka has a Victorian air, most likely because you'll see Victorian architecture all over the place. Thanks to its confluence of resources, the folks of Eureka enjoyed a pretty high standard of living back in the day; the miners out along the Trinity and Klamath Rivers found enough gold to keep things interesting, while those who didn't strike it rich got into logging—there were seven mills processing lumber in the town only four years after its founding. Fishing was also an important industry, and even today the Humboldt Bay off Eureka's coast plays host to more than 300 fishing vessels, which land hundreds of tons' worth of salmon, shrimp, oysters, and Dungeness crab every year. Even whaling was an

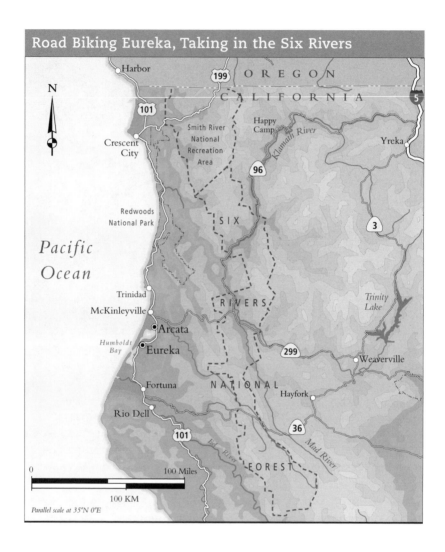

Road Biking Eureka, Taking in the Six Rivers

Harbor

199

O R E G O N

C A L I F O R N I A

5

101

N

Smith River
National
Recreation
Area

Happy
Camp

Klamath River

Yreka

Crescent
City

96

Redwoods
National Park

S I X

3

Pacific

Ocean

Trinidad

R I V E R S

*Trinity
Lake*

McKinleyville

Arcata

*Humboldt
Bay*

Eureka

299

Weaverville

Fortuna

N A T I O N A L

Hayfork

Rio Dell

36

101

Eel River

Mad River

F O R E S T

0

100 Miles

100 KM

Parallel scale at 35°N 0°E

economic pastime, until the residents figured out that the giants were worth far more alive than annihilated.

The city's attractions evoke these former lives in different ways. The Victorian architecture stems from the general prosperity of the place, as well as the ample lumber supply running through the bay on a daily basis. The area's old-growth redwood stands also demonstrate the lumbering appeal of the place—you can cull an unbelievable amount of lumber out of just one huge redwood, and the wood you get is fire resistant, rot resistant, strong, and extremely durable even under tough outdoor conditions. It's no wonder, then, that these beautiful buildings are still standing today, ready for photographing or just simple gawking. Make sure to check out the Carson Mansion, built in 1885 by lumber entrepreneur William Carson—he started the house to keep his mill workers busy during slow times, and their labor paid off in one incredible structure.

The fishing industry has given Eureka another storied heritage: one of excellent seafood. Head to most any good restaurant in town, and you'll get fantastic crab, rockfish, shrimp, and salmon fresh off the dock. And take it from me—you haven't eaten great seafood until you've done so after an all-day bike ride up and down streets as pretty as those of Eureka. Don't let your taste buds miss the experience. And after your meal, take a ride along the Eureka boardwalk to check out boats hauling in the catch, as well as the birds, harbor seals, and other wildlife that call Humboldt Bay home.

Once you're finished tooling around Eureka and you're ready to ride elsewhere, head out to the Smith River National Recreation Area and give yourself a sample of what northern California's outdoor reaches have to offer. In a region rich with nature's treasures, the Smith ranks as one of the most authentic and unspoiled; it's the only major river in California that flows without a dam for its entire length, and more than 300 miles of its length is federally protected— more than any other river in the United States. You may even want to forgo the bike, as this wilderness begs for slow, meandering contemplation.

In any case, whether you decide to stick with your bike or dismount for some hiking, you have mucho trail options to choose from; Little Bald Hills Trail, for example, begins in Jedediah Smith Redwood State Park, near Hiouchi, and travels into the South Fork of the Smith River. The more difficult Elk Camp Ridge Trail was originally a pack train trail between Crescent City and the gold mines of the Illinois Valley in Oregon, and it offers amazing views of sky-reaching mountain peaks, the Pacific, and the Smith River's North and Middle Forks. Bring the fishing rods, too—the steelhead and salmon run heavy here, and the natural isolation of the place makes for a very Zen, placid fishing experience.

Sure, it's a tad isolated, but you'll still find ample draw in and around Eureka—in fact, that isolation isn't such a bad thing, given the relaxed state of affairs it breeds. Sure, the town is a bit touristy— but there's not a lot of reason to come through here unless you're looking for that sort of thing. In other words, if you don't live here, chances are you sought the place out, which makes you a tourist

Bikers enjoying the temperate Eureka summer. CHRIS BECKER

whether you like the designation or not. So enjoy the atmosphere, and don't worry about the tag you'll earn there—just throw that camera around your neck, put your feet on the pedals, and get to touring. **Price: $50–$200 (depending on bike rental and accommodations)** *(Summer, Medium)*

DRIVING DIRECTIONS

Eureka is located at the intersection of Highways 101 and 299 (which leads to Redding, California). Smith River NRA is a bit farther north, close to Crescent City. Head up Highway 101 to Highway 199 east and enter the forest area.

OUTFITTERS

SIX RIVERS NATIONAL FOREST
Eureka, CA
(707) 442–1721
www.fs.fed.us/r5/sixrivers/

FOR MORE INFORMATION

EUREKA CHAMBER OF COMMERCE
(707) 442-3738
www.eurekachamber.com

RECOMMENDED READING

Burdick, George. *California's Smith River Steelhead and Salmon.* Portland, Ore.: Frank Amato Publications, 1993.

Fragnoli, Delaine and Robin Stuart. *Mountain Biking Northern California's Best 100 Trails.* Anacortes, Wash.: Fine Edge Productions, 2000.

Newcombe, Jack. *Northern California: A History and Guide—From Napa to Eureka.* New York: Random House, 1986.

SLEEP CHEAP

Smith River NRA has four campgrounds, which make for ideal accommodations during the summer. Prices run from $8.00 to $14.00 per night. If you're not too worried about cost, look into reserving the Bear Basin Butte Lookout, an old fire lookout with a 1930s-style cabin on the ground below. It's $75.00 per night, and you still need to bring all your camping supplies (though firewood is provided). You can also bring up to eight people, which makes the price better than right. This super-unique living arrangement gives you the chance to see some incredible scenery, as well as camp in a one-of-a-kind environment. Call (707) 457-3131 for questions and reservations.

Learning to Surf in Santa Cruz

The Birthplace of Cool

Golf makes its home at Pebble Beach. Alcatraz is a triathlete's mecca, while the Yosemite wilderness draws photographers from around the world eager to follow in the footsteps of Ansel Adams. Yet among the superlatives of California, where all kinds of outdoor activities find their greatest expression, one native adventure defines the state for millions around the world. I'm talking about surfing, of course, and its place of pilgrimage along the NoCal coast: beautiful Santa Cruz, home of the Santa Cruz Surfing Museum and the perfect place to catch your first swell.

Polynesians started riding the waves way out in the Pacific as early as 1500, according to petroglyphs found on volcanic stone in Hawaii. The Hawaiian kings used surfing to assert their dominance over their subjects and to test their strength and agility. Modern surfing was born from a resurgence of the sport on Waikiki Beach back in the early twentieth century, a movement that led the way for surfing's rise along beaches all over the Pacific. In 1907 Californian Henry Huntington brought a board to Redondo Beach down in Los Angeles, and the California surf culture was born. The scene soon evolved into one of intense innovation and experimentation; California saw the first short boards (earlier boards were more than 15 feet long), along with Styrofoam boards and fins. The 1950s and '60s saw California surf culture begin to explode, with Dick Dale and the Beach Boys picking out the tunes while Frankie and Annette brought the lingo, style, and attitude to Middle America. Beyond all the hype, though, was a challenging, liberating sport coming into its prime and poised to grow through the next few decades into a pastime and lifestyle that would attract people from around the country and the world to California's swells and sand.

Santa Cruz came by its stellar reputation via some spectacular surf. Its location on the north end of the Monterey Bay puts it right in the middle of a huge variety of waves, from the massive pounders at Half Moon Bay to the gentle, friendly surf of Cowells Beach, a beginner's paradise. The water is fairly chilly year-round, never rising much above 50 or 60 degrees; as a result, you'll want to bring your wet suit if you already have one (all the surf schools mentioned here will provide you with one if you're just getting started). The days are pleasant in the summer, with temperatures edging a bit over 70, but the winters can get pretty chilly—obviously, you want to hit the area in the summertime for maximum surf potential, but a few of the schools below teach all year. Just get in touch after you know when you'll be in town, but count on the best time being the warmer months.

Before you set out to learn to surf, decide what exactly you want from your surfing experience. Each outfitter in Santa Cruz offers different programs for nascent beach bums; some are longer and involve a lot of perks, while others are simply a few hours of lessons, with rental equipment available if you feel like continuing on your own.

Santa Cruz Surf School, for example, conducts its classes on Cowells Beach and provides both private and group lessons. Beginners are, for the most part, better off in the group setting; more experienced surfers should get into private education, as should small children who might hold back a larger class of older surfers. In the intro phases, you'll learn how to stand up and control your board, as well as rules and etiquette of the surf, very important things to know when a bunch of people with large, heavy boards complete with sharp fins are sharing the same water. More advanced students will take on more specific maneuvers like cross-stepping and duck-diving.

The Richard Schmidt School of Surfing offers two-hour lessons in a small group setting, along with longer surf camps for both adults and the kids. These camps require a bit more commitment on your part—they last five days—but by the time you're done, you'll be

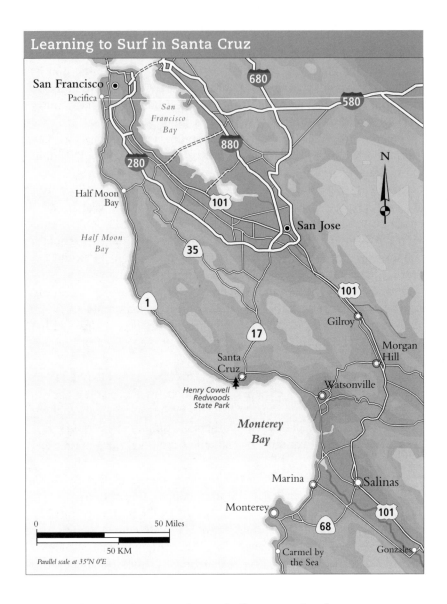

too cool for school, having learned all you need to know to get surfing on your own. You don't have to be a beginner to enjoy the surf camp, though, as even more advanced surfers can benefit from instruction in technique, fitness, and diet. You won't concentrate solely on the surfing, either, as camping, nature hiking, and surf industry tours are also on the menu. You'll have to bring your own sleeping bag, but all the food and equipment is provided—it makes for a pretty inexpensive five days, all told.

Club Ed is another Santa Cruz school that will take you on for a longer period or just give you lessons for the day you decide to hit the waves. Ed himself has been the surfing instructor at the University of California—Santa Cruz since 1991 and has more than sixteen years of teaching experience under his belt. Club Ed's surf camp is a seven-day affair, complete with a surfboard factory tour, a massage on the fourth day (great for working out surfboard soreness), and video coaching methods that will have you seeing exactly what you want to do better on your next wave. These few aren't the only schools in town, either—check with all the schools listed below to see which one suits you best, and don't be afraid to ask questions.

For a history lesson after your surf lesson, head over to the Mark Abbott Memorial Lighthouse, home to the Santa Cruz Surfing Museum. Here you'll find one hundred years of California's surfing history laid out before you, much of it directly related to Santa Cruz itself. Check out old-school longboards, video clips demonstrating the sport's evolution over the years, and other artifacts of all kinds. You'll also get a spectacular view of Steamer Lane, one of the world's most famous surf spots, as well as the rest of the heartbreakingly gorgeous Monterey Bay.

The surfing lifestyle represents one of California's everlasting contributions to the world. Though Hawaii may have been its birthplace, California made surfing the huge, multi-million-dollar industry it is today and brought the culture into the spotlight of notoriety. A trip to Santa Cruz, along with a few hours of surf school, will put you into close contact with this famous community of wave shredders and perhaps persuade you to pick out a board of your own and start owning beaches nearer to you.

Price: Starting at $70–$90 for your first lesson. Follow-up lessons are typically cheaper, though, so if you go for the weekend and take two or three lessons, you'll get a better deal. Multiple-day surf camps can get a little more pricey—more than $1,000 for Club Ed, for example—but you'll be a much better surfer when you come out the other end of the training.

(Summer, Medium)

Heading out to rip some curls. © BRAND X PICTURES/ANDREW SARNECKI

DRIVING DIRECTIONS

Santa Cruz is located on the northern part of Monterey Bay, about 74 miles south of San Francisco and 30 miles from San Jose. Just hop on Interstate 17 from San Jose, and you're there; from San Francisco, take Highway 101 south to Highway 85 south, then take the exit for I–17 headed south.

OUTFITTERS

CLUB ED SURF SCHOOL
(800) 287–7873
www.club-ed.com

GIRLSADVENTUREOUT (GEARED MORE TOWARD WOMEN, THOUGH MEN AND KIDS ARE ALSO WELCOME)
Pacifica, CA (lessons in Santa Cruz)
(650) 557–0641
www.girlsadventureout.com

RICHARD SCHMIDT SCHOOL OF SURFING
Santa Cruz, CA
(831) 423–0928
www.richardschmidt.com

SANTA CRUZ SURF SCHOOL (LESSONS AT COWELLS BEACH)
Santa Cruz, CA
(831) 426–7072
www.santacruzsurfschool.com

FOR MORE INFORMATION

SANTA CRUZ SURFING MUSEUM
Santa Cruz, CA
(831) 420–6119
www.santacruzsurfingmuseum.org

RECOMMENDED READING

Afcari, Kia and Mary Osborne. *Sister Surfer: A Woman's Guide to Surfing with Bliss and Courage.* Guilford, Conn.: Lyons Press, 2005.

Duane, Daniel. *Caught Inside: A Surfer's Year on the California Coast.* New York: North Point Press, 1997.

Earle, Sylvia. *Sea Change: A Message of the Oceans*. New York: Ballantine Books, 1996.

Guisado, Raul and Jeff Klaas. *Surfing California*. Guilford, Conn.: Falcon, 2005.

MacLaren, James. *Learn to Surf*. Guilford, Conn.: Lyons Press, 1997.

Werner, Doug. *Surfer's Start-Up: A Beginner's Guide to Surfing*. Chula Vista, Calif.: Tracks Publishing, 1999.

SLEEP CHEAP

Henry Cowell Redwoods State Park is located just outside Santa Cruz—a perfect place to rest when you're done shredding waves. Campsites are available all year except in the winter for a great price ($13 to $16 a night), along with some nice amenities (visitor center, showers, bookstore). Call (800) 444-7275 for reservations or (831) 438-2396 for campground information.

Northern California Dude Ranching

Get Along, Li'l Dogies!

After doing some gold panning, observing the beautiful mustangs of Pizona, or just delving into California's frontier history, you might feel a small twinge of disappointment, as if you've missed out on something special. You might say to yourself, "I could have ridden the range, broken wild steeds, driven an ocean of steer 200 miles! If I'd only been born a century and a half earlier!" Well, put your money where your mouth is, pilgrim, and saddle up at one of northern California's dude ranches. Go ahead and prove you're not the city slicker everybody takes you for. And while you're at it, bring the whole clan—there's something for everyone at these cowboy-style getaways, even if not everybody's as ready to take on the range as you are.

Northern California boasts some great ranches, places that cater to just about any group of vacationers you can think of. What's more, most of them go out of their way to draw families of would-be riders and ropers (though you single adventurers looking for an authentic Old West experience can have a grand old time, too). These ranches dot the vast, wild landscape and are usually a little drive away if you're staying in more urban surroundings, but they are well worth your time and the effort to reach them.

Be prepared to spend a little money on this adventure, as rates can run somewhat high. The upside is that nightly or package prices

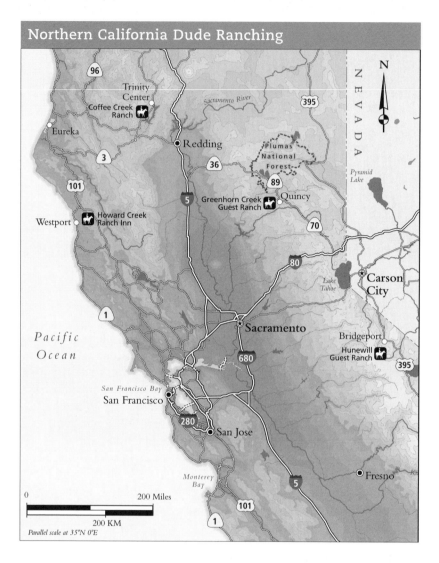

often include a lot more than the roof over your head—all three meals (home-cooked by your hosts at most places) are usually provided, as are a majority of your activities (riding, learning to brand, even throwing a lasso). Be aware, though, that some ranches will charge extra for certain activities, so make sure you know what you're in for wallet-wise before you go. The best way to keep your costs down is to round up as many people as possible to take on the adventure; usually, rates drop significantly when you bring a team of cowpokes with you.

When looking for the perfect ranch, don't stop after one phone call. Northern California boasts a few high-quality ranches, all of which have different things going for them. You've got everything from authentic, working ranches that allow you to drive cattle with the wranglers to Western-style resorts that offer a variety of tourist-related amenities along with their ranch activities. Coffee Creek Ranch, for example, definitely falls into the resort category, but with great Western ambience to boot. It boasts a gaggle of non-horse related activities—pool, spa, pedal boats, shuffleboard—as well as great nearby attractions like historic Weaverville and the Trinity Alps wilderness. You can enjoy hiking, mountain biking, hunting, and trout fishing right down the road, if you need some respite from life at the ranch.

And let's not forget about the riding! Coffee Creek offers overnight wilderness pack trips on horseback, as well as morning and afternoon rides just about every day. As far as the kids' stuff goes, you won't be disappointed, either—all summer, kid-specific programs decorate the calendar. Your very little ones will get pony rides, story times, and gold panning adventures; older kids have the chance to learn roping and riding and can even try their hand at trapshooting if they're up to it.

Another ranch with great kid skills is Greenhorn Creek, located just outside of Quincy. The million-acre Plumas National Forest will serve as your playground here; you'll have two rides every day to see as much of it as you can. You can do it all with a clear con-science, too, because the kids are in good hands—there's an on-ranch petting zoo, as well as the "Kiddie Corral," where little ones who can't hit the trail yet will enjoy pony rides, crafts, and enough fun to beat the band. Grown-ups looking for a different type of Western fun will be happy to know that no fewer than nine quality golf courses lie nearby, thanks to the ranch's proximity to Reno and Lake Tahoe. This location is also a bonus when night falls, though you can have a heckuva time without leaving the ranch, too—it boasts an on-site saloon, square dancing, friendly card games, and other welcome forms of "city" entertainment once the sun sets, along with more traditional campfire sing-a-longs.

For those of you without children, Howard Creek Ranch Inn, located on the incredible Mendocino coast, provides a more romantic yet adventurous vibe. Horses are available courtesy of nearby Ricochet Ridge Ranch, which has a stable full of beautiful Arabians, Russian Orlovs, and Appaloosas, among others. You can ride along the surf or

To ensure your most authentic cowpoke's pose, please remember to bring your hat and the spurs that jingle-jangle. FRANCINE GARRIGUS

up into the redwood-studded mountains, and if you're already an experienced rider, Ricochet offers steeds with both Western and English riding experience. Once you've taken your ride, Howard Creek will impress you with its other offerings—beautiful farm-style surroundings complete with livestock, German massage services, delectable breakfast menus, and excellent bird-watching. Head here, and bring your significant other, if you're the "gentleman rancher" type with more on your agenda than just good horsebacking.

Finally, those looking for more authentic, less touristy ranching should call on Hunewill Guest Ranch, founded in 1861 and eager to bring you out on the cattle drivin' trail. Hunewill is a working ranch, with more than 1,200 head of cattle and 120 horses in its stable. More advanced riders will love the chance to learn how to rope, part out, and track the cattle, as well as the rare opportunity to learn about "cow logic" from people who deal with it every day. For maximum authenticity, you should tag along for the ranch work that takes place a few times throughout the year, in which the cowboys drive the cattle with a little help from you. Keep in mind that these drives are not for the weak or the novice; typical days involve a lot of time in the saddle through some rough country, and you need to know what you're doing on horseback before you think about going. (You may even want to bring your own horse, if you have one and it's well broken.) However, it is hardship well worth the memories, the skills, and the incredible backcountry pictures you might capture on the way.

There are other ranches throughout California, both in the north and south. Again, keep in mind that each ranch caters to a certain customer, and their facilities and emphases are geared in specific directions. This is mostly because ranches tend to be small, family-run operations that work best with their preferred clientele. Just do your homework, and you'll have no trouble finding just the right ranch for your particular set of needs.

Rides on the range, home-cooked meals, and more fun diversions than you can shake a stick at—that is what California's ranches are all about. So come out and experience the West firsthand, and the next time you see a rodeo while you're flipping through the channels, you'll be able to say, "I could do that," and mean it.

Price: $200–$500-plus
(Summer, Medium)

DRIVING DIRECTIONS

The ranch you choose will give you detailed directions on how to reach it.

OUTFITTERS

COFFEE CREEK RANCH
Trinity Center, CA
(530) 266–3343, (800) 624–4480
www.coffeecreekranch.com

GREENHORN CREEK GUEST RANCH
Quincy, CA
(530) 283–0930, (800) 334–6939
www.greenhornranch.com

HOWARD CREEK RANCH INN
Westport, CA
(707) 964–6725
www.howardcreekranch.com

HUNEWILL GUEST RANCH (SUMMER)
Bridgeport, CA
(760) 932–7710;
winter number: (775) 465–2201
www.hunewillranch.com

FOR MORE INFORMATION

GUEST RANCHES OF NORTH AMERICA
www.guestranches.com

RECOMMENDED READING

Erickson, John R. and Fay E. Ward. *The Cowboy at Work: All About His Job and How He Does It*. Norman, Okla.: University of Oklahoma Press, 1987.

Morris, Michele. *The Cowboy Life: A Saddlebag Guide for Dudes, Tenderfeet, and Cow Punchers Everywhere*. New York: Fireside, 1993.

Starrs, Paul F. *Let the Cowboy Ride: Cattle Ranching in the American West (Creating the North American Landscape)*. Baltimore: Johns Hopkins University Press, 2000.

Sea Kayaking Tomales Bay

Paddling on Your Own Time

You've done everything you can think of on land—you've hiked over hill and dale, rode your bike down all the right single tracks, and even climbed a few sheer rock faces. But you somehow feel like you're missing something, namely the spectacular scenery right out there, where the Pacific meets the California coast. Sure, you've spent some time on the beach—California law requires it, you think—but you haven't got much past that, haven't explored the possibilities that await you out there beyond the breakers.

You won't find a much better way to start your offshore adventuring than kayaking, or sea kayaking, more specifically. Sea kayaking is exactly what it sounds like—take a kayak and start paddling out into the deep blue water until the vestiges of civilization peel away, and you're left with a whole lot of wild seashore and yourself, all alone and in each other's company. You'll get the opportunity to camp in places that are unreachable via land routes, as well as the ultimate backwoods responsibility: You'll have to pack in everything you need and pack out everything you'd normally leave. There are other ways to camp in true backcountry style, but none that lets you see the same combination of scenery and wildlife you'll get on an overnight kayaking trip into one of California's prettiest backcountries.

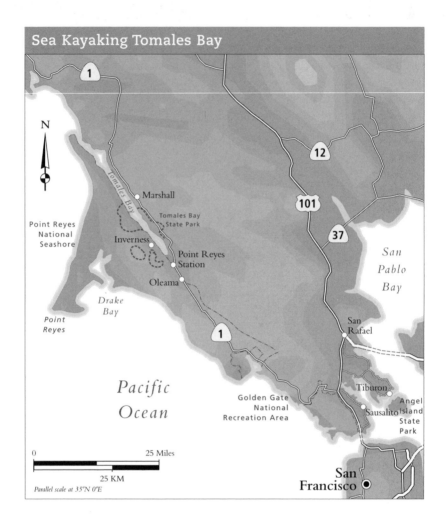

N

Tomales Bay

1

12

Marshall

Tomales Bay
State Park

101

37

Point Reyes
National
Seashore

Inverness

Point Reyes
Station

San
Pablo
Bay

Oleama

Drake
Bay

Point
Reyes

San
Rafael

Pacific

Ocean

Golden Gate
National
Recreation Area

Tiburon

Angel
Island
State
Park

Sausalito

0   25 Miles

25 KM

Parallel scale at 35°N 0°E

San
Francisco

Right off Point Reyes National Seashore, you'll find this piece of paradise open for business: Tomales Bay, a 15-mile tidal water that happens to be the largest unspoiled coastal embayment on the California coast—an impressive distinction, given California's many beautiful and pristine bay areas. On the west banks, you'll find the national seashore, but tucked within it, and across the bay on the east side, you'll find another smaller jewel: Tomales Bay State Park, 2,000 acres featuring four beautiful surf-free beaches. These are worthy stops on your kayaking tour, though you can't spend the night; for your campsite, you'll be sticking to the west bank, namely the six beaches that allow overnight boat-in camping.

These beaches provide different levels of amenities, and a few may see closures due to wildlife use (namely Blue Gum Beach, where harbor seals give birth to their pups). Check with the Seashore reservation office for the status of every beach, as well as to buy your permit. Also: Do *not* camp anywhere but these six beaches—they are broken in for your use. Breaking in a new area damages the ecosystem in that area, and it's not your job to do that. Follow the regulations—some rules are made to be broken, but not these.

That goes for the rules of low-impact camping, too. When you get to your campsite, a quick look around will tell you how to conduct yourself. If there's an outhouse, for example, go ahead and use it; if not, you're packing out *all* the waste you create. To build a campfire, you'll need to acquire a free permit at the national park's visitor centers, though you can never use the driftwood you'll find to fuel such fires. Instead, bring along pine or almond wood to burn, but don't bring any oak because there's no way to know if the logs you're carrying are free of organisms that carry sudden oak death. Also, don't build your fire near overhanging branches or large piles of driftwood. (Yes, it's common sense, but the fact that I need to say it demonstrates that there are enough idiots who have done it to warrant the warning.) And make sure you keep a careful eye on your food supply, including the scraps. The campsites you'll be nesting in are true backcountry, and leaving food lying around is tantamount to tempting the beasties to get a little too close.

Obviously, the best defense against emergency is common sense—bring enough to drink and eat, and make sure all your equipment is good to go before you set out. Bring extra dry clothes, and pay attention to your traveling partners—at the first signs of exhaustion, sunstroke, or any other adventure-related ailment, get yourself to shore. Be smart on the water, and you'll come through your escape with exactly what you want: a good time.

Kayaking Tomales has become more and more popular over the last couple decades, and today quite a few companies conduct guided day and overnight tours into the bay. Blue Waters Kayaking, for example, offers a variety of ways to help you camp Tomales, from weekend kayak rentals (kayaks with storage for your gear, of course) to guide services and motorboat support, meaning they will motor your gear in to your campsite. Blue Water also offers lessons, if you want to get your kayaking skills up to par before taking on longer paddles. Kayak Connection out of Santa Cruz offers overnight trips, too—just give a call for the details—as does Current Adventures, along

Paddling out to the good stuff. Make sure you pack out everything you pack in when you camp out of your boat—mom doesn't work on the Tomales Bay beaches.
ROBERT HOLMES/CALTOUR

with a variety of other kayak tours in California and beyond. As usual, talk to all the companies below, see who offers what you want, and start planning for your paddle. Twilight trips, moonlight paddles, all-day sessions—check out the offerings first, then start deciding.

You won't want to hit Tomales unguided if you've never done any kayaking before, at least not for the kind of overnight trip I'm talking about here. If you do have some paddling experience, though, just remember to be careful. First off, don't paddle too hard—you'll disturb the wildlife beneath and around you. Don't get yourself out too far away from shore, either, and keep open water crossings as direct as possible—you never know when conditions can drop out on you. Wind can change quicker than you think, and the tides in and around Tomales, particularly at the mouth of the bay, can create some strong currents. With conditions like this, you'll want to make sure you set out with the right information in hand; keeping a transistor radio with you to monitor the weather is a good call, and checking the tide charts before you set out will help you stay out of the mudflats at the lower end of the bay when the water level drops.

Tomales Bay and Point Reyes represent everything great about California's coastal backcountry—beautiful scenery, prominent and plentiful wildlife, and activities that keep you young. Particularly if you're looking for an alternative to your backpack and bike rack, check with the outfitters below and book a trip. And if you already have the kayaking bug, there's no better place to get your first experience in boat camping than out here, where the shore meets the ocean. Throw that boat in the back of the truck and head out.

Price: Kayaking—even with a guide-isn't that pricey. Lessons run between $50 and $100, while guided day trips are about $100 on average. Multiple-day trips will obviously run you a little more, but you're usually getting your food included, too, along with a big helping of recreation courtesy of your guide and the folks you're paddling with.

(Summer, Medium)

DRIVING DIRECTIONS

Tomales Bay and Point Reyes National Seashore lie just off Highway 1, north of San Francisco. Call the outfitter you decide to go with to see where they'll be launching from. If you're bringing your own kayak, you can launch from four areas: Miller County Park, also known as Nick's Cove; Tomales Bay State Park, which has two launch sites (Millerton Point on the east side of the bay and Hearts Desire Beach on the west); Golden Hinde Inn and Marina, also located on the west side (you can leave your car overnight here, too); and Lawson's Landing, where you'll find gas, a dump station, and boat rentals, as well as a parking lot where you can park overnight (for a fee).

OUTFITTERS

BLUE WATER KAYAKING
(415) 663–1743 (reservations)
www.bwkayak.com

CURRENT ADVENTURES
Lotus, CA
(888) 452–9254
www.kayaking.com

KAYAK CONNECTION
Santa Cruz, CA
(831) 479–1121
www.kayakconnection.com

SEA TREK OCEAN KAYAKING CENTER
Sausalito, CA
(415) 488–1000
www.seatrekkayak.com

FOR MORE INFORMATION

POINT REYES NATIONAL SEASHORE
(415) 464–5100
www.nps.gov/pore

TOMALES BAY STATE PARK
(415) 669–1140
www.parks.ca.gov/?page_id=470

GOLDEN HINDE INN
Inverness, CA
(800) 339–9398
www.goldenhindeinn.com

RECOMMENDED READING

Alderson, Doug. *Sea Kayaker's Savvy Paddler: More Than 500 Tips for Better Kayaking*. New York: Ragged Mountain Press, 2001.

Glickman, Joe. *The Kayak Companion*. North Adams, Mass.: Storey Books, 2003.

Pike, Charlie. *Paddling Northern California.* Guilford, Conn.: Falcon, 2001.

SLEEP CHEAP

The best way to go about camping is to do it from your boat, either with a guide or without one if you think you're ready. Otherwise, camping is available in Point Reyes, though all the campsites are backcountry, meaning there are no drive-up spots. For your boat camping privileges, call (415) 663–8054 for information on getting the proper permit (they'll send it to you). Beach fire permits are also required; you can get these for free at park visitor centers.

Llama Trekking in the Marble Mountains

Have Camelid, Will Travel

Horses, mules, and donkeys, dogs and cats, cows and pigs, llamas...
Llamas?

The noble llama, favorite pack animal of the South American
Andes, suffers from a credibility gap here in the good old USA compared to better-known domestic animals. Though most 5-year-olds
have seen llamas at their local petting zoos, and most adults could
describe the beasts if you asked them to, few people here really
know anything about them. Everyone knows what pigs are good for,
and what horses can do, and how to act around dogs. But llamas
are a different story. Even worse, much of what we do know is
tainted by ignorance—they spit, they're nasty, they smell bad. In
other words, they're good for not biting the little kids who want to
pull on their coats for a few minutes but little else.

If you are thinking these thoughts as you read this, or have
thought them, I have only one thing to say: how wrong you are.

Llamas are members of the camel (Camelid) family and are
descended from wild creatures called guanacos, which still roam the
planet today. About 5,000 to 6,000 years ago, man domesticated the
first llamas, making them among the world's oldest domesticated
animals and an important part of the local economy at that time
and since. While their humped cousins headed to sunnier climes and
evolved their famous water storage systems, the llamas developed

thick, warm coats to deal with the cold weather that buffets the mountainous reaches of the Andes. The natives used their flesh for food, their hides for shelter and clothing, and their manure for fuel, but only after they served their purposes in life as beasts of burden.

Today, the estimated seven million llamas in South America serve a variety of purposes, from traditional pack animal to source for mass-produced wool. There are somewhere around 100,000 in the United States, too, many of which are involved in one of the llama's oldest professions: trekking.

Generally, camping is a minimalist experience. You put a lot of energy into deciding what *not* to take with you, and make sure that your pack is filled only with the stuff you'll absolutely need. In fact, many of us, particularly those with children or physical limitations, would love to hit the backcountry but can't because it means carrying far more than our bodies can handle. In a llama trek, however, there's not much need to limit your load; llamas can comfortably carry between a quarter and a third of their body weight, and they weigh in at a stocky 300 to 450 pounds. As a result, you can bring in all the food you want, all the camp supplies you want, and even some fun things that might never make it into a pack that's going on your own aching back.

What's more, llamas are more environmentally friendly than other domestic animals—because they walk on soft, padded feet akin to sneakers, llamas won't clip up the plants they tread on or leave the significant trail damage some other animals do. They also possess great agility and can leap over obstacles that might stymie other pack animals. These factors, coupled with their intelligence and composure on the trail, make llamas great hiking companions and allow for a completely new and different wilderness experience.

One more thing: Llamas spit primarily at each other to assert dominance and otherwise communicate, though occasionally they may spit at people who mistreat them. Unless you are either a llama or an idiot, you have little to worry about. As a precaution, however, pay attention to where you are—this way, you will likely avoid getting caught in the middle of a llama debate complete with flying fluids.

Northern California presents great opportunities for llama trekkers—there's plenty of unspoiled wilderness, along with cooler temperatures that keep the llama's heavy coat useful. For a llama primer, try a day or half-day excursion, meant to demonstrate the benefits of traveling with a creature that can carry a whole lot more

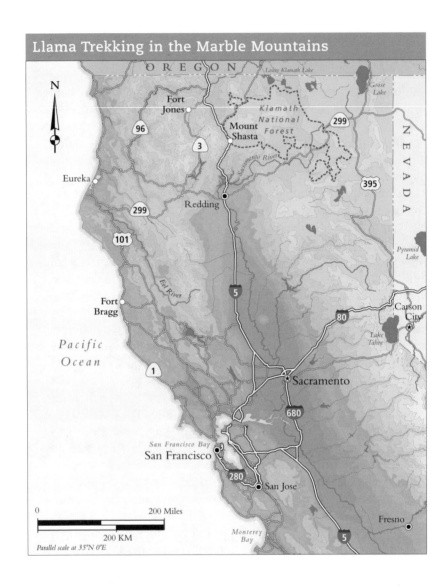

than you can. Full gourmet lunches are a frequent perk, complete
with tables and chairs; large camera rigs, art supplies, and even
musical instruments are all A-OK, too, provided that they fit in the
llama's pack and fall within the aforementioned weight requirements. Typically, each participant will be permitted about 15 to 20
pounds of gear, as there are generally more people than animals.
However, given that your weight allowance won't include food or

other camp gear, you should be able to bring everything you want to and more.

Northern California's llama outfitters offer a variety of hiking options. At Lodging and Llamas, located near Fort Bragg on the coast, you'll get cozy cottage rentals with your llama adventure. Rather, you'll get your llama adventure with the rental—a one-week stay comes complete with a free trek on Ten Mile Beach, located along a protected stretch of northern California's incomparable coast. If you can't stay that long, no problem: Their llama treks are still quite reasonable and include truly wonderful lunches (when was the last time you ate veggie lasagna on the trail?).

If you're looking for more intense person-to-llama bonding, check with the wonderful folks at the Broken Wheel Ranch, located near the Klamath National Forest and Mt. Shasta. Owners and guides Judy and David Inghram offer catered trips for extremely reasonable daily rates, given that you're getting all the food and supplies you need without having to carry much of anything. They operate by special permit in the Klamath National Forest area and present trekkers with a variety of trips to choose from, ranging from fairly simple jaunts to more strenuous hikes. Broken Wheel advertises shorter day hikes and three- to five-day trips but can customize trips according to the needs of the trippers.

Hiking can be a pain in the back, especially if you want to live the good life while on the trail. Why not enlist some help, so you can have your trail mix and maybe eat some gourmet chicken pesto, too? It's about time you made a new hiking buddy anyway.

Price: $100–$500-plus

(Summer, Medium)

DRIVING DIRECTIONS

Broken Wheel Ranch runs a number of trips into the Marble Mountain Wilderness, a part of the Klamath National Forest in Siskiyou County. You can access this area via Highway 96 between Hamburg and Somes Bar, Highway 3 from the Scott River Road between Scott Bar and Fort Jones, or from Highway 3 via the Etna-Somes Bar Road.

Llamas might smell a little funny to you, but imagine how you smell to them. *Ewww.* CHRIS BECKER

OUTFITTERS

LODGING AND LLAMAS
Fort Bragg, CA
(707) 964–7191
www.lodgingandllamas.com

BROKEN WHEEL RANCH
Fort Jones, CA
(530) 468–2559
www.llamapacktrips.com

RECOMMENDED READING

Daugherty, Stanlynn. *Packing With Llamas*. Broadview Heights, Ohio: Pine Grove Publishing Company, 1994.

Green, David and Greg Ingold. *Marble Mountain Wilderness*. Berkeley, Calif.: Wilderness Press, 1996.

Lewon, Dennis. *Hiking California's Trinity Alps*. Guilford, Conn.: Falcon, 2001.

SLEEP CHEAP

It may not be the cheapest place you've ever stayed, but for all you get, Lodging and Llamas is a great choice. There are two cottages to choose from, each of which features a lovely garden setting, outdoor spas, and enough room to sleep seven or eight (depending on which one you choose). Remember—the more llama packers you bring, the lower the price. Call for availability and to make reservations.

Off-roading the Rubicon Trail

Boulders like Volkswagens

There's off-roading—dirt roads to the campground, stone pathways to trailheads, and such. Then there's *off*-roading, or driving on paths that barely resemble roads, conquering rocky slopes as you test both the vehicle and yourself. Trails that present this sort of challenge are more rare than the former kind, but they present a unique opportunity to traverse terrain that, from a distance, looks like only rock climbing gear could get you over.

The undisputed king of these bad country trails, located between Lake Tahoe and Georgetown, is the Rubicon, perhaps the best-known off-road trail in the country and certainly one of the toughest. Taking your vehicle of choice to the Rubicon is sure to stretch your backcountry driving skills to their limits and push the vehicle you drive to its breaking point. But know what you're doing going in, follow the rules, and be careful along the trail, and you'll be in for the commute of a lifetime.

Off-highway vehicles (OHVs) come in all kinds of different shapes and sizes. Dirt bikes and ATVs fall in here, as do Jeeps, dune buggies, SUVs, and trucks suited up for the backcountry. Even snowmobiles fall into the OHV category, with good reason—when the snow falls, it's the only one of these vehicles worth its salt off the plowed and salted byways. Obviously, you need a fair amount of gear (i.e., an OHV) and some skill to navigate any of these machines over rough roads or white drifts; driving the Rubicon is possible in just about any of them. Obviously, the more off-road customizing you do, the better, and there are companies out there that can help you do it (see outfitters below). But people have driven the Rubicon with basic SUVs, trucks, and even mountain bikes, as well as with customized, badass backcountry machines. Don't be afraid to bring the old grocery getter out here, but be careful, and don't try to do anything you can't handle.

The time you choose to run the Rubicon is vital, as certain seasons are more likely to cause trail damage. July and August are the most popular months and the best time to make the drive—there's no snow, and conditions tend to be pretty dry. Wet conditions mean you'll be carving the ground and messing it up for people who come after you. Set out too early in the year, even in late May, and you take the chance of degrading the road and maybe even getting into danger. Run in the high season, and the trail will thank you. Another side benefit is the companionship you'll find out there; four-wheeling is best done in a social setting, where you can depend on other people for help if you need it, and vice versa.

A few words of caution, especially if you haven't driven your SUV or truck in off-road conditions like these: Those big boys may be rugged, but they are not invincible. They cannot go everywhere, and you absolutely should not blaze side trails through the wilderness, even if you think you can. Not only might you smash up your prized ride, but you also may end up destroying some of the very wilderness you came to see.

The various Rubicon gurus mentioned at the end of this chapter can provide you with proper guidelines, but they're mostly common sense—stay on paths, pack out everything you pack in, etc. Contrary to beliefs in some environmentalist quarters, it's possible to enjoy off-roading without destroying the environment you're moving through. A few bad apples have managed to turn large parts of the conservationist community against off-roaders, putting them in the same category as hunters—a bit misunderstood at best, demonized at worst. To avoid adding to this confusion, get educated and follow all the rules of the trail. Don't prove the critics right, and off-roaders who follow you may have an easier time hitting the trail.

As if you didn't know, there are few things worse than running out of fuel 50 miles from the nearest major road—forget to bring the essentials, and you may find yourself in serious trouble. One gallon of water per person per day is the minimum. Several military MREs

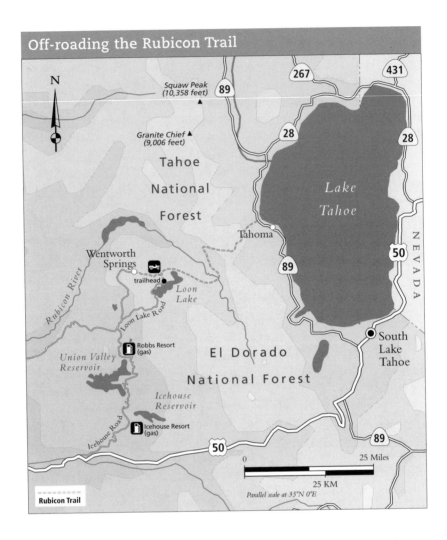

Squaw Peak
(10,358 feet) 89

267

431

Granite Chief ▲
(9,006 feet)

28

28

Tahoe

National

Forest

Lake
Tahoe

Tahoma

Wentworth
Springs

50

trailhead

Loon
Lake

89

Rubicon River

Loon Lake Road

Robbs Resort
(gas)

El Dorado

South
Lake
Tahoe

Union Valley
Reservoir

National Forest

NEVADA

Icehouse
Reservoir

Icehouse Road

Icehouse Resort
(gas)

50

89

0

25 Miles

- - - - - - - - - -
Rubicon Trail

25 KM

Parallel scale at 35°N 0°E

(Meals Ready to Eat), high-energy bars, and other long-shelf-life foods should have a place in your vehicle, too, in addition to whatever trip goodies you tote along in the cooler. Finally, if you don't know how to change a tire, the spare won't do much good—so know basic maintenance procedures if you don't already. For these reasons, I repeat: Make your off-roading a social activity. Having a couple fellow OHVs along will help if you need towing or (worst-case scenario) you need a ride home.

You don't need any special permits on the Rubicon—after all, it's just a backcountry road in really, really bad shape, when you get down to it. Any street-legal vehicle with a California plate is okay; if you've got an off-road-only vehicle, you'll have to get a sticker from the Department of Motor Vehicles. Green stickers allow vehicles to operate on public land all year, while red ones apply to motorcycles and ATVs that can only run during certain times of the year due to their emissions. Contact the state's off-road rec authorities to make sure you have the permissions you need to run the trail and others like it.

If you're not too keen on bringing your own ride out to the Rubicon, Lake Tahoe Adventures can lead you on a one-day excursion over the trail, using ATVs rather than larger rock crawlers. These vehicles will let you avoid some of the bigger travails out there, and the company runs the trail just about every day in the summer and fall. They've got tons of experience out there, and as a result they can show you the safest, best way to get down the road. After this ride, you'll have a nice start on trail knowledge and the ability to come back with an idea of what you'll face.

Off-roading is fun no matter where you are, but certain trails are more than just a pleasant drive through the woods. Take on the Rubicon if you and your vehicle are ready for it, and be prepared for a true challenge. When you're done, highway potholes will feel smooth as silk.

Price: Free–$100 (provided you've got the vehicle)

(Summer, Difficult)

DRIVING DIRECTIONS

The Rubicon Trail is located in northern California near Lake Tahoe. The beginning of the trail is off Highway 50 near Loon Lake and ends on the rear side of Lake Tahoe at Tahoma. Most people start the Rubicon at Loon Lake, as this route is a little less stressful on the vehicles, but you can also begin at Wentworth Springs. Take the Ice House Road/Crystal Basin exit off Highway 50, about 20 miles east of Placerville; then follow it for 28 miles until you see Loon Lake Road, which goes to the right. Follow that another 4 miles across the second dam to the start of the Rubicon.

Try not to attempt anything your vehicle can't handle out there. If it looks like you're not going to make it through or over, there's a pretty good chance you won't. DAVID ROSE/ISTOCKPHOTO.COM

OUTFITTERS

LAKE TAHOE ADVENTURES
South Lake Tahoe, CA
(530) 577–2940
www.laketahoeadventures.com

FOR MORE INFORMATION

CALIFORNIA OFF-HIGHWAY MOTOR
VEHICLE RECREATION DIVISION
Sacramento, CA
(916) 324–4442
www.ohv.parks.ca.gov

EL DORADO NATIONAL FOREST
(LOCATION OF THE RUBICON)
Placerville, CA
(530) 622–5061
www.fs.fed.us/r5/eldorado/index
.html

DEL ALBRIGHT, RUBICON TRAIL
ACTIVIST (GOOD FOR TRAIL INFO AND
LAND USE RESOURCES)
www.delalbright.com

RUBICON4X4.COM (OFF-ROADING
PARTS AND SUPPLIES)
(800) 905–4294
www.rubicon4x4.com

OFFICIAL RUBICON TRAIL WEB SITE,
www.rubicon-trail.com

RECOMMENDED READING

De Long, Brad. *4-Wheel Freedom: The Art Of Off-Road Driving.* Boulder,
Colo.: Paladin Press, 1996.

Evans, Lisa Gollin. *An Outdoor Family Guide to Lake Tahoe.* Seattle:
Mountaineers Books, 2001.

Teie, William. *4 Wheeler's Guide to the Rubicon Trail.* Rescue, Calif.:
Deer Valley Press, 1998.

SLEEP CHEAP

You can finish the Rubicon in two days; however, taking it in three
will let you enjoy the environment more and perhaps take a few
diversions back there (e.g., fishing, hiking, etc.). Most camping along
the trail is free, so spend that cash on extra water and food. In order
to legally have a campfire or even operate a flame burner stove
anywhere in the Rubicon area, you must obtain a fire permit, available at ranger stations free of charge. Get one before you set out
(contact the El Dorado Forest at the number above for ranger station
locations).

Extreme Mountain Biking in Northern California

Flexing Those Fat Tires

Sure, your muscles are burning. Sure, you've got scrapes on your legs courtesy of a thousand little branches and needles, and a few drops of dry blood decorate your shins. And sure, your bike has mud caked in every spoke, nook, and cranny, along with rocks jammed between every other knob.

And it goes without saying that you wouldn't trade a speck of that mud, or a drop of the blood, for anything in the world. After all, this is mountain biking for the hard core—no room for regrets.

Mountain biking comes in all flavors; those of you looking for a smooth, creamy vanilla might want to check out the Angel Island escape in this book (Escape 7). But if boulderish Rocky Road agrees with your taste buds a bit more, northern California offers loads of places to get your ride on and beat your quads into submission. These trails stretch across the state, from Marin to the far northern reaches of Siskiyou County, and present an array of single-track challenges for you and your bike to conquer. So throw on that bike rack and head out—you're going to hit it hard and fast.

A few words about where you can and cannot pull out your bike: Though hiking can take you just about anywhere, many parks limit access for mountain bikes, as bikers tend to rip up trails a bit more than on-foot folks. Many national park areas are strictly off-limits; don't head to Yosemite with your mountain bike in tow, for example, as you won't find any off-road paths within the park for you to attack (road biking is, of course, a different story). Do your homework ahead of time, and use the resources listed below to find out where to hit the trails—you'll save yourself some aggravation and make more time for the good stuff, namely riding.

Of course, you can help keep more trails open for bikers by maintaining decorum out there on the trail. First off, stay on the single track; heading out to traipse through the woods where you're not supposed to go is a sure way to mess up beautiful wilderness and limit the access of future bikers. Also, pay attention to who else is on the trail and respect their presence as you'd expect them to respect yours. Bikers often get a bad rap for rudeness out there, but it's for a reason: Some riders are freakin' rude. Don't be one of them.

In the San Francisco/Marin County area, Camp Tamarancho represents the best single track around. The camp, affiliated with the Boy Scouts of America, requires a small fee to ride but presents beautiful coastal landscape over 8 miles with around forty switchbacks and 2,100 feet of elevation change thrown into the mix. Mount Tamalpais, where the camp is located, features a ton of additional bike areas, too, among its 50 miles of official trails. Point Reyes National Seashore also offers some pretty rides, though they are a little easier than the winding Tamarancho trails.

Those of you who don't have the time or inclination to put together your own bike tour in the SF/Marin area might want to contact Escape SF Tours, a local company that runs tours to a number of local mountain biking meccas. Though many of these tours are for the less experienced biker, a few gear toward rough riders who already know what they're doing. Just give them a call and find out what's going on during your window of opportunity.

Take your bike up to the northern reaches of the state and you'll find friendly environs in the Shasta-Cascade region, home to seven national forests and a smattering of national and state parks. With only a few hundred thousand people living in the area, you'll have lots of space to move around in. Whiskeytown National Recreation Area offers some of the best routes for roughneck riders—paths like the Shasta Bally ride, a constant climb to the 6,200-foot summit of Shasta Bally Mountain. Or the Three Rivers ride in Shasta-Trinity National Forest, a punishing 70-mile loop of single track and gravel that takes you over and through a whole lot of water. You might want to consider doing this one over two days, as the campsites

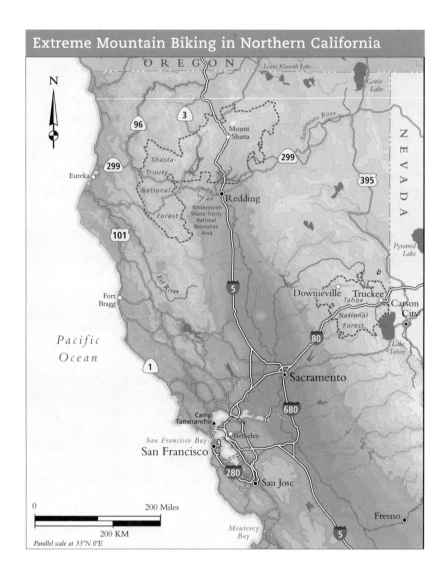

along the McCloud River and Hoffmeister Creek look mighty tempting after a few dozen miles.

For real hardcore riding, though, Tahoe National Forest might be the best pick in all northern California, particularly the areas around Downieville and Truckee. Downieville doesn't look like much; it covers only a few blocks, and the population was just forty-six in 1990. However, biking represents a kind of religion here, and one look at the landscape will tell you why—the town sits at the confluence of the Downie and Yuba Rivers, among streams, green woods, and incredible biking trails.

Because of Downieville's north-country location, you'll want to hit the trails during the summertime when snow stays well away. And why would you want to miss out on all that green, anyway? Butcher Ranch Trail, for example, represents a tough 4-mile trek through spectacular Sierra country and parallel to beautiful Pauley Creek. Take the trail in July and you'll get an incredible dose of wildflower color along with your workout. The Chimney Rock Trail gives you 28 miles of single track, with liberal sprinkles of quad-punishing uphill climbs at elevation. The trail options give you literally hundreds of miles to bump over, miles that will bring you entire days of pleasure.

Luckily, not being familiar with the Downieville trails is no reason to forgo them. You've got a few options for bike rentals and guided tours, as this tiny town boasts two high-quality bike operations. Downieville Outfitters runs a daily shuttle to Packer Saddle, Chimney Rock, and Lakes Basin, among other trailhead destinations, as well as epic rides out to Mount Ellwell, where an incredible technical ride awaits you. Yuba Expeditions also runs a trail shuttle service, as well as bike rental operations. Both companies keep their shuttle services fairly cheap, making a Downieville-area ride well worth the $20 or so you'll drop.

Keep in mind that these rides won't agree with you if it's your first time on two knobby tires. However, even if you haven't done a lot of riding before, you can consult the recommended readings below and get some practice on more basic trails through similarly breathtaking countryside. Then, when you get your skill level up, hit the tough stuff, and it won't be long before you understand the rush. It's the scratches, the speed, and the slopes you'll be craving, and the better you get the more you'll find.

Price: Next to nothing outside of gas if you plan your own trip; $70–$90 or so if you need a shuttle ride and rental.

(Summer, Difficult)

DRIVING DIRECTIONS

These bike sites are scattered across the state. Contact the outfitter of your choice for specific directions to where they want to take you; otherwise, check with the "Recommended Reading" at the end of the chapter for trail locations and directions.

Yosemite is great for road biking, but you won't be able to get your knobbies on any trails—mountain bikes are forbidden on almost every dirt path. CHRIS BECKER

OUTFITTERS

CAMP TAMARANCHO
San Rafael, CA
(415) 454–1081
www.boyscouts-marin.org

DOWNIEVILLE OUTFITTERS
Downieville, CA
(530) 289–0155
www.downievilleoutfitters.com

ESCAPE SF TOURS
Sacramento, CA
(866) 372–2735
www.escapesftours.com

YUBA EXPEDITIONS
Downieville, CA
(530) 289–3010
www.yubaexpeditions.com

FOR MORE INFORMATION

NORTHERN CALIFORNIA MOUNTAIN
BIKE ASSOCIATION
www.norcamba.org

SHASTA–TRINITY NATIONAL FOREST
Redding, CA
(530) 226–2500
www.fs.fed.us/r5/shastatrinity

TAHOE NATIONAL FOREST
Nevada City, CA
(530) 265–4531

WHISKEYTOWN NATIONAL
RECREATION AREA
Whiskeytown, CA
(530) 242–3400
www.nps.gov/whis

RECOMMENDED READING

Bicycling Magazine. Mountain Bike Magazine's Complete Guide to Mountain Biking Skills. New York: Rodale Press, 1996.

McGehee, Roger. *Mountain Biking Northern California.* Guilford, Conn.: Falcon, 2001.

Nealy, William. *Mountain Bike!: A Manual of Beginning to Advanced Technique.* Birmingham, Ala.: Menasha Ridge Press, 1992.

SLEEP CHEAP

If you're biking around Downieville, camping in the Tahoe National Forest is your best bet. The sites are first-come, first-served, with fees at $12 to $15 per night. Most developed sites have trash cans, and fire permits are not required there, but be sure to pack out your trash if there are no cans, and get a fire permit for camping in undeveloped forest areas. For more information, call the Downieville Ranger District at (530) 288–3231.

The Escape from Alcatraz Triathlon

The Pinnacle

Every difficult activity in this book challenges would-be athletes to take on more than they might be able to handle. Many present tests well above and beyond what you might be used to in your outdoor adventures, from mustering up the courage to hurl yourself from an airplane to pushing your knobby-tired grocery getter to the limit on off-road trails. Of course, to do these activities, you have to take all the time you need to practice, get educated, or otherwise get yourself in a position to accomplish the goal you're setting out for. If you aren't willing to put in that time, there's no reason to bother—just pack up and go home.

This adventure is just like those in that respect—you need to put in the time. However, more than any other, the time you put in for this one is above and beyond what you might do in preparation for skydiving or rock climbing. Triathlons require *training,* a regimen that's going to get you into shape and prepared for the most grueling competitive event in sports. However, unlike many of the aforementioned difficult activities, training for such an event will impact every part of your life, as you watch your physical fitness spike up to a rarified level mysterious to all but those few people who earn the right to call themselves "athletes." What's more, you'll be able to do your training just about anywhere and anytime—all you need is some pavement and a pool.

I know—that's a whole lot more than a weekend, all that training. But the adventure, the activity of the title, is a little thing called
the Escape from Alcatraz Triathlon, an event that, if you can get
there, will make every other escape in this book seem like a short
walk in the park.

The Escape from Alcatraz is one of the few triathlons in the
world that receives the full sporting event treatment—TV coverage,
DVDs, crowds to watch along the route, all that. This coverage is, in
large part, what makes this particular triathlon so popular, and thus
so difficult to get into. The race begins with a paratrooper-like jump
into the ice-cold water between the San Francisco Piers and
Alcatraz itself; the wet suit–clad triathletes deal with obstacles like
tough currents and massive, curious sea lions on their way to the
Marina Green beach, where a short warm-up run leads into an 18-
mile bike ride out into Golden Gate Park and back. The final leg is
an 8-mile run to Baker Beach Battery, punctuated by the 400-step
Sand Ladder, a punishing cliffside feature that takes the wind out of
even the strongest sails. Finally, you'll finish up by crossing back
under the Golden Gate, reaching sea level and a celebration you'll
certainly deserve.

Now I sense the question—why include such an involved, exclusive quest in a book about short little weekend jaunts? Answer: If
you're already in peak physical shape, you might not be that far off.
Many of us who spend a lot of time outdoor adventuring are pretty
fit anyway—the triathlon simply represents a next logical step,
another challenge to overcome. For anyone who's done the majority
of what I've presented here, triathlon simply symbolizes another
mountain to climb, wall to scale, or air current to catch. This is the
peak, the tops, the max—the ultimate adventure for the few who can
handle it.

You can't just sign up for the Alcatraz Triathlon and expect to
get in, however. Though there are a few random drawings to fill out
the field, many of those in the race make it to Alcatraz through a
system of qualifying races, which take place around the country and
even in Europe. Your weekend escape in Alcatraz symbolizes a cul-
mination, unless you're very lucky, so look into the triathlon culture
near you before simply making plans and setting out for San
Francisco. Again, this adventure is the most exclusive one here—
what makes it so cool is that you *can* get in, if you put in the work
ahead of time.

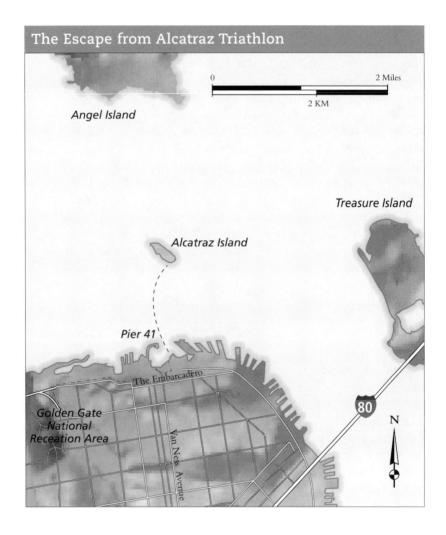

The Escape from Alcatraz Triathlon

Angel Island

0 — 2 Miles

2 KM

Treasure Island

Alcatraz Island

Pier 41

The Embarcadero

Golden Gate National Receation Area

80

Van Ness Avenue

N

Of course, to take on something as demanding as a triathlon— any triathlon—you need to get yourself primed up physically, and that's not easy to do. It requires hard work and dedication just to get reasonably healthy; imagine the efforts involved in honing your body to a razor's edge. Luckily, the "Recommended Reading" section below provides some proven triathlete's training regimens, steps which you can follow to bring yourself up to snuff. The best part is that those of us who work out regularly have time for these activities already built into our schedules; you might end up just having to alter your program a little to work on the right things.

Diet matters, too, so follow their advice on that front, particularly in the couple months before a race. This sounds like obvious advice, but I think we all know how easy it is to diverge from a successful diet when presented with a box of Krispy Kremes at company birthday parties and such. Resist the urge, maintain discipline, and you'll probably shave just a few hairs off your times.

And above all, enter local triathlons to get a feel for what they require. The list of qualifying triathlons is posted at the Escape from Alcatraz Web site; there are seven of them. You probably won't be running/swimming/biking under some of the extreme conditions you'll find in the Escape from Alcatraz—the Sand Ladder is a one-of-a-kind beast, thankfully—but you will get a good sense of what you'll need to work on training-wise, as well as what your strengths are. You'll also whet your competitive appetite and begin to understand how to compete: etiquette, preparation, etc. The final Alcatraz escape depends on your getting there, and doing other triathlons is the surest way to do it.

Check the Escape from Alcatraz Web site for more information on requirements for getting in, applications, and more general information on the race. Getting a spot won't be easy, but if you leap over the required hurdles, you're in for one of the most physically demanding, intensely rewarding experiences of your entire life. If you're already in great physical shape, just pick up the training pace, enter a few triathlons, and you're on your way. If, however, you're not yet up to the physical par, you can certainly aspire to great things. All triathlons, after all, begin with the first mile you ever run, swim, and bike. After that one, it's simply a matter of working upward.

Price: The registration price for the Triathlon varies from year to year. Contact the race authorities to get the current price.

(Summer, Difficult)

DRIVING DIRECTIONS

The race takes place along the San Francisco coast, starting out in the waters off Alcatraz and finishing up at Marina Green. Spectators can watch the proceedings from Marina Green or just above the St. Francis Yacht Club, where the swimmers are in full view.

Alcatraz and San Francisco. COURTESY OF THE SAN FRANCISCO CONVENTION & VISITORS BUREAU

OUTFITTERS

TRI-CALIFORNIA (RACE ORGANIZERS)
Pacific Grove, CA
(831) 373-0678
www.tricalifornia.com

FOR MORE INFORMATION

TRIATHLETE MAGAZINE
www.triathletemag.com

ONTRI.COM (GREAT ORGANIZATIONAL,
TRAINING, COMMUNITY RESOURCE)
www.ontri.com

RECOMMENDED READING

Aronson, Virginia and Steven Jonas. *Triathloning for Ordinary Mortals.*
New York: W.W. Norton & Company, 1999.

Harr, Eric. *Triathlon Training in Four Hours a Week*. New York: Rodale Books, 2003.

Mora, John M. *Triathlon 101*. Champaign, Ill.: Human Kinetics Publishers, 1999.

SLEEP CHEAP

If you get to compete in the Escape from Alcatraz, you deserve a splurge. Try the Mandarin Oriental in the middle of the city, within walking distance of Union Square. It's one of the top hotels in the world, and you'll have access to the best views of the city (the hotel is the city's third-tallest building). The on-site restaurants are exquisite, too—perfect for a post-race treat. Call (415) 276–9600, or visit www.mandarinoriental.com for more information.

Fall

Soaring/Gliding

No Motor, Will Travel

If you've ever been to an airshow, you know that jet-powered hijinks require a few things: fuel, fire, and a big fat dose of noise, for starters. Stunt squads like the Blue Angels don't skimp on the monstrous, muscular engines, and with good reason—the rules of nature don't bend without a fight, and often those engines are the only things standing between flyers and the inevitable, powerful yank of the ground.

If airshow antics are an all-out shooting war against gravity, glider flight is a gentle, silent, more graceful dance with it. Strap into the passenger seat of a glider, and you're heading up to play with the elements rather than beat them into submission, embarking on a flight that promises both peace and some Gs to help break it up. It always starts out calm—a few bumps as the tow plane brings you to the proper altitude, punctuated by the metallic *clink* of the tow hook letting go—but once there's nothing between you and terra firma but a few well-wrought pieces of wood and fiberglass, adventure is not too strong a word.

Gliding (or soaring, as it's often known) involves flying in a motorless sailplane propelled by nothing more than the atmosphere itself, via the phenomenon called lift. Luckily for soarers like you, California boasts all three forms of lift energy: columns of warm, rising air called thermals; ridge lift, where air currents following the terrain rise over the windward side of a hill and create momentary gusts upward; and wave lift, the powerful result of winds hammering their way off mountains and other large land formations and

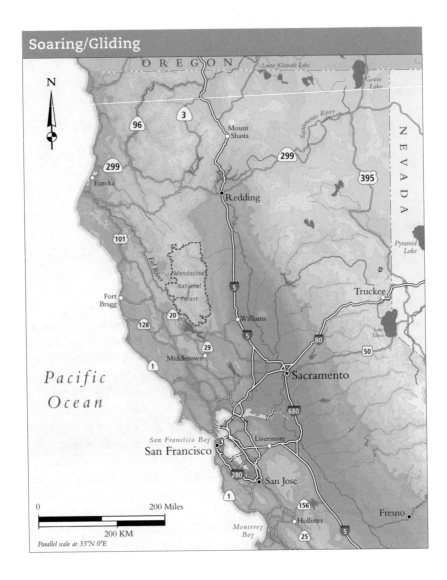

surging up with massive force. Good sailplane pilots move in and out of these various lifts and use them to remain airborne for hours at a time. Wave lift is best for expert-level soaring, and wave flights can reach altitudes of nearly 50,000 feet.

These primal forces provide all the gas you'll need for aerobatic excursions to rival anything you'll see the Blue Angels do. Hit the right wave of air and you can find yourself shooting straight up, *Top Gun* all the way into any number of aerobatic moves. If you really dig moving just a little faster than you probably should, aerobatic flying is the way to go—loops, rolls, and humpty bumps await the courageous flyer. (Want to know what a humpty bump is? Take to the sky and find out!) Nervous first-timers or anyone with fear of heights should probably pass up these raw thrills, at least for the first flight, and opt instead for a simple beginner's glide. You won't be missing out if you elect to go slow on your early flights; cutting through the air in a plane without an engine will be excitement—and buzz—enough for your maiden voyage. Even experienced jet pilots get a little weirded out when there's no engine noise to keep the plane in the air, so just ease into it at your own pace, and pick the flight that makes you most comfortable.

You can take your first glider flight for a pretty modest price, though cost does depend on how long you fly and what kind of flight you want. Northern California is full of good commercial gliding operators; in fact, soaring is a pretty popular pastime in the Bay area. The Bay Area Soaring Associates (BASA) and the Pacific Soaring Council (PASCO) are two local soaring organizations dedicated to soaring as a sport and passion, and they offer an excellent batch of resources if you're interested in taking up the wing. You'll find outfitters all over the state, too, though there's a big concentration of them around the San Francisco/Sacramento corridor. Williams Soaring Center, for example, is literally minutes off Highway 5, making it a great diversion during a longer trip or a convenient training facility whether you live in the Bay or gold country. (Sure, it's a little ways outside of San Fran, but the drive's all highway. Not bad, take it from me.) Williams offers many flying options, from mile-high flights to the top of the world to aerobatic stunt flights that will keep you rolling and diving. Crazy Creek Soaring offers similar flights among the eastern foothills of the Mayacamus Mountains, the inland-most part of the Northern California Coastal Range. You'll have 4,000-foot mountains within just 10 miles of your takeoff point, with some 7,000-foot peaks off farther in the distance, making for some spectacular in-flight scenery. Just be sure to call all the outfitters listed below and find out the differences between them. Then choose the one that's best for your situation and location and go to town.

Flight length depends on flying conditions, but introductory trips are generally long enough to enjoy yourself and short enough to leave you wanting just a few more barrel rolls. The cockpit, a bubble of glass allowing for incredible views, is well suited for

Preparing to take off. CHRIS BECKER

enjoying the scenery thousands of feet below. The visuals, along with the silence, make for an almost spiritual experience on calmer flights. You may even want to share the beauty with your significant other; if your combined weight is less than 300 pounds, the two of you can enjoy a quiet mile-high together, maybe to kick off a night out, or down, on the town.

When you do finally land, the pilot will enter your flight information in a logbook, which works well as a souvenir or as the first step on your way to full-fledged glider pilot training. Try booking additional training flights to fit your schedule, and see how far you get—a whole hierarchy of milestones awaits, from simple certification to a chance for competitive aerobatics if you can't get enough of that upside down, turned around feeling. Stay relaxed during your lessons, take your instructions to heart, and have the time of your life—you could find yourself certified to fly solo after only twenty to thirty flights.

But if you get the gliding bug, the wait is worth it. Once you have your license, you may find yourself saving a few bucks each week toward your very own set of wings. And since introductory soaring flights are within everyone's skill set, even the kids can enjoy the air up there—in fact, you may even catch sight of a younger pilot or two while you're out at the gliderport. Gliding is a rewarding, relatively inexpensive hobby for teenagers and young adults, and if anything's going to build up a young person's confidence, it's flying at the top of the world with his own hand on the stick.

Whether you are looking to get your kicks on a one-shot thrill ride or trying to find a regular route into the wide blue sky, soaring is the perfect answer—you'd be hard-pressed to find a better balance of wild times and relaxing, contemplative pleasure. Give it a try, no matter what your intentions, and see just how accommodating gravity can be.

Price: $60–$150, $500-plus if you want lessons

(Fall, Easy)

DRIVING DIRECTIONS

Williams Soaring Center: Minutes from Interstate 5; just take the second Williams exit, go east for a half mile, and you're there.

Crazy Creek: From Middletown, take Highway 29 three miles north, then turn right on Grange Road. Continue about half a mile, and turn right at the GLIDER RIDES sign.

Bay Area Glider Rides: Located at the Hollister Municipal Airport. Take Highway 101 to Highway 25 in Gilroy, head south about 8 miles to Highway 156. Turn left on Highway 156, and then turn right on San Felipe Road. The airport is about 2 miles along on the right.

Attitude Aviation: From the Bay area, take Highway 580 toward Livermore. Take the Airway Boulevard exit and drive toward the control tower. Follow it until you pass the tower on your right and start seeing hangars. Turn right at the light (Kitty Hawk Road), and then turn right at the signal onto West Jack London Boulevard. As you approach the hangars, turn right into the second driveway.

If you're in the Lake Tahoe area between May and September, try **Soar Truckee,** at the Truckee/Tahoe Airport: Take Interstate 80 to Truckee (Highway 267); exit heading south. In town center, cross both the railroad tracks and the river. Continue on Highway 267 toward Kings Beach and pass the Airport Road. Watch for Martis Creek Dam Road on your left about a half mile in, then turn left and follow the road to the gate at the end. Turn left into the gliding site.

OUTFITTERS

ATTITUDE AVIATION
Livermore, CA
(925) 456–2276
www.attitudeaviation.com

BAY AREA GLIDER RIDES
Hollister, CA
(888) 467–6276
www.bayareagliderrides.com

WILLIAMS SOARING CENTER
Williams, CA
(530) 473–5600
www.williamssoaring.com

CRAZY CREEK SOARING
Middletown, CA
(707) 987–9112
www.crazycreekgliders.com

SOAR TRUCKEE
Truckee, CA
(530) 587–6702
www.soartruckee.com

FOR MORE INFORMATION

BAY AREA SOARING ASSOCIATES
Sunnyvale, CA
(831) 801–2363
www.flybasa.org

PACIFIC SOARING COUNCIL
Fremont, CA
(925) 639–1110
www.pacificsoaring.org

RECOMMENDED READING

Piggot, Derek. *Understanding Gliding: The Principles of Soaring Flight.*
London, England: A&C Black, 1998.

Thomas, Fred. *Fundamentals of Sailplane Design.* College Park, Md:
College Park Press, 1999.

SLEEP CHEAP

How about sleep free? Head to the Mendocino National Forest, just
north and east of Middletown and Williams, and you have your pick
of campsites in the forest's southern section. You have to pack your
trash out, and the facilities are somewhat primitive, but the price is
most certainly right. Call (530) 934–3316 for more information and
directions, or visit www.fs.fed.us/r5/mendocino for a list of campsites and their locations.

Scenic Driving Redwood National and State Parks

Rolling among the Giants

You look up, and the sight almost knocks you to the mossy ground: trees like skyscrapers, towering around you up into infinity and mist, their trunks as wide as barns. They crowd around you, both directly and by extension, covering hundreds of square miles in every direction, stretching up and down the coast. This isn't even the first time this trip that you've looked up at the trees, but every time you do, the feeling of awe creeps over you. You pull out your camera, then put it away again—you've already got at least a hundred shots stored, and you think you can't possibly improve on the photos you've already got, can't possibly capture any more of the beauty around you.

"Maybe up the road a ways," you decide finally, and head back to your car, ready to truck on to your next destination and find that shot you're looking for. After all, you're not even midway through the first day of your redwood country tour.

Northern California's redwoods stand as one of the state's most precious natural resources. They can reach more than 300 feet in height, and live 2,000 years or more. They have seen more history than almost any living thing in the world, and their superlatives lend them a larger-than-life status. This is not to say that the trees haven't hoed a difficult row at times; in the 1800s, loggers began chopping down the trees, taking advantage of a seemingly inexhaustible wood supply. Within a scant one hundred years, the logging industry had

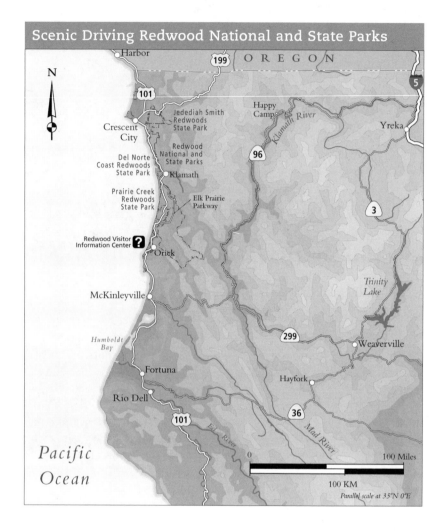

eliminated such acreage of old-growth forest that the future of the entire redwood population in California fell into doubt. Luckily, organizations like the Save-the-Redwoods League, founded in 1918, came forward to stop this wanton destruction and save the remaining forests from the axe. The organization began purchasing old-growth redwood forest land then and continues to do so today, thus saving that land from development, logging, and other destruction courtesy of human neighbors.

The labors of these organizations have created a long stretch of redwood forests along the northern California coast, comprising three state parks and one national park—Prairie Creek Redwoods State Park, Del Norte Coast Redwoods State Park, Jedediah Smith Redwoods State Park, and Redwood National Park. This large conglomeration holds about 45 percent of the remaining old-growth redwood forest in all of California, and their worldwide importance is sufficient to warrant the area being named a World Heritage Site and International Biosphere Reserve. The parks don't just hold redwood forests, either; you'll find prairie and oak woodlands, huge rivers and trickling streams, and 37 miles of untouched Pacific coastline. Because they stretch over such a large area, the best way to get around, see everything you want to see, and do everything you want to do is to pack up the family car (or a rental) and set out on the scenic roadways winding through the big groves, stopping along the way whenever the fancy strikes you. This isn't a very difficult adventure, but it's one you can share with the whole family and a ride you're sure to remember years down the line.

You'll find a whole bunch of places worth stopping for. Along the Howland Hill Road, a beautiful 6-mile drive, short walks through the astounding redwoods abound; a few paths will even take you out to incredible ocean overlooks and the tide pools that dot the coastline. The Coastal Drive takes you past another set of fantastic ocean views, then into Prairie Creek, while you just might catch sight of some Roosevelt elk, one of the largest members of the deer family and a frequently sighted denizen of the parks. If you visit the parks during the gray whale migrating seasons (late fall and early spring), you may spy some of these magnificent creatures as they make their way to or from their breeding grounds. Visit the Klamath River Overlook for the best viewing, and take a walk down to the lower overlook for truly spectacular seascapes.

Looking for a bit more of a hike? The various parks boast hundreds of miles in hiking trails, from the easy, paved route at Stout Grove up in Jedediah Smith State Park to the glorious coastal trail that takes you along the shoreline for as long or as short a stroll as you'd like. More advanced hiking parties regularly take on the whole 70-mile stretch of California Coastal Trail that runs through the parks; less extreme adventurers, however, should feel free to sample the trail over the course of just a few miles. (For more on the California Coastal Trail, check out Escape 36.) Hiking the park will give you firsthand knowledge of just how the many ecosystems here interact with each other; some trails will take you from deep in the redwood groves out to the pristine Pacific within a matter of a few miles.

It should go without saying, but be sure to pull off frequently when you're driving through redwood country; the trees are even more impressive when you're standing next to them. CHRIS BECKER

If you're having trouble coming up with things to do as you make your way through the parks, never fear—the collective parks' staff and other local outfitters offer quite a few guided tours and field seminars, covering everything from kayaking on the Smith and Klamath Rivers to photography, astronomy, and wildflower identification. Pride Enterprises out of Eureka provides narrated five-and-a-half-hour tours to the beautiful stands of redwood north and south of the city, along with additional points of interest. The ranger-led programs are offered only in the summer season, though, so make sure you call ahead to find out just what's going on when you're going to be in the area.

Camping is obviously the most cost-effective lodging option in the parks. I'm not talking about the hard-core backcountry variety, either—you'll find a number of developed campgrounds in the area, though you won't find trailer hookups at any of the parks' campsites. If you do decide to camp, keep in mind that bears lumber through those big trees, and they would love nothing better than a free lunch on your account. To avoid unnecessary contact with these big guys, make sure you use the bear-proof lockers at your campsite and keep your area nice and clean.

Taking in the redwoods and the country they call home makes for perfect family weekend escaping. In fact, this escape is a great one to bring the kids along on, especially if they generally spend the better part of the weekend in front of the TV or computer. There's nothing quite like the look on a kid's face the first time she lays eyes on a grove of leafy behemoths. It's a sight that will stay with you forever, just as the trees themselves will.

And who knows? A few more journeys into pretty country like this, and the kids might be choosing next weekend's escape—with a little help from this book, of course!

Price: Pretty cheap—just gas, food, camping, and a $5.00 daily fee for the state parks (nothing for Redwood National Park itself). This is a great adventure for families feeling a little stretched in the wallet.
(Fall, Easy)

DRIVING DIRECTIONS

The Redwood National and State Park system stretches from just north of Eureka (about 20 miles above the city by Humboldt Bay) all the way up to Crescent City. Highway 101 cuts through big parts of the forest, so just jump on that highway and follow it into red-wood country. From there, choose your diversions as you wish, using information from the parks and the "Recommended Reading" below.

OUTFITTERS

REDWOOD NATIONAL AND STATE
PARKS (ENCOMPASSES ALL THE
PARKS MENTIONED ABOVE)
Crescent City, CA
(707) 464–6101
www.nps.gov/redw

FOR MORE INFORMATION

SAVE-THE-REDWOODS LEAGUE
San Francisco, CA
(888) 836–0005
(415) 362–2352
www.savetheredwoods.com

RECOMMENDED READING

Barbour, Michael G., John Evarts, and Marjorie Popper. *Coast Redwood: A Natural and Cultural History.* Los Olivos, Calif.: Cachuma Press, 2001.

Brett, Daniel. *Hiking the Redwood Coast.* Guilford, Conn.: Globe Pequot Press, 2004.

Dunning, Joan and Doug Thron. *From the Redwood Forest: Ancient Trees and the Bottom Line.* White River Junction, Vt.: Chelsea Green Publishing, 1998.

Lorentzen, Bob. *The Hiker's Hip Pocket Guide to the Humboldt Coast,* 3rd ed. Mendocino, Calif.: Bored Feet Publications, 1998.

Noss, Reed F. *The Redwood Forest: History, Ecology, and Conservation of the Coastal Redwoods.* Washington, D.C.: Island Press, 1999.

SLEEP CHEAP

There are four developed campgrounds in Redwood National and State Parks. These sites go for $20 per night in the summertime and $15 per night in the off-season. You can make reservations up to six months ahead of time by calling (800) 444–7275. Three of the four (Jedediah Smith Campground, Mill Creek Campground, and Elk Prairie Campground) have many sites, though Mill Creek is only open in the summertime. However, I would still call ahead to make sure I had things wrapped up before I hit the road.

The Nakoma Spa and Dragon Golf Course

High Sierra Pampering

Never had a Swedish massage, eh? A rice scrub? A volcanic lava wrap? Not even an antioxidant facial? Too bad.

If you've never paid a visit to a spa or had a session with a professional masseuse, you're missing out on a wonderful way to treat your body and mind to relaxation in its purest form. There are few other places where another person—at least a perfect stranger—can cater so completely to you, putting your body and mind into such an ideal state of repose that they bleed over into each other, the mind experiencing only the body and pleasant sensations. There's nothing quite like it, and no better place to feel those sensations than the Nakoma Spa in northern California's High Sierras.

Nakoma offers a lot more than mud wraps and facials, too. An escape to this wonderful destination offers equal doses of history, architecture, and recreation, much of it thanks to the spa's design, based on actual plans drawn by the great Frank Lloyd Wright. In case you aren't familiar with Mr. Wright, here's a little background: Born in 1867, Wright holds a revered place among American architects, perhaps the most revered place. His buildings around the country still stand as monuments to his innovation and genius; visiting them is well worth it if you ever find yourself in Pennsylvania (Falling Water), New York City (the Guggenheim Museum), Phoenix (Taliesin West), and any number of other regions that bear some mark of Wright's influence. (Check the "Recommended Reading" at the end of the chapter for a more complete list of Wright's works, along with how to get to them.)

Nakoma isn't one of Wright's original works, in that he never actually saw it built. In 1923 Wright was commissioned to build a golf clubhouse in Madison, Wisconsin, which he named Nakoma. Unfortunately, it was never built there, thanks to the high costs the project would probably have meant for the country club. So the plans languished in a drawer at Taliesin Architects, the firm that continues the architectural practice Wright founded in 1893. In 1995, however, the new Nakoma's founders got permission to use the plans for their own spa-to-be, and the rest is history. The Nakoma Country Club was completed at Gold Mountain, a recreation community in Graeagle just 50 miles north of Reno, in 2001—forty-two years after Wright's death.

And what a place it is. Nakoma, a Chippewa Indian word meaning "I do as I promise," is a tribute to Native American culture and lifestyle, and the architecture shows it; the structure consists of a series of contrasting shapes—octagons, squares, rectangles—which culminate in a tepeelike roof 55 feet high. The Native American theme continues in the giant, open fireplace, labeled "campfire" on Wright's original plans and rising up through the central core of the open interior.

The architecture is something to behold, a history lesson writ large. However, the reason you're making this trip is to give your aching muscles a well-deserved rest and take your mind away from the day-to-day routine you deal with back in your version of the real world. The spa works with a few themes, from Asian spa rituals to more Native American–focused activities, emphasizing harmony between the four elements (earth, air, fire, and water) along with therapies that highlight our connection with the beautiful land of the Sierra Nevadas. There's also a broad selection of traditional European treatments on hand—things like thermal mineral water bathing, aromatherapy, and herbal treatments.

In fact, your choices are literally overwhelming. Moor mud wraps, natural spirulina wraps, Jamu massage, thalassobath, aromatherapies of all scents—this is just a tiny sample of the spa activities available to you. Go ahead and peruse Nakoma's offerings and pick out what sounds best to you; then call and ask all the questions you need to. The preparation will be worth it once you're lying on that table or in that bath, feeling the toxins and stress of everyday living draining out of your very pores. The body offerings

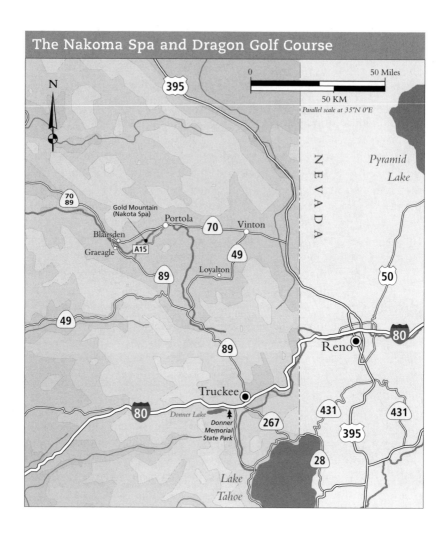

aren't the only reason to hit Nakoma, either. Skin care, facials, hair, and cosmetics are all here, as is a full slate of participatory fitness activities like tai chi, personal training, water aerobics, and yoga. If the outdoors are your bag, you can get in some hiking, bird-watching, tennis, even fly-fishing on the spa grounds, taking in the awe-inspiring landscape that makes the High Sierras so famous.

You don't want to miss the other major reason to visit Nakoma, either: the Dragon golf course, eighteen holes of pure links pleasure. The Dragon is a par-72 course on which every hole has its own name—names like Deception, Teeth of the Dragon, Defiance, and

Audacity (perfect titles when you're talking about a golf course, as any golfer knows).

The course's motto—"Send me your heroes"—gives away the fact that this isn't an easy place to play. You won't have a lot of trouble with major water hazards, but don't let that reprieve comfort you; there's nothing to take for granted here, from the narrow fairways to sneaky bunkers, rocks, little trickles of stream, and ravines. You'll have to bring your A game, or a whole box of balls you aren't afraid to lose. What you will get, regardless of your skill level, is a mind-blowingly beautiful course that seems to rise from the fertile green Sierra landscape, a course that sets a high standard for harmony with its surroundings. You'll get all this without having to mortgage anything, either—rounds run between $120 and $140, which isn't terrible if you know anything about greens fees on truly impressive courses. What's more, you'll get to use a bunch of the spa's amenities when you pay to play, like the indoor Jacuzzi, the saunas, the steam room, and the workout room if you're looking for some physical exercise after the mental paces you've just gone through on the course.

Nakoma presents a host of opportunities for escaping your daily grind through history, relaxation, sport, or some combination of them all. It's a little expensive but well worth the splurge if you've got some celebrating to do—think anniversary, birthday, or simple "let's get out of here for the weekend" trip. Save up a bit, then head out where the air's clean, the buildings inspire, and the escaping is of the purely relaxational variety. Throw in the High Sierra environment, and you've got the whole package. Start pinching those pennies!

Price: $500-plus for accommodations, spa treatments, golf, etc.

(Fall, Easy)

DRIVING DIRECTIONS

From the Bay Area: Exit Interstate 80 at Highway 89 north and turn left towards Sierraville. Leaving Sierraville, turn left at the stop sign to continue on Highway 89. Within 5 miles, Highway 89 will split; take the right turn on Highway 89 to Graeagle/Blairsden/Quincy. Continue on for 10 miles, where the road will split again, then turn right on Plumas County Road A-15. Within 5 miles you will see the entrance to the Nakoma Resort and Dragon Golf Course on your right at Bear Run Road.

You might want to look into a facial, massage, makeover, or any number of other treatments available at Nakoma. LEAH-ANNE THOMPSON/ISTOCKPHOTO.COM

OUTFITTERS

NAKOMA RESORT & SPA
(877) 418–0880
www.nakomaresort.com

RECOMMENDED READING

Bonds, Ray. *Frank Lloyd Wright Field Guide: His 100 Greatest Works*. Philadelphia, Pa.: Running Press Book Publishers, 2002.

Leavy, Hannelore R. *The Spa Encyclopedia: A Guide to Treatments & Their Benefits for Health & Healing*. Clifton Park, N.Y.: Thomson/Delmar Learning, 2003.

Storrer, William Allin. *A Frank Lloyd Wright Companion*. Chicago: University of Chicago Press, 1993.

Wright, Frank Lloyd. *Frank Lloyd Wright: An Autobiography*. New York: Barnes & Noble, 1998. (reprinted)

SLEEP CHEAP

Donner Memorial State Park, located right down the road near Truckee, offers great accommodations, including a 154-space campground, showers, and a host of recreation options from fishing to windsurfing. Call (530) 582-7892 for more information.

Calaveras County's Caverns

The Subterranean Playground

The great outdoors stretches in all directions, a canvas in front of you. Northern California's beautiful treasures—its landscape, its crisp air, its hundreds of fantastic activities—beckon to you the way they always do. You're hooked as soon as you leave the house, but this time you aren't looking forward to another great hike or a wheeled jaunt through the tall trees. Instead, you're headed down another road, one that leads out of the sunlight and into another, deeper world.

Prepare yourself to go underground—literally. Calaveras County is home to one of California's most valuable natural resources: an extensive network of caverns, accessible from a few different points throughout the countryside. After tooling around aboveground for a while, the journey downstairs will take you into a strange, fantastic place where natural beauty is no less prevalent, even if you need a flashlight to see it.

Amador and Calaveras Counties, located just east of Sacramento, offer four excellent cave complexes, which in turn offer all kinds of adventures for every skill level and age group. Visiting a few of the caves within a few days makes for terrific weekend escaping, particularly when you throw a tent in the back of the car and spend your aboveground hours enjoying the stuff on top of those extensive tunnels.

There is probably no environment more self-contained than the subterranean world of the cave. The creatures that live underground make do with so few resources that it's amazing they manage to survive at all; think about how *you*'d do with no sunlight (thus no green plants), no wind, and no temperatures above chilly—ever. Of course, what you do get underground is a chance to see the forces of moisture and geology work together to create awesome formations that seem to defy all the natural laws. The static air down there lets delicate pipes and flutes form free of the forces that might crumble them topside, preserved forever—or until the water and stone form them into different works of art.

Starting spelunkers can head to any of the four caves introduced here and get a pretty nice primer on the underground realm; every one offers a simple, short tour meant for families. Sutter Gold Mine, for example, offers a great initiation into the world of gold mining, from the practical modern angle rather than the—admittedly more romantic—classical 49ers direction. Sutter is a modern hard-rock mine and saw use up until very recently. Today, however, the mine is open just for perusal by folks like yourself. You can take a one-hour tour during which you'll don a hard hat, descend into the mine, and learn all about the mining industry and Gold Country geology. You'll also see a ton of cool mining equipment, from tiny drills to gigantic rock-hauling trucks.

Black Chasm, located right down the road from the Sutter mine, also offers a short tour—the 50-minute Landmark Family Tour, which follows a defined path designed to give the best vantage point of the cave and all its glories. The setup disturbs the natural environment as little as possible and culminates in the Landmark Room, where you'll find a beautiful collection of helictite crystals, curving, angled formations that evoke delicate underwater creatures. There's a Hollywood connection here, too—at the visitor's center, you'll find props from the *Matrix* trilogy, namely huge stalagmites from the underground city of Zion. You'll also find information about the structures down in the cave, as well as just how the heck those pretty chambers got discovered in the first place.

Moaning Cavern in Vallecito boasts its own claim to fame: the largest publicly accessible vertical chamber in California. You could fit the Statue of Liberty in there, and then rappel right down past it thanks to the 165-foot dangle-and-drop the cave staff takes visitors on. You'll find family-friendly tours here too, but the rappel is the big thing—you don't need prior experience, but you beginners will

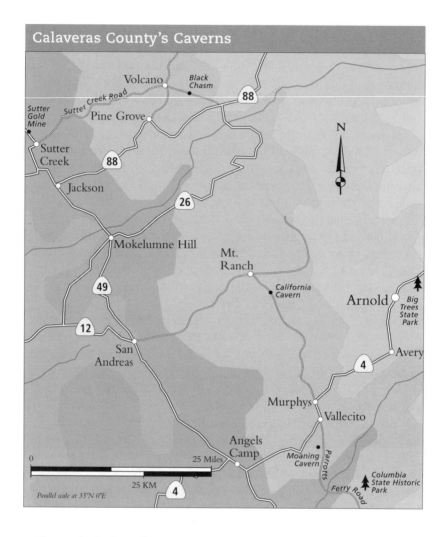

still get the feeling that the master spelunkers got the first time they descended into unknown darkness.

If you'd like to get even farther down the rabbit hole, sign up for Moaning Cavern's three-hour Adventure Trip, which starts with the rappel and continues with a few hours of squeezing through the cavern's deeper recesses. You won't find lights or walkways down here—instead, you'll be belly crawling through damp passages with a lamp mounted on your head. It's a great intro taste of cave exploration, though you'll have the distinct benefit of experienced guides and a traveled passage to cut your teeth on.

The deepest adventuring awaits you at California Cavern, discovered in the mid-nineteenth century when Captain Joseph Taylor was taking target practice by the cave's entrance and noticed a breeze from the rocks that seemed to move his shots. Thereafter, the cavern was the first in the state to be opened to the public for guided tours. Today, California Cavern plays host to two longer cavern tours, the three-hour Mammoth Cave journey and the ultimate: the five-hour Middle Earth Expedition, which will take you about 80 percent of the way through the entire California Cavern system. The first hour of the trip leads you through the original part of the system, the so-called Mammoth Cave area; after that, you'll move into Middle Earth, where you'll walk through knee-deep clay (make sure you bring your high-tops). You'll spend the rest of the trip exploring horizontal fissures and finish up with a 79-foot rafting trip across Tom's Lake, a subterranean body of water that evokes all kinds of movie sets, and crawling through a few more gorgeous caverns. You have to be at least 16 to take this trip, but it's well worth your time if you can swing it—especially if you think that underground exploration might be where it's at for future weekend escapes.

You don't have to feel the sunlight on your face to feel like you're exploring. In fact, descending into the underground will put you into some places that not too many people get to go, particularly if you take the more "spelunky" of the tours above. If the caving bug bites you, get together with some more experienced spelunkers courtesy of the National Speleological Society and take up spelunking on a more full-time basis. And as time progresses and you know more and more what you're doing, descending deeper and deeper into the welcoming dark, you'll always remember that weekend, back in California, when you decided to strap on your helmet light and head down under.

Price: Basic tours are only $12 or $15 for adults and less for kids, making the cave journey a super-inexpensive escape at the basic level. More involved tours cost more, of course; the pinnacle Middle Earth tour at California Cavern, for example, runs about $130.
(Fall, Easy)

DRIVING DIRECTIONS

All of these caverns are located fairly close to one another; all directions are given from Stockton, the nearest large town (and

Checking out an upside-down garden in Black Chasm. COURTESY OF CALIFORNIA CAVERNS

near the "Sleep Cheap" option, the Stockton/Lodi KOA).

California Cavern: Take Highway 4 east to Angels Camp, then Highway 49 north to San Andreas. Take a right turn on Mountain Ranch Road and go approximately fifteen minutes (9 miles). Turn right on the second Michel Road turnoff at the California Historical Landmark sign that says CALIFORNIA CAVERNS.

Sutter Gold Mine: From Highway 99 north in Stockton, take Highway 88 east to Martell. Turn left in Martell, taking Highway 49 north through Sutter Creek. Look for the entrance on the right approximately 1 mile north of Sutter Creek.

Moaning Cavern: Take Highway 4 east. Turn right at Angels Camp; continue about 1 mile through historic downtown Angels Camp. At the Highway 4 east sign, turn left. Travel approximately ten minutes, then turn right on Parrotts Ferry Road at the Moaning Cavern sign. Go 1 mile, then turn right on Moaning Cave Road. Take the road to the end and park.

Black Chasm: From Highway 99 north in Stockton, take Highway 88 east to Jackson. Turn left at the lights to continue on Highway 88 east to Pine Grove. Make a left turn toward Volcano on Pine Grove-Volcano Road and continue 2½ miles to the bottom of the steep hill. Make a sharp right turn onto Pioneer-Volcano Road and continue about 1,500 feet. Turn right at the Black Chasm National Natural Landmark entrance.

OUTFITTERS

BLACK CHASM NATIONAL NATURAL
LANDMARK
Volcano, CA
www.caverntours.com/BlackRt
.htm

CALIFORNIA CAVERN STATE
HISTORICAL LANDMARK
Mountain Ranch, CA
www.caverntours.com/califrt.htm

MOANING CAVERN
Vallecito, CA
www.caverntours.com/MoCavRt
.htm

SUTTER GOLD MINE
Sutter Creek, CA
www.caverntours.com/sgmt
.html

*One company manages all
four caves:*
SIERRA NEVADA RECREATION
CORPORATION
Vallecito, CA
(209) 736–2708
www.caverntours.com

FOR MORE INFORMATION

NATIONAL SPELEOLOGICAL SOCIETY
www.caves.org (check out the
links to the local chapters,
too—in Cali and beyond!)

RECOMMENDED READING

McClurg, David R. *The Adventure of Caving.* Carlsbad, N. Mex.: D&J Press, 1998.

Taylor, Michael Ray. *Caves: Exploring Hidden Realms.* Washington, D.C.: National Geographic, 2001.

Taylor, Michael Ray. *Cave Passages: Roaming the Underground Wilderness.* New York: Scribner, 1996.

SLEEP CHEAP

The Stockton/Lodi KOA is located right off Highway 99, the road that leads you to all the caves mentioned here. It's got both tent and RV sites and makes a great base of operations for your underground weekend escape. If you feel like frolicking aboveground for a while, check out the swimming pool (in season, of course) or rent a couple bikes and take a ride. Call (800) 562–1229 for reservations, or visit www.koa.com/Where/CA/05175.htm.

California River Panning

There's Gold in That Thar Mud

They may be the most American adventurers of all—people who set out for a strange land in pursuit of their fortunes, put their hands into the earth, and pulled out their dreams. They have a football team named after them and have inspired both heroic tales and comedy-sketch stereotypes. You may even catch yourself speaking like one—ever say "Eureka!" after a particularly brilliant idea?

Everyone raise a pan and shovel, please, to California's own homegrown heroes, the diggin' 49ers—and when you're done, set out to follow their footsteps on an expedition of your own along one of California's still-rich rivers of gold.

In January 1848, James Marshall discovered gold along northern California's very own American River, kicking off the following year's exodus west and the explosive immigration that still continues unabated. Wagonload followed wagonload, and who can blame them? Ten pounds of the yellow metal was worth a small fortune back in those days, and California's cheap real estate meant you could strike a vein and find yourself owning your very own gentleman's ranch.

Prospecting was a common pursuit across the entire West back then, but a small, dedicated group of prospectors continues the hunt today, plying rivers and deserts alike in their search for leftover nuggets. With advancing technology, some of their methods have also advanced; some other search-and-extract processes, however, have remained the same since the old days. Lucky for us, a few of the more enterprising and successful of these prospectors have

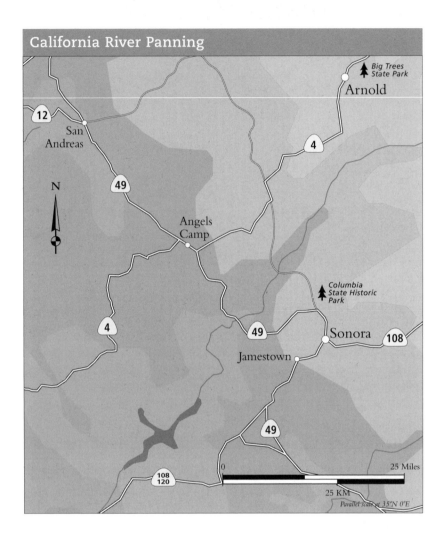

California River Panning

decided that sharing the wealth isn't such a bad idea. These kindly folks happily take novices on gold hunting expeditions, allowing any one of us to feel their fever for the Mother Lode, if only for a couple precious days.

In a way, these folks are on to something—prospecting is a much surer bet than Vegas, and weekend diggers often find significant amounts of gold on their two- and three-day excursions. If you pan away for a few hours and come up empty, just keep two things in mind: there's always time to find what you came for if you're patient, and it most certainly is there, waiting to be found. In 1992, for example, California's Jamestown Mine yielded a massive, 45-pound nugget that would be worth about $270,000. That's right—a quarter mil, just lying around underground!

You may not be quite that lucky, but with the right guidance and techniques, you could find a whole new reason to shout "Eureka!" Up in northern California, river prospecting is the best way to do this. In simple terms, river prospecting involves moving silt through sluices either by hand or machine, and separating the gold from everything else. Desert prospecting, on the other hand, involves more use of high-tech metal detectors, which are capable of finding treasures up to 18 inches down in the ground. This is not to say that river prospectors don't get into the high-tech stuff; there's just more earthmoving involved, and hands get just a bit dirtier as a result.

If you're ready to get your feet wet, Get Gold Adventures & Outfitters specializes in stream prospecting, and they are definitely worth checking out no matter what level of digging you're looking to get into. Come with the whole family and get a test drive, with one- to four-hour excursions meant to introduce you to gold fever. Or, if you really want to find some riches, take a one- to five-day overnight tour around the California River that boast mucho gold, as well as some great chow (Get Gold boasts the best sourdough in the Mother Lode). Get Gold even offers claims-for-rent; for a small fee, you can buy the right to prospect on the company's claims as much as you want for a whole year. It's well worth it if you plan on prospecting as a hobby, and at the very least you'll have exclusive access to some beautiful California camping land for a whole year.

Gold Prospecting Adventures, located in Jamestown southeast of Sacramento, offers some great prospecting classes and has been teaching people to prospect for more than twenty-five years, from introductory three-day courses on using hydrology to determine where the gold is in the stream to advanced courses on making and keeping claims. They also can teach you to use metal detectors more effectively, for when you decide to use one for more than finding bottle caps at the beach. The teaching facilities are done up like an authentic 1849 miner's camp, with the guides decked out in period costume—just another way to get you in the mood to dig up your fortune. Nearby Jamestown has its own attractions, too—shopping, restaurants, concerts, even two theater companies.

After all, total involvement is really what prospecting is all about. The more dirt you move or ground you cover, the better your

Though desert prospecting makes more use of advanced technology (e.g., metal detectors, etc.), river panning is just as fruitful, if not more so. Go ahead and get your hands dirty. ROBERT HOLMES/CALTOUR

chances for striking—by some estimates, the 49ers left behind about 85 percent of the gold in those California hills and streams. That being said, don't forget about immersing yourself in the countryside, too. You'll have time to sit back and enjoy the scenery in between loads of silt, so don't pass up the opportunity. There's also a lot of time to get to know your comrades and guides; look forward to sharing good company, acquiring a new skill, and spending a weekend learning one of the most American pursuits there is. Prospecting is adventure for fun *and* profit, the kind of activity that pays for itself if you're lucky but is relaxing even if you find nothing but more mud.

Price: $100–$500-plus

(Fall, Easy)

DRIVING DIRECTIONS

Get Gold Adventures will tell you how to get to your mining destination. Because claims "dry up," your site could be different every trip. Gold Prospecting Adventures is located in Jamestown, just off Highway 49 (which you can reach by taking Highway 50 east from Sacramento). Call for street directions once you roll into town.

OUTFITTERS

GOLD PROSPECTING ADVENTURES
Jamestown, CA
(209) 984–4653
www.goldprospecting.com

GET GOLD ADVENTURES & OUTFITTERS
Sonora, CA
(209) 588–1523
www.getgold.com

FOR MORE INFORMATION

OAKLAND MUSEUM OF CALIFORNIA
(510) 238–2200
www.museumca.org/goldrush

MUSEUM OF THE CITY OF SAN FRANCISCO, ONLINE GOLD RUSH EXHIBITS
www.sfmuseum.org

RECOMMENDED READING

Alt, David and Donald W. Hyndman. *Roadside Geology of Northern and Central California*. Missoula, Mont.: Mountain Press Publishing Co., 1999.

Angier, Bradford. *Looking For Gold: The Modern Prospector's Handbook*. Mechanicsburg, Pa.: Stackpole Books, 1982.

Basque, Garnet. *Gold Panner's Manual*. Guilford, Conn.: Lyons Press, 1999.

SLEEP CHEAP

If you take a Get Gold tour, you'll be camping during the trip. If you're in Jamestown, head over to Columbia State Historic Park, located 3 miles north of Sonora, off Highway 49. It's an actual town, once known as "the Gem of the Southern Mines," and it offers regular lodging, as well as civilization's perks, in a very cool historical environment. Call (209) 532–0150 for more information.

Exploring Mount Tamalpais and Golden Gate

Lost in the 'Frisco Wilderness

San Francisco is a hell of a town for all kinds of reasons, from its funky culture to the many examples of urbanized beauty you'll find there. You won't come across another place like it, this wild, fun buddy of a city.

Nor will you find another large urban area that manages to fit in so well with the natural world surrounding it. Another San Fran distinction: The place is simply enveloped by great outdoor adventure. I'm not just talking about gentle walks on paved or gravel trails, either; within mere minutes of the city, you'll find some bad mama-jamma hikes, stuff that you'll need to break out the knobby boots for. The good people of the Bay area—and northern California in general—decided a long time ago that nature is better enjoyed if you keep it close by, rather than pave over every tree in a 60-mile radius. Instead, the Bay's first outdoorspeople thought ahead and set aside big chunks of land so their children's children might have some places to play.

The result? That you can take a short drive over the Golden Gate into Marin County and enjoy all sorts of outdoorsy activities, even strenuous ones, in a true backcountry environment, rather than a cheap approximation of one. Fill up the canteen and get

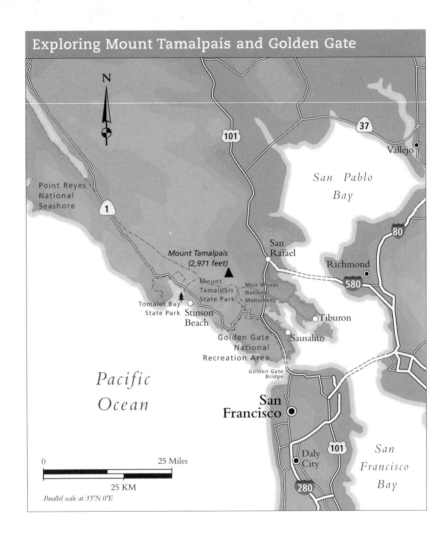

N

Point Reyes
National
Seashore

San Pablo
Bay

Vallejo

Mount Tamalpais
(2,971 feet)

San
Rafael

Richmond

Mount
Tamalpais
State Park

Muir Woods
National
Monument

Tomales Bay
State Park

Stinson
Beach

Tiburon

Golden Gate
National
Recreation Area

Sausalito

Golden Gate
Bridge

Pacific

Ocean

San
Francisco

Daly
City

San
Francisco
Bay

0   25 Miles

25 KM

Parallel scale at 35°N 0°E

ready for a sweat, because it's time to hike the challenging trails
just north of the city, where you can forget all about the bustling
life for a while and put your mind a thousand miles away from the
urbanization you just left.

Step one: Don't take this escape on the weekend when everybody else does. To feel like you're out there by your lonesome, you
have to time things correctly and hit the trail when there are just a
few other adventurers out there willing to do so. Take a couple days
off work if you have to—the more open country you'll experience
will be worth it. After all, the city is close by, and the people of the

Bay love their countryside. They're great folks, for sure, but try to dodge them just this once.

The next thing you want to do is get your lungs up to the proper capacity. Sure, there are simple trails that even your grandmother can handle (not that there's anything wrong with those trails, either), but this escape is about the backcountry in your backyard, so make sure you're ready for it. Lastly, pick up a few of the books listed at the end of this chapter as recommended reading. There's not enough room here to discuss all the great trails that stretch through Marin County, but the recommended books will provide you with a bunch of great trails in the areas I'll mention.

Much of the peninsula just north of the city is protected wilderness area of some kind. The Golden Gate National Recreation Area and Mount Tamalpais State Park, home to Marin's signature promontory, lie right over the big bridge, and Muir Woods National Monument actually lies inside the rec area, just south of Mount Tam's east peak. In all three of these areas, you'll find some spectacular hiking through country that seems to lie hundreds of miles from civilization, rather than just a short hop. Throughout the entire area, you're looking at more than 200 miles of hiking trail, some of which you'll share with mountain bikers and equestrians.

Golden Gate NRA opened to the world in 1972 as part of a trend to bring wilderness resources closer to city populations. The park contains loads of historical and cultural resources—think Alcatraz, the Presidio, and the Nike Missile Site—along with the aforementioned land, more than 75,000 acres in all for your perusal. I'm talking 59 miles of total bay and ocean shoreline, attracting sixteen million visitors every year. Of course, the majority of these folks never make it to places like the Olema Valley, rolling grassland that offers wonderful views and an amazing natural and human history.

Muir Woods, tucked up in the middle of Mount Tamalpais State Park, will probably end up being another focal point of your search for backcountry, both because of its incredible beauty and its isolation in comparison to Golden Gate NRA. The area wasn't logged out because the trees are somewhat hard to get to—always a good sign for hikers. The land, more than 550 acres in all, has been federally protected since 1908, and it encompasses quite a few wonderful areas. Take Muir Beach, for instance: This sandy ribbon marks the area where Redwood Creek empties into the ocean, and it comes complete with towering bluffs and astounding views. Throw in some nearby wetlands, a lagoon, and the fact that you can jump in the

Marin County from the high points of Mount Tamalpais. ROBERT HOLMES/CALTOUR

chilly ocean to cool off (provided you can swim—no lifeguards on duty), and you've got a great spot to spend a few outdoorsy hours.

Don't forget to hit Mount Tamalpais, either, the 2,571-foot main peak of Marin County that rises up to provide some great, and some-times strenuous, hiking. Mount Tam, as the locals call it, has served in its recreational role for almost a century and a half now; 49ers started tooling around the area between expeditions, and the habit stuck in later denizens of the Bay area. Today, it's a day hiker's paradise, with more than 50 miles of trail that link into a larger, 200-mile system at multiple points. From the summit on a clear day, you'll see the Farallon Islands 25 miles out at sea, along with the city and the bay. If you're really lucky, you might even glimpse the Sierra Nevada's snowcapped peaks, more than 150 miles away.

The Mount Tamalpais Interpretive Association offers a ton of guided hikes every month, ranging in difficulty from fairly low-impact to hard-core difficult. The type of hike depends on the day you go; Sunday hikes are longer and more difficult, generally rang-ing from 7 to 12 miles and taking in a lot of elevation. Night hikes are a cool idea, too—monthly astronomy programs and specially scheduled night hikes for taking in the various stages of the moon are fun and provide the rare treat of seeing the park after dark. Just visit the association's Web site or give them a call, and they'll let you know what's going on and when.

Backcountry is wherever you find it, even if the highway back into the city is only a scant few miles away. Head north to Marin County and the trails that burrow through its forests and beaches, especially when the crowds have other things to do, and you'll get that lost-in-the-woods feeling. Now lace up those knobby boots!

Price: Next to nothin'—admission to the Golden Gate NRA is free unless you're headed to Alcatraz or Kirby Cove to camp, and Muir Woods is only $3.00. Mount Tamalpais is accessible with only a small fee, too.

(Fall, Medium)

DRIVING DIRECTIONS

Mount Tamalpais and the wilder areas of Golden Gate NRA are both located just over the Golden Gate Bridge in Marin County. Simply cross the bridge and stay on Highway 101 for Golden Gate, or take Highway 1 to get to Tamalpais.

OUTFITTERS

GOLDEN GATE NATIONAL RECREATION AREA
San Francisco, CA
(415) 561–4700
www.nps.gov/goga

MUIR WOODS
Mill Valley, CA
(415) 388–2595 (recorded message)
(415) 388–2596 (headquarters)
www.nps.gov/muwo

MOUNT TAMALPAIS STATE PARK
Mill Valley, CA
(415) 388–2070
www.parks.ca.gov/default.asp?page_id=471

FOR MORE INFORMATION

MOUNT TAMALPAIS INTERPRETIVE ASSOCIATION
San Rafael, CA
(415) 258–2410 (taped message about upcoming hikes)
www.mttam.net

MARIN TRAILS
www.marintrails.com

RECOMMENDED READING

Brown, Ann Marie. *Foghorn Outdoors' 101 Great Hikes in the San Francisco Bay Area*. Emeryville, Calif.: Avalon Travel Publishing, 2003.

Martin, Don, Kay Martin, and Bob Johnson. *Hiking Marin: 133 Great Hikes in Marin County*. Marin County, Calif.: Martin Press, 1999.

Martin, Don, Kay Martin, and Bob Johnson. *Mt. Tam: A Hiking, Running and Nature Guide*. Marin County, Calif.: Martin Press, 1993.

Salcedo-Chourre, Tracy. *Exploring Point Reyes National Seashore and Golden Gate National Recreation Area*. Guilford, Conn.: Globe Pequot Press, 2002.

Sprout, Janine and Jerry Sprout. *Golden Gate Trailblazer: Where to Hike, Stroll, Bike, Jog, Roll in San Francisco and Marin County*. Markleeville, Calif.: Diamond Valley Company, 2001.

SLEEP CHEAP

Mount Tamalpais offers first-come, first-served camping up the mountain on the Panoramic Highway, as well as reserve camping down at Rocky Point, a mile south of Stinson. Call (800) 444–7275 to reserve a site, or visit www.reserveamerica.com; for questions about the first-come sites, call the park at (415) 388–2070. The cost is $15 per night in both places.

Fly-fishing for Salmon and Steelhead

Treasures of the Trinity

Imagine a place where the water runs clean. Valley walls, coated with thick, green life, shoot up on either side of you, bringing your focus down on the river like a tunnel. The water bubbles by and beneath you, around your legs, pausing for nothing. Imagine then that you're wielding a long, whippet-thin fishing rod, slicing the air and kissing the water with your fly until you hear a small *tish,* the sound of a 2-foot steelhead breaking the surface and grabbing your line. As you reel him in, one thought keeps popping into your head: "This would make a heckuva beer commercial."

And so it would–fly-fishing in the Trinity National Forest is the real-life version of the vibe all those "head for the mountains" and "cool as a mountain stream" pitches are shooting for. For getting in touch with northern California's primal wilderness, as well as some extremely tasty fish, you won't find a better escape.

The Trinity River starts in the Trinity Alps National Forest and flows down to Trinity Lake, which is in turn created by Trinity Dam. It's the largest tributary of the Klamath River system and serves to drain a watershed consisting of a few hundred thousand acres of Trinity Alp snowmelt. It holds a legendary status among fly fishermen and reigns as California's preeminent steelhead and salmon fishery. What's more, you can drive right along its whole length (with every hole and pool visible) on California's State Highway 299

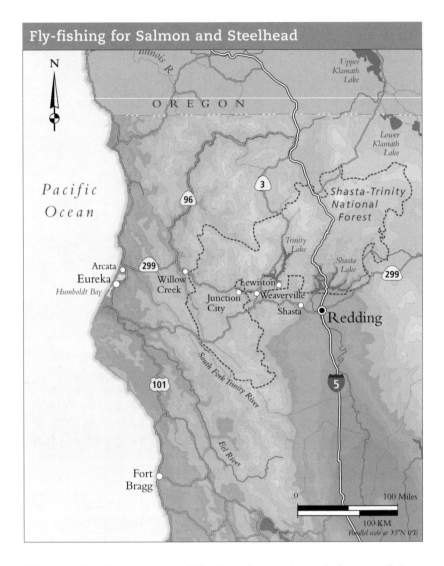

West, making it more accessible than those primeval, faraway fishing holes in the middle of the woods. Just about every pull-off along the highway has a trail leading down to a holding area, so even you novice steelheaders will find pretty nice fishing by just driving along, looking down to the right, and pulling off when you see a still, quiet pool below.

Just as the leaves are beginning to blush a little, the main stem of the Trinity comes into its most abundant season; from September all the way through until March, the fish are running, though it's not terribly uncommon to land a rogue steelhead in the dead of summer. Throw in the gaggle of campsites you'll pass along the way, and you've got one of the quietest, most leisurely weekend drives around.

Hooking a steelhead can be a whole lot easier than landing one. Steelies average around 6 pounds, with the occasional 12-pounder thrown in for good measure, and they put up a heck of a fight. These aren't the only fish you'll be looking for, either; the river supports an annual migration of salmon, as well as a decent population of resident brown trout. You can fish for steelhead from November thru February, sometimes into March, and the salmon run around the same time. Chinook (king) salmon make their way up the river by the thousands, seeking spawning grounds, and the Coho (silver) salmon follow close behind. Fly fishers using eight- or nine-weight rods can pull these fish out of the drink with little trouble, provided your technique is good and you have some idea about where to go—or you have someone along who can *tell* you where to go.

If you have no fly experience whatsoever, never fear—the Trinity still holds huge possibilities for fish-finding adventure, even if you've never performed a roll cast in your life. There are a number of guide services operating here, any of which can help you land a few of these legendary fish while you take in the natural splendor around you. Regardless of your skill level, these folks can get you out there and teach you what you need to know—whether it's how to start casting or what type of fly to use in February, when the steelies begin to focus on hatching aquatic insects and become more susceptible to dry flies.

Trinity River Adventures, for example, based outside of Lewiston, can help you catch a few no matter what your fishing game, conventional or fly. They run well-outfitted boats on the upper Trinity, a 20-mile stretch from the Old Lewiston Bridge down to Junction City. Jack Trout Fly Fishing & Guide Service operates on some other California rivers in addition to the Trinity, as well as in international locations—if you happen to be in another part of the state and can't make the drive, they'll take you to the Sacramento River in search of rainbow trout or the Pit River up by Lake Shasta if you want to stick to that area. There are other guides, too (see "Outfitters" later in the chapter), so just give them all a call and see which one offers the most of what you're looking for.

Obviously, your guide will help you navigate the Trinity's complicated fishing regulations. However, if you're already a well-versed

Just driving down Route 299 will give you a great show as fly fishermen up and down the river look to land big steelies. CHRIS BECKER

fly fisherman, and you want to hit the river yourself, make sure that you grab a copy of California's Fish and Game Regulation booklet. The state's fishing regulations are constantly evolving to meet the fishery's needs; make sure you know the current version of those rules. You'll need to have a valid California fishing license on you at all times, as well as special punch cards for salmon and steelhead. You can pick up all this paperwork at most California sporting goods stores or from the California State Department of Fish and Game. Regulation booklets are free, so you can spend your cash on yet another cool fly.

Those of you who already fish with flies should know the following (beginners, you'll get this paragraph after your trip): use weight-forward floating lines on a seven- to nine-weight rod (though you can go down to five). The floating line will let you switch from nymphing with a weighted fly to swinging the fly, or switching completely to a dry if you want to. Go with this setup, and you won't have to bring an extra rod or spool. Wading is a big part of fishing here, even if you're in a boat, so bring your best pair of waders along (and the water is cold, so dress accordingly).

No matter what your skill level, fly-fishing the Trinity is a treat. Don't be intimidated by the folks you see out there, with their beautiful casts and perfect form; just start slow, get a terrific guide, and start fishing. Go ahead and crack a beer, too, if the urge to "head to the mountains" strikes you.

Price: $250–$500-plus

(Fall, Medium)

DRIVING DIRECTIONS

Trinity country is about five hours north of the San Francisco Bay. The fastest way to get there is to go north on Interstate 5 to the city of Redding, then west on Highway 299. A longer, more scenic route from the Bay area is along the Pacific Coast through the Redwood Empire on U.S. Highway 101 to Eureka/Arcata; from there, go east on Highway 299.

OUTFITTERS

TRINITY RIVER ADVENTURES
Scott Stratton, owner/guide
Lewiston, CA
(530) 623–4179
www.trinityriveradventures.com

JACK TROUT FLY FISHING & GUIDE SERVICE
Mt. Shasta, CA
(530) 926–4540
www.jacktrout.com

ANDREW HARRIS FLYFISHING
(530) 632–3465
www.andrewharrisflyfishing.com

KING'S GUIDE SERVICE
Douglas City, CA
(530) 623–3438
www.timkingsfishing.com

THE FLY SHOP
Redding, CA
(800) 669–3474
www.adventuresinflyfishing.com

FOR MORE INFORMATION

SHASTA-TRINITY NATIONAL FOREST
Redding, CA
(530) 226–2500
www.fs.fed.us/r5/shastatrinity

RECOMMENDED READING

Combs, Trey. *Steelhead Fly Fishing*. Guilford, Conn.: Lyons Press, 1999.

Lord, Macauley, Dick Talleur, and Dave Whitlock. *The L.L. Bean Ultimate Book of Fly Fishing*. Guilford, Conn.: Lyons Press, 2002.

Stienstra, Tom. *Foghorn Outdoors: California Fishing Sixth Edition: The Complete Guide to More Than 1,000 Fishing Spots in the Golden State.* Emeryville, Calif.: Avalon Travel Publishing, 2001.

SLEEP CHEAP

There are a ton of camping options along Highway 299—just keep your eyes open and turn off when you feel like it. Call (530) 623–6106, the Big Bar ranger station, for more information on the Trinity, camping in the area, or anything else regarding the area.

Scuba in Monterey Bay

The Strange Country Down Under

The water closes over your head, and the gear you're wearing threatens to pull you down farther. You simply pull in a breath, then continue pulling and pushing your lungs, looking around and taking in the sights all the while. To your left, the faint outline of a California sea lion drifts by. His entrance underwater was marked by a blunt *poof* in your ears. He descends toward some large crevasses and rocks below, bubbles jetting from his mouth. You grin widely behind your own regulator as you follow him. *It's going to be a good dive,* you muse as he darts by, setting up for another pass.

Scuba diving might be the best example of man conquering the natural world that all of us have a chance to experience. A skydiver can interact with the wind and sky on the drift downward; a surfer can cut and ride on waves that would otherwise knock you under. But a scuba diver can actually become part of a totally alien environment, no less so than astronauts in space suits do. However, unlike space travel, anyone can go to their local dive shop—or a dive shop in any part of the world—and get under the water. Anyone can train to dive under more difficult conditions, too, provided they have the physical ability to do so. Above all, diving allows you to see a world you could never otherwise take in, which makes it a perfect adventure for those of us looking for new places to explore.

Getting certified is fairly easy; just take an accredited introductory diving class to learn the basics, take a few certification dives, and you'll receive a card from either the Professional Association of Diving Instructors (PADI) or the National Association of Underwater

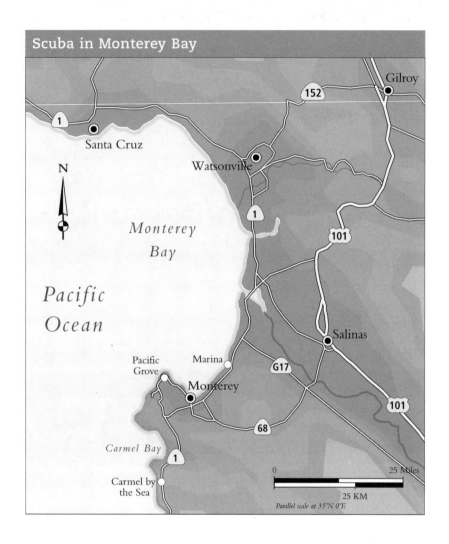

Gilroy

152

1

Santa Cruz

N

Watsonville

Monterey

Bay

1

101

Pacific

Ocean

Salinas

Pacific
Grove

Marina

G17

Monterey

101

68

Carmel Bay

1

0   25 Miles

25 KM

Carmel by
the Sea

Parallel scale at 35°N 0°E

Instructors (NAUI), which will allow you to dive anywhere in the
world, with any certified shop. This intro class is fairly inexpensive,
too—generally around $200 in the Monterey area—but you need a
bit of equipment to start, namely a mask, booties, fins, and a
snorkel. That package will run you a couple hundred more, depending on the level of equipment you buy; however, once you have
that starting package, you'll be able to rent the rest of the equipment you need just about anywhere you're likely to go.

The California Coast boasts a proliferation of terrific dive destinations, and Monterey Bay stands out as one of its finest. The water

is a little cold, particularly if you have previous experience with tropical diving; you'll be wet-suiting up pretty much all year long. What's more, you'll want to head to Monterey in late fall or early winter for the best dive conditions, so the water is certain to be a tad chillier than it would be at the height of summer. The coolest thing about this cool water is the explosion of life it facilitates; while tropical waters are generally dominated by a few groups of organisms such as coral, cold water attracts a little bit of everything, from jellyfish and shelled creatures to the aforementioned sea lions. Oh, and then there are the great white sharks...

Yes, Monterey does have some of those big guys swimming around—not a lot, but a few. The Monterey Peninsula sits at the southern end of the so-called Red Triangle, an area of water that stretches from just above San Francisco 120 miles down the coast. This zone accounts for 45 percent of the great white attacks ever recorded worldwide, so while you stand about as much chance of seeing a great white as you do of getting hit by lightning, know that they are there.

Another quick word about safety, namely shop certification: diving is a potentially dangerous activity. You're dealing with pressurized gases, and an adventure that takes place up to 100 feet away from your nearest breath of naturally occurring air. All this being said, diving with professionals is incredibly safe, and you shouldn't fear when you're in good hands. However, be sure you put yourself *in* good hands—you don't ever want to sign up for a class, or a dive of any kind, with an outfit that does not have certification from either NAUI or PADI. To get these certifications, dive outfitters must conform to certain regulations governing tank filling, instruction, and insurance. Any company missing this certification is certainly not worthy of trusting with your safety, as they're operating under the radar of any regulation or authority. Don't put your safety in such a fly-by-night organization's hands.

Around the Monterey Bay, you won't have any trouble finding outfitters with all their ducks in a row. The Monterey Bay Dive Center, Bamboo Reef Scuba, Aquarius, and Manta Ray Dive Center are all local dive shops that teach the basics if you need them, as well as bring you up to speed on more advanced skills and take you out into the open water for certification dives or just-for-fun dives. Monterey has its share of charter dive boats, too, which will take you out into the bay and the ocean beyond, where you can experience the one-of-a-kind adventure dive boat excursions represent.

Here comes the sun. COURTESY OF THE NATIONAL OCEANIC AND ATMOSPHERIC ADMINISTRATION (NOAA)

Though the boats listed below are not of the live-aboard variety, they do offer you the chance to get out into the water a ways before you suit up and jump in. You'll have access to a whole new seascape beyond what you can access from the shore.

For beginners and experts alike, Monterey delivers the goods. You pros already know the drill; just call up the dive shops and see what they can do for you. As for you beginners, the best way to get your certification taken care of is to sign up for your classes, take them, then head out for a weekend escape to get your certification dives out of the way. The shop you take your classes with can bring you out into the open ocean to complete these certifications, so check on the trips each one offers before you sign up for instructional classes—those are probably the jaunts you'll be on when you earn the right to carry your certification proudly to the next submerged destination you pick out.

Diving requires its share of precautions—you have to get the right training and pay attention when you're out there on your own. But if you do decide to take the plunge, you'll get to experience something very few people ever do: an alien world, wholly different from the one you wake up to and live in every day. For any potential explorer, how much better does it get than that?

Price: $250–$500

(Fall, Medium)

DRIVING DIRECTIONS

The Monterey Peninsula is located right off the Pacific Coast Highway, a little more than 100 miles south of San Francisco and just a stone's throw (or 30 miles) from Big Sur. Just head to the peninsula, and your dive outfitter will guide you from there into the Monterey Bay.

OUTFITTERS

Dive Shops

AQUARIUS DIVE SHOP
Monterey, CA
(831) 375–1933
www.aquariusdivers.com

BAMBOO REEF SCUBA
Monterey, CA
(831) 372–1685
www.bambooreef.com

MANTA RAY DIVE CENTER
Monterey, CA
(831) 375–6268
www.mantaraydive.com

MONTEREY BAY DIVE CENTER
Monterey, CA
(831) 656–0454
www.montereyscubadiving.com

Dive Boats

DIVE CENTRAL
(877) 462–3483
www.divecentral.com

MONTEREY EXPRESS
(888) 422–2999
www.montereyexpress.com

DIVER DAN'S
(800) 247–2822
www.diverdans.com/trips/
montereyboats.htm

FOR MORE INFORMATION

MONTEREY BAY NATIONAL MARINE
SANCTUARY
http://bonita.mbnms.nos.noaa
.gov

MONTEREY PENINSULA CONVENTION
AND VISITOR'S BUREAU
www.monterey.com

RECOMMENDED READING

Emory, Jerry. *The Monterey Bay Shoreline Guide.* Berkeley, Calif.:
University of California Press, 1999.

Jaconette, Lucinda. *Monterey Bay: The Ultimate Guide, From Santa Cruz
to San Simeon.* San Francisco, Calif.: Chronicle Books, 1999.

Owens, Tom and Melanie Chatfield. *Insiders' Guide to the Monterey
Peninsula.* Guilford, Conn.: Globe Pequot Press, 2004.

Rosenberg, Steve. *Diving & Snorkeling Monterey Peninsula and Northern
California.* Oakland, Calif.: Lonely Planet Publications, 2000.

SLEEP CHEAP

Since you're right up the road from Big Sur, why not enjoy camping in that fabled, beautiful region? Head to Pfeiffer Big Sur State Park and settle back into the big trees after checking out the underwater scene. If you want a more domesticated experience, the Big Sur Lodge is right there, too. Call (831) 667–2315 for park information, or (800) 424–4787 for the lodge. Obviously, even though the prices at the lodge aren't outrageous, the less pricey route is the campsite. There's a grocery store on-site too, if you forget anything (though *that* part of the lodge is abnormally pricey).

Ansel Adams Photo Tours

Making Photographs with the Master

"You don't take a photograph, you make it." This is just one of many bits of wisdom you might collect from the legendary Ansel Adams, photographer extraordinaire, patron saint of Yosemite National Park, and all-around American icon. More than anyone else in the history of photography, Adams defined the genre, and people around the world recognize his photos even today, fifty years after they were taken.

Though you may not believe your skills could ever match Adams's, there's no reason to think you can't learn something from his legacy. Luckily, his artistic descendants are more than happy to share their secrets (and his secrets) with you through frequent seminars held in the great photographer's name. So grab your camera, your best artist's eye, and the first ride to Yosemite, because it's time to learn from the legend—and maybe even shoot like him, too.

Adams was born in 1902, and his life coincided with, and in many ways reflected, the rise of the conservationist movement. He grew up in San Francisco and spent much of his life in California, but Yosemite in particular had a hold over him; Adams first visited the park in 1916 and spent significant time there every year until his death in 1984. Many of his most famous photographs were taken among Yosemite's waterfalls and forests, and through his association with the Sierra Club and similar organizations, he fought tirelessly to preserve the park and pristine wilderness areas like it.

However, as much as he did for conservationism—and one could argue that he is personally responsible for saving some of America's best-known wilderness areas—his first calling was photography for the art of it, rather than for its political/environmental ramifications. He was a technical photographer of the highest order and served as a consultant for Polaroid, among others, while he plied his trade throughout America's most pristine natural vistas.

Today, Yosemite is Ansel Adams Central, both for those who want some of the master's own work and others who want to create a few masterpieces themselves. For would-be *artistes,* the Ansel Adams Gallery in Yosemite offers a broad range of photography instruction—in fact, they offer just about everything a photographer looking to improve could want, whether that shutterbug is a first-day beginner or a seasoned, self-developing pro. Adams himself wrote ten technical manuals on photography, still widely regarded as some of the best literature in the field, and his intellectual descendants run the various photography programs at the Yosemite Gallery.

Keep in mind that all these programs have limited space available—most classes have space for eight or ten students, and they fill up fairly quickly. If you don't know when you're going to be in Yosemite yet, give the gallery a call before you plan anything, and see what's going on before you lock yourself into dates. Otherwise, you might miss a class that's right up your alley because you left two months earlier than you should have.

Just starting out? You'll be happy to know that there's a place for you, too: the Gallery schedules camera walks on Tuesday, Thursday, and Saturday (weather permitting). These jaunts provide a little guidance through Yosemite's photographable sites, a 1- to 2-mile stroll with one of the Gallery's staff photographers. The walks are free, and provide a basic camera review along with some composition suggestions, generally lasting about two hours. If you're going to Yosemite for a visit and want to get a few pointers that will make your snapshots a little better, this is a great option; you can be taking the best vacation shots of your life within a couple hours' time.

More advanced photographers will definitely want to sign up for one of the Gallery's many workshops, held throughout the year in the Yosemite Valley and at nearby Mono Lake. These seminars teach Adams-specific subjects and are best for those folks who already know their way around a camera. Many, for example, teach different

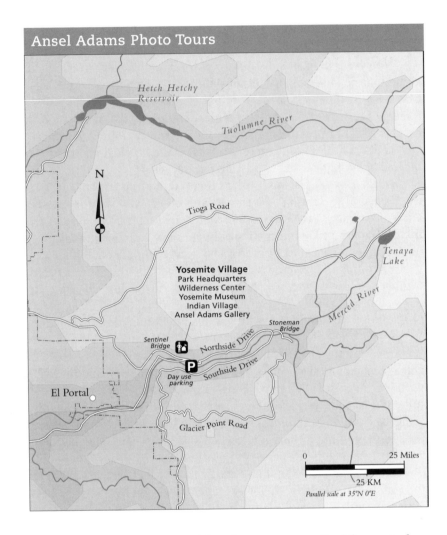

Hetch Hetchy
Reservoir

Tuolumne River

N

Tioga Road

Tenaya
Lake

Yosemite Village
Park Headquarters
Wilderness Center
Yosemite Museum
Indian Village
Ansel Adams Gallery

Merced River

Stoneman
Bridge

Sentinel
Bridge

Northside Drive

Day use
parking

Southside Drive

El Portal

Glacier Point Road

0   25 Miles

25 KM

Parallel scale at 35°N 0°E

aspects of the Zone System, Adams's very own method for control-
ling and linking exposure to development. Though this system is
quite complicated in some ways, the Gallery workshops try to teach
easy ways to use it, both in the field and in the darkroom. Along
with the Zone, there are classes on color management, landscape
photography in general, and black-and-white photography, as well as
more advanced sessions on platinum printing and digital photography.
And speaking of digital—some classes are more geared toward film
than others. There's not much reason to take a darkroom-intensive
class, for example, if your "darkroom" is a computer desktop. Make

sure to do your homework and take the right class for the format you're shooting.

Compared to photography classes you might take at the local community college, these multiday seminars are fairly reasonable, at around $450 to $700 a pop. As you might expect, beginner's classes tend to stay at the low end of that range, while more advanced skills cost a bit more to develop. (Advanced materials tend to be more expensive, too, as you probably already know if you've done some photography.) If you really want to learn a ton, and you've got some serious scratch lying around, think about signing up for one of the Gallery's private workshops—as the only student, you'll have the chance to pursue those topics of most interest to you with skilled instructors who are sure to give you the tools you need to bump your skills up a few notches.

Good photography skills can make every adventure you take a little better. Just think of how many bad photos you've taken over the years, and about how you'd have loved to capture this mountain's majesty, or that ocean vista's beauty, if only you knew how. To move beyond taking photographs and start making them, let Adams's legacy benefit you. At the very least, you're getting the chance to photograph one of the nation's most beautiful wilderness sites. But if you take your lessons to heart, pay attention, and internalize what you are taught, you'll reap the rewards every time you snap the shutter or develop a print. Choose this route and experience the joy of creation for yourself.

Price: $0–$500-plus, depending on the class you take
(Fall, Medium)

DRIVING DIRECTIONS

There are four entrances to the park: the south entrance on Highway 41 north from Fresno; the Arch Rock entrance on Highway 140 west from Merced; the Big Oak Flat entrance on Highway 120 west from Modesto and Manteca; and the Tioga Pass entrance on Highway 120 east, from Lee Vining and Highway 395. The Tioga Pass entrance is closed from the first major snowstorm in November until late May to June due to snow. All other park entrances are open all year but may require tire chains because of snow anytime between November and April.

Yosemite's Half Dome, one of the big rocks that make even the best rock climber's knees quiver. ROBERT HOLMES/CALTOUR

OUTFITTERS

THE ANSEL ADAMS GALLERY
Yosemite National Park, CA
(209) 372-4413
www.anseladams.com

YOSEMITE NATIONAL PARK
www.nps.gov/yose

FOR MORE INFORMATION

YOSEMITE AREA TRAVELER INFORMATION
www.yosemite.com

RECOMMENDED READING

Adams, Ansel. *Yosemite.* New York: Bulfinch, 1995.

Alinder, Mary Street. *Ansel Adams: A Biography.* New York: Henry Holt & Company, Inc., 1998.

Schaefer, John P. *The Ansel Adams Guide: Basic Techniques of Photography, Book One*. Manhattan: Watson-Guptill Publications, 1999.

SLEEP CHEAP

Obviously, Yosemite features a slew of camping options. For sites close to the Gallery, check in the Lower, Upper, or North Pines Camping areas, which are all located in the Yosemite Valley (800–436–PARK or www.reservations.nps.gov). Even closer, you'll find ready-made campsites at the Housekeeping Camp; these sites are for folks who don't feel like pitching a tent, and as a result they're a little more per site (depending on season). However, the cost is the same for one person or four, so bring a group to drop that cost down. Check out www.yosemitepark.com for details; go to the accommodations link. And reserve early no matter what you pick, as these are all prime sites in one of our most visited national parks.

Hiking the California Coastal Trail

The Lost Coast

If there's anything that makes the California coast a little less fantastic than it should be, it's the overabundance of buildings and people that coat its larger urban areas. In this day and age, seaside property is expensive, hard to come by, and, as a result, mostly snapped up. You won't find a lot of untouched real estate on a journey up the Cali coast; that highway you're driving on is evidence that even in seemingly untouched coastal areas like Big Sur, a fleet of heavy machinery preceded your passage.

Would you like to get an untouched sample of California's oceanside essence? A dose of what the seashore ought to look like? Then grab your backpack and set out for the Lost Coast, the longest stretch of untouched seaside wilderness in California and a breathtaking yet relaxing journey into backcountry that, unlike the dense forests of interior California, spreads out before you like infinity.

The Lost Coast lies in Humboldt County and stretches about 80 miles along the Pacific. A chain of small mountains runs along the spine of the coast, with 4,087-foot King Peak the highest of them; they all reach up over 2,000 feet, though, adding another landscape and climate dimension to the area. These mountains, along with two dozen year-round streams and steep canyons, serve to isolate the coast, making it all but unreachable except for four roadways, two of which are one-lane dirt, more path than road.

If you burn easily, make sure you bring ample shade gear and/or sun block. There's not a whole lot of shade when you're walking out on the beach. CHRIS BECKER

Camping the Lost Coast is fun, and the scenery is first-rate, but you're going to be roughing it. You won't find many showers or beds—or even tables and chairs—during your journey, so come prepared with a full pack and all the contingency plans that requires. This trip doesn't make a good first outing with a backpack, simply because if you forget something, you're mostly screwed. Take on the coast after you've already got a few miles on your hiking boots; the experience will serve you well out there. You're operating without a net back here, where forgetting your camp stove or matches can lead to a few miserable days rather than a few inconvenient hours.

Just a few words about the hiking conditions and distances, and you'll see what I mean. The California Coastal Trail—your main artery through the Lost Coast—runs for 64 miles, taking you into Kings Range National Conservation Area and the Sinkyone Wilderness State Park. Firm footing awaits you over some of the trail, but most of the way you'll be treading on beach sand that presents a decent foothold in places and nothing but stereotypical sinking softness in others.

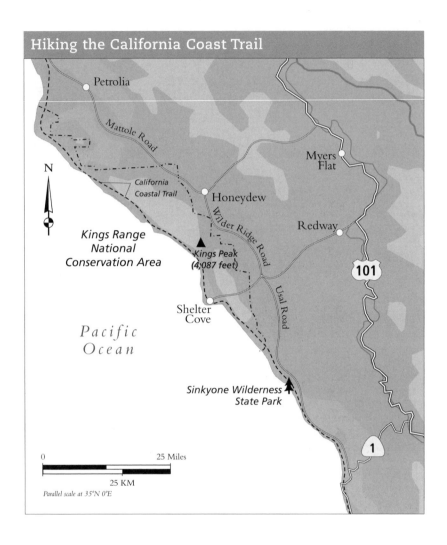

If you decide to take the alternative route, you're in for even more difficulty; it is steeper and leaves you taking the high country, since there is no continuous route along the beach, where 1,000-foot cliffs break things up. You'll see a total elevation gain of about 8,000 feet, though there's never a climb of more than 1,450 before a descent.

Again, you shouldn't take on the Lost Coast without some prior experience with a pack on your back—that 64-mile stretch can take seven days to complete. Even if you do know what you're doing, you'll probably want to slice off just a piece of the trail if you're planning for a simple weekend escape. Unfortunately, I don't have the room here to outline a recommended trail in all the detail you'll need, so check out the recommended reading section for books that are dedicated to navigating you along the Lost Coast and the California Coastal Trail.

You should know, too, that the California Coastal Trail, or CCT, does not simply run through the Lost Coast. Far from it—this trail is one of the more massive ones in the nation, running for 1,194 miles along the Cali coast. Private property and simple geography sometimes force the trail inland, but on the whole there's no better way to get in some beachside hiking than to find your way to the trail and start exploring. Along with the Pacific Crest Trail and the venerable Appalachian, the CCT is one of America's great long-distance routes, a passage from the deserts down south to the rain forests of the great Northwest.

Perhaps the coolest things about the CCT are its length and versatility; the trail stretches from Mexico to Oregon, and thus presents a multitude of hiking possibilities. You can take it on in small chunks—probably the best way to do it if you've got other obligations in your life—or eat up large swaths at a time, cutting off 100- or even 500-mile chunks and setting off. Of course, you might even want to take on the through-hike, though you'll obviously need a lot of time for that. No matter what you decide, the CCT stands out as one of California's most precious recreational resources, and in hiking it you'll be taking part in an adventure far bigger than just the steps you're taking today. For some people, this trail represents a whole lifetime of recreational bliss, a resource that, thanks to its great size and versatility, never gets old.

Whether you find yourself in this group, or simply use the trail for one great weekend escape, the Lost Coast is probably the most beautiful, isolated, and amazing section of the whole trail—indeed, of the whole fabled California coast. Whether you head up to Humboldt County for a weekend or pass through the coast on a much longer trek, its many wonders are sure to stay with you long after you've returned home.

Price: Not much—just the cost of shuttle service and camp supplies, plus any fees the parks might charge. Account for about $20 per day in food and fees, and you should be in good shape, provided you already have all your camping equipment.

(Fall, Medium)

A hike along the Lost Coast will take you past some of the least-viewed coastline in the entire United States—count yourself among the lucky ones. CHRIS BECKER

OUTFITTERS

LOST COAST TRAIL TRANSPORT
SERVICE
(707) 986–9909
www.lostcoasttrail.com

BLM CAMPFIRE PERMITS
(707) 986–5400

FOR MORE INFORMATION

KINGS RANGE NATIONAL
CONSERVATION AREA
(707) 986–5400
www.ca.blm.gov/arcata/king_
range.html

SINKYONE WILDERNESS STATE PARK
Whitehorn, CA
(707) 986–7711 (recorded
message)
www.parks.ca.gov/?page_id=429

RECOMMENDED READING

California Coastal Commission. *California Coastal Access Guide,* 6th ed. Berkeley, Calif.: University of California Press, 2003.

Lorentzen, Bob and Richard Nichols. *Hiking the California Coastal Trail, Volume Two: Monterey to Mexico.* Mendocino, Calif.: Bored Feet Publications, 2000.

Spitz, Tullan and John A. Vlahides. *Lonely Planet Coastal California.* Oakland, Calif.: Lonely Planet Publications, 2004.

SLEEP CHEAP

Camping along the Lost Coast is all about finding a spot (one that's already been impacted) and setting up. Just keep in mind that there's a bit of a bear problem in the area—bring a bear-proof canister for your food, and keep a lookout for big furry critters in and around your camp. Above all, *don't* give these big guys a reason to pay you a visit—put your food away, and leave nothing out that the bears might enjoy sniffing around.

Paragliding Northern California

Blue Sky Country

Have you ever thought about what birds must feel like—wheeling through the air on thermals and gusts, floating above all creation? Did you ever think, sitting in your cramped airline seat, that the view must be better without the window—and the 135 other passengers—in the way?

If you've had these thoughts, or thoughts like them, it might be time to introduce yourself to a brand-new way to grab air: the Zen float known as paragliding.

Don't confuse paragliding with parasailing. The latter is fun, but it doesn't involve actual flight per se; it's more of an assisted tow through the air, with power supplied by the boat below. If that boat stops, so does the parasailer. Para*gliding,* on the other hand, is a brand of real aerial transportation, complete with intense training and licensing for certified pilots.

And when I say pilots, I *mean* pilots. You should be prepared both mentally and physically before you take on such an intense adventure. Physical fitness comes into play when you're getting off the ground, toting the so-called wing behind you and steering it once you're up. However, strength is secondary to mental prepara- tion—make sure you're well rested and that you've got a clear head going. Even as a student, you'll have to think clearly and quickly to keep yourself aloft and out of trouble, so be ready to listen to instructions, process what you hear, and execute. Otherwise, you're just asking for the bad mojo. Always remember: Paragliding is serious business, and though it's the fun-filled rush of your life, it's also a big-time challenge.

For some folks, height will be an issue—recreational pilots begin by just skimming over the ground, but as they gain experience they can soar upwards of 10,000 feet and stay aloft for two or three hours. At bottom, it's a judgment call on your part—are you prepared to take on the big air, fear be damned? Willing to at least give it a shot and see what happens? Bear in mind, while you're considering, that takeoffs and landings are gentle and that, once in the air, most people are amazed by how calm and quiet the whole experience is. Unlike some other flight, you won't have major velocity behind you, so you're free to enjoy yourself a little more. But in the end, it's up to you—just follow directions, keep your mind open, and you may find yourself wanting more.

Paragliding works like this: You strap yourself to an aerofoil canopy similar to a parachute but designed to fly rather than float. Paragliders are far lighter than parachutes, as they don't have to withstand the shock of opening, and they generally contain more air-retaining cells. Once you're all strapped in, you run downhill, and the paraglider billows out behind you. As air works its way under the canopy, it lifts into the air, taking you with it. Now the cool part: You steer with two brake cords that also control your speed, and coast along the winds silently and without the kind of speed you can accumulate in a hang glider. This simplicity and mellow nature make paragliding easier to learn than hang gliding and a modicum safer, too. And once you're aloft, the comfort level is pretty high, adding a relaxing dimension to a pretty extreme activity.

Northern California boasts first-class paragliding conditions up and down the coast and all the way through the interior. As a result, people take to the skies with surprising frequency. San Francisco in particular has a vital and large paragliding community, complete with a bunch of outfitters who will be glad to teach you how to get up, up, and away. All will start you off with a tandem flight, in which you fly attached to an instructor. This type of flight will show you the bare essentials and establish whether paragliding is something you'd like to get a bit more of. After that, the pace at which you proceed is up to you, though it's a very good idea to take a concentrated introductory course. These courses run anywhere from seven days straight through to three or four days a month for a

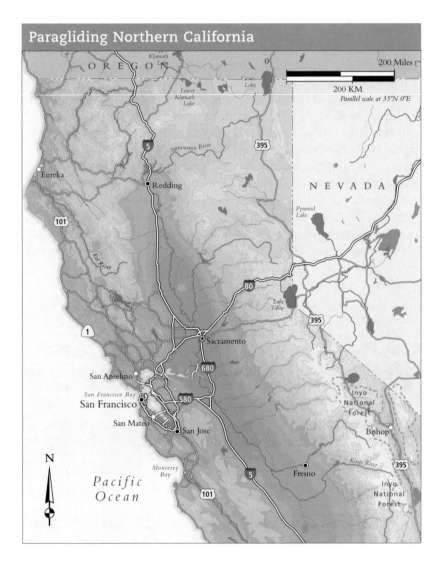

couple months; the goal is to install an intense training regimen before bad habits can develop, rather than to turn as many paraglider pilots as possible loose on the skies. All of these outfitters know that 10,000 feet of altitude is nothing to mess around with, and they are more than happy to do whatever is necessary to ensure your success as a pilot. Often, outfitters screen potential pilots in the first few lessons—in other words, your instructors will know if you're serious about learning this stuff, so show them that you are.

You'll find some prime soaring locations scattered throughout California's northern reaches, the most famous of which is Owens Valley. The 100-mile-long, 20-mile-wide valley produces some of the strongest lift found anywhere in the world, at least during the summertime. In the winter, spring, and fall, however, the air is smooth and perfect for training. Kari Castle, one of the best-known paragliders in the world, runs her operation in the Owens Valley and is glad to teach you what she knows. Just pay her a visit and take advantage of the knowledge she's got. Access coastal paragliding from San Francisco or points north if floating over scenic ocean vistas is your thing. Just remember—and I can't emphasize this enough—follow directions and go only where you're supposed to. One of paragliding's strengths—how easy it is to learn—can also fool you into thinking you're ready for more than you actually are. Steer clear of this trap, and fly within your limits.

Paragliding's basic techniques—launching, turning, landing—won't take you long to pick up. The time, the good part, is in perfecting those techniques and advancing to new ones. Advanced licenses await those of you who can't get enough of the gentle sky; really get into it, and you'll find yourself hitting intermediate levels after a few dozen flights, and expert status after a bunch more. You can get used equipment through northern California's developed network of fellow fliers, not to mention some first-class flying partners. The community is established, supportive, and enthusiastic, so get patched in if your first few glides get your blood flowing.

Nonmotorized flight is one of the world's greatest outdoor adventures. If you think you can handle the challenge—the altitude, the tough training, the mental discipline—then take the first step and get your earthbound butt up there!

Price: $50–$350, $500-plus for pilot certification training
(Fall, Difficult)

DRIVING DIRECTIONS

The paragliding school you choose will give you directions to your flight grounds. Some flight outfitters conduct training classes at a certain flight facility, while others move to different locations, depending on weather, time of year, availability, etc.

Learning to paraglide isn't horribly tough; just pay attention and do what you're told, and you'll be off to the friendly skies. CHRIS BECKER

OUTFITTERS

ADVANCED PARAGLIDING (BAY AREA)
www.advancedparagliding.com

KARI CASTLE (FLIGHT INSTRUCTION,
GUIDE SERVICES)
Bishop, CA
(760) 872–2087
www.karicastle.com

MERLIN FLIGHT SCHOOL
San Anselmo, CA
(415) 456–3670
www.merlinflightschool.com

SAN FRANCISCO TANDEM
PARAGLIDING
San Mateo, CA
(415) 310–7411
www.sftandem.com

ZEPHYR PARAGLIDING (BAY AREA)
(510) 748–0451
www.flyzephyr.com

FOR MORE INFORMATION

U.S. HANG GLIDING ASSOCIATION
(ORIGINALLY THE SOUTHERN
CALIFORNIA HANG GLIDING
ASSOCIATION)
(719) 632–8300
www.ushga.org

SAN FRANCISCO BAY AREA
PARAGLIDING ASSOCIATION (SFBAPA)
Pacifica, CA
www.sfbapa.org

RECOMMENDED READING

Cook, Matthew and David Sollom. *Paragliding: From Beginners to Cross-Country.* North Pomfret, Vt.: Trafalgar Square, 1998.

Pagen, Dennis. *The Art of Paragliding.* Spring Mills, Pa.: Sport Aviation Publications, 2001.

Whittall, Noel. *Paragliding: The Complete Guide.* New York: Lyons Press, 2000.

SLEEP CHEAP

If you're paragliding in the Owens Valley, Inyo National Forest makes a great camp destination in between flights. Inyo offers a huge variety of wilderness to see—this is, after all, John Muir country, and Ansel Adams himself took a number of photos here. What's more, there are campgrounds literally all over the place, though some close up by the beginning of September thanks to snow and colder temperatures. Call (760) 873–2400 for more information on camping and anything else regarding the area.

Diving with Great White Sharks

No Kidding

California is a land of superlatives and "bests"—the best rock climbing, the best surfing, the best whatever you can think of. Part of the
reason for writing this book (and its companion, *52 Great Weekend
Escapes in Southern California*) is to bring attention to California's
many natural and man-made adventures, a whole slate of activities
that could, conceivably, keep you occupied for not just one, but a
dozen lifetimes.

Among these escapes, though, are a few that are themselves
adventures of a lifetime. That is, things you might get to do once, if
you ever get to do them at all, things that you generally have to set
off for more exotic destinations to experience. California offers a
few adventures like these among the wonderful hiking, biking,
climbing, and riding that you'll find in every corner of the state.
But one in particular draws attention from the others—a journey
that takes you away from the shore and into the primal jaws of
another world, an ancient one in which giant sea creatures (rather
than giant conglomerations of humanity) dominate the Earth.

It's the chance of a lifetime: getting into the water with
possibly the greatest predator the world has ever seen. Welcome
to the domain of the great white shark—keep your hands inside the
cage, please.

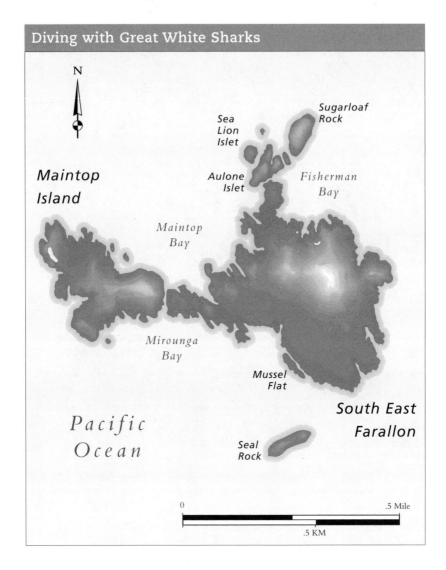

N

Sugarloaf
Rock

Sea
Lion
Islet

Maintop
Island

Aulone
Islet

Fisherman
Bay

Maintop
Bay

Mirounga
Bay

Mussel
Flat

South East
Farallon

Pacific
Ocean

Seal
Rock

0   .5 Mile

.5 KM

Great White Adventures, operating out of Emeryville, offers this once-in-a-lifetime chance to scuba divers looking for perhaps the greatest thrill in the natural world: the chance to witness a great white shark attacking prey, or even just swimming by. Among undersea predators, the great white occupies the top position— there's pretty much nothing out there eating these giant beasties. Only the killer whale can lay any claim to a similar position in the ocean's food chain.

You'll find great whites around the world, from Europe and northern California to South Africa and Australia. They'll swim as far south as the tropics, and occasionally into the colder waters off Alaska and Canada. In fact, their population is hard to nail down in part because they range so widely. Whatever the population is, however, we do know that it's fairly small, and great white protection is a worthy goal for many organizations advocating protection of sea life.

These massive beasts can measure up to 20 feet in length and weigh up to three and a half tons. Their eating habits tend mostly toward other fish and rays when they're younger, but as they grow, they invariably move on to mammals, namely seals, sea lions, and even small whales. Their chosen method of attack is a quick surprise strike from below that (hopefully for the hungry shark) leaves its prey dead or incapacitated. Occasionally, you'll see an ocean mammal with the telltale scars of a great white attack—they're usually gruesome and huge, commensurate with the horrifying mouth that left them.

One could go on and on about the great white—their ability to detect tiny biological electrical currents; the fact that they can smell drops of blood in the water from 3 miles away; the ridiculous number of razored teeth they sport in ever-replenishing rows. They are truly fascinating to read and think about, but this chapter isn't in here to give you food for thought. It's food for *action*, folks, and getting into the cage and seeing one of these creatures up close is about ten times better than talking about them all day.

Great White Adventures will take you into that rarified, eerie water, just a few miles off the coast of San Francisco near South East Farallon Island, where elephant seals make great meals before the shark's grueling trans-Pacific migration. You'll drop down into the cage without tanks—air will run down to you straight from the boat—and usually in groups, though no more than four at a time. You'll rotate in and out of the cage throughout the day in thirty-minute intervals, during which the crew will use decoys to draw great whites closer to the cage. As you wait topside on GWA's *New Superfish,* the only great white–specific dive boat operating in U.S. waters, you'll get your fill of chow and drinks, as well as beer and wine if you so desire.

A word of caution: You won't be in any danger when you're in the water or on the boat, but the mammals in the water might be if there's a hungry shark nearby. If you do happen to get lucky and see a 20-foot great white shark attack and eat a 200-pound elephant

Up close and maybe too personal with a great white. Bill Stableford

seal, you should know that it's a brutal, awesome, bloody—yet completely natural—event. If you don't think you have the constitution to handle watching such a thing, you might want to think twice about viewing it. (You won't be spared if you're on the boat, either, as most predation takes place right on the surface.) The whole point of this adventure is to find and observe the ocean's most implacable predator doing what it does best, so you can't be disgusted, offended, or otherwise put out when you're actually fortunate enough to see what you came to see. Keep in mind, too, that the great white shark season is short—mid-September through mid-November. Plan well ahead to take advantage of the time window.

Those of you who don't dive can get in on the action, too, for a much lower price to boot. You can go this route if you'll be accompanying a buddy who's down in the cage or if you just want to see a great white from the distance the boat provides. Since most feedings take place on the surface, you might actually see some action akin to what the divers are taking in. Whatever route you decide on, you'll be in good hands onboard the *New Superfish,* so ask any questions you might have about the sharks themselves or anything else about the region—the crew is knowledgeable and willing to help out any way they can.

Great white sharks are, for most people, the stuff of fantasy. To know something so mythical, misunderstood, and mighty is for real, you have to get up close and personal just to see what all the press is about. With a little help from Great White Adventures, you've got the chance to do just this, within 25 miles of the beach. The cost, while high in terms of dollars, can't begin to quantify what you get out of an awe-inspiring experience like this one.

Price: $775 for divers, $375 for topside observers. That cost includes your diving, air, weights and belts, continental breakfast, lunch, snacks, drinks, and alcohol should you choose to indulge.
(Fall, Difficult)

DRIVING DIRECTIONS

You'll be leaving from Emeryville.

From San Francisco: Take the Bay Bridge east. Then take Interstate 580 west/Interstate 80 east toward Sacramento. At the first exit (Powell Street), turn left and cross under the freeway. Follow it 1 mile to the Emeryville Marina and park at the harbor offices and the Emeryville Sportfishing dock.

From Oakland or the South Bay: Take Interstate 880 north, then Interstate 980 toward downtown Oakland. Then follow the signs to I–580 west, and exit 80 east to Berkeley. Get off on Powell Street, and follow the directions above.

OUTFITTERS

GREAT WHITE ADVENTURES
Alameda, CA
(510) 814–8256
www.greatwhiteadventures.com

FOR MORE INFORMATION

SAN FRANCISCO OCEANIC SOCIETY
San Francisco, CA
(800) 326–7491
www.oceanic-society.org

RECOMMENDED READING

Cousteau, Jean-Michel. *Cousteau's Great White Shark*. New York: Harry N. Abrams, 1995.

Ellis, Richard and John E. McCosker. *Great White Shark*. Palo Alto, Calif.: Stanford University Press, 1995.

Matthiessen, Peter. *Blue Meridian: The Search for the Great White Shark*. New York: Penguin, 1997.

SLEEP CHEAP

After diving with the big beasts, you deserve a relaxing place to unfold your camp chair and put your feet up. No place fits the bill (despite its name) like Mount Diablo State Park, a beautiful patch of country a little ways east of Emeryville. The camping's great year-round, and if you do a little hiking, the view from the top of the mountain is unbelievable—you can even catch sight of Half Dome in Yosemite with a pair of binoculars and a clear day. Call (800) 444-7275 or visit the ReserveAmerica Web site (www.reserveamerica.com) to get a spot of your own.

Windsurfing San Francisco Bay

Batten Down the Hatches!

Windsurfing is one of those hybrid activities that combines a number of disciplines to create something equal to, or even better than, any of them. Take the crazy thrills of surfing, mix in a few dashes of sailing's tranquility, top with a back-to-nature experience that rivals California's sweetest hikes, and you've got it—a watery challenge that pays off in spades for anyone willing to give it a go.

If you're going to step up to this particular plate, there's no better place to pick up the bat than the San Francisco Bay, a huge expanse of windy water that plays host to some of the world's nicest windsurfing. You'll also find a bunch of windsurfing instructors here, along with loads of equipment for rent (or purchase, if you really get the bug). In all, the Bay is to windsurfing what Yosemite is to rock climbing: a great place to learn it, as well as a playground for the expert.

When you see windsurfers on TV, they inevitably make the whole thing look easy. Seeing pros in action might plant thoughts of extreme shredding in *your* head, which can be a somewhat dangerous thing—windsurfing is a tough nut to crack on your own, no matter how effortless it might look. This isn't to say that you can't learn it; under the right conditions (namely under the direction of a qualified instructor), you can get yourself sailing with the best of

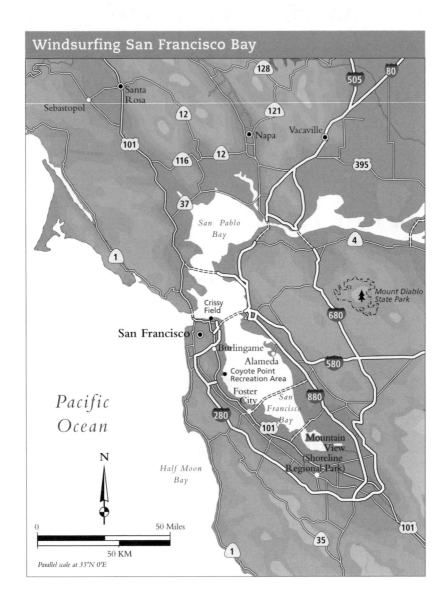

them. And if you're just learning to windsurf, you'll be well served by the numerous windsurfing instructors around the Bay, all of whom can get you up and on your board in a couple hours, even if you don't know a rig winch from a boom.

Start windsurfing and you'll quickly find out that a few things you've heard about the sport are a little off-base. First thing: It's not as hard as people might have you believe. After a few hours with an instructor and some attention on your part, you should find yourself upright and mobile for fairly long periods of time. Another common myth is that you have to be Hercules to maneuver the thing around. One need only look at the typical windsurfer to see that this is not true—finesse is the name of the game, and women windsurf every bit as well as guys do. You don't need hurricane gusts to be out there, either, as breezes of less than 10 mph will keep you moving.

The Bay is blessed with wind of all kinds, from these low-grade gusts to more intense storm winds—something for windsurfers of all stripes. The local sailing season begins in March or April, depending on how the weather behaves, and runs all the way through to September. You can sail almost every day during these months, particularly if you don't mind driving around the picturesque Bay area. Keep in mind, though, that the water is never tropical. At the beginning of the season, it's pretty chilly, though nothing a fairly heavy wet suit can't handle; as the weather picks up, the water warms up enough to accommodate a lighter wet suit, and a lot of windsurfers get by on shorties in the summertime. The degree of warmth you'll need depends on how far out you'll be sailing and where you begin (sailing the coast is always chillier). Just make sure that you prepare yourself for colder conditions, especially in the early season—equipment problems can occasionally result in slow going and leave you spending a few hours in the water. You don't want to deal with that kind of chill in nothing but your skivvies.

Beginners should have a pretty easy time finding their way to simple surfing grounds, thanks to the instructor you eventually decide to go with. However, if you don't feel like you're quite ready for the big Bay, Shoreline Regional Park down in Mountain View has a nice, progressive training program that starts you with a two-day class and brings you all the way up through the advanced intermediate level. Shoreline Lake, a cozy, fifty-acre saltwater lake filled with San Francisco Bay water, boasts predictable summer breezes, and it will prepare you for the more difficult conditions on the Bay. What's more, the lake is a whole lot warmer—all the way up in the 70s during the summer.

Unfortunately, the Bay water itself isn't the cleanest you'll find in the state of California. After heavy rains, though, the water quality gets worse because runoff from the storm sewers—containing insecticide and all sorts of other things it's best not to think about—

Windsurfing isn't a test of strength, but of finesse. Once that thing's up and running, the wind will provide the muscle. MATTHEW SCHERF/ISTOCKPHOTO.COM

gets overloaded and spills into the Bay. Now, before you write off your Bay adventure completely, remember that swimming in any body of water this big is a little dicey—especially one as urban as the San Francisco Bay. Just take simple precautions, don't fill your canteen out there, and surf away. (Local agencies will usually post warnings if the overflow problem gets particularly bad.)

Once you get a few hours of instruction in, you're ready to head out on your own and explore the Bay. The options boggle the mind—take Coyote Point, for example, over in San Mateo, probably the most popular windsurfing site in the Bay area. Access is easy from the Coyote Point Recreation Area, and stable, constant wind makes the place a gold standard for windsurfers. Unfortunately, these very benefits help make the place one of the more crowded sites in Northern California, so keep an eye out for traffic as you sail. Or if you've already got some windsurfing experience—repeat, *if you've already got some windsurfing experience*—you many want to visit Crissy Field, one of the more challenging and dangerous sailing spots in the Bay area. You'll find muscular currents, cold water, strong winds, and heavily traveled shipping lanes, which create large wind shadows, or zones where air movement is nearly zero. You'll find a bunch of other sites, too, so ask around when you're getting your outfitter squared away—they'll point you to their own favorites, which all offer their own special features.

No matter where in the Bay you decide to get your sail on, and no matter what your skill level happens to be, you'll get a huge kick out of feeling the wind whip you along as the most beautiful city on the West Coast scrolls by. You could spend an awful long time sailing the Bay before you expend its possibilities, too, so it's the kind of place—like the rock walls of Yosemite—that grows with you as your own skills expand and require new challenges. Happy sailing!

Price: $100–$300 (for a day or two of lessons, with equipment included)

(Fall, Difficult)

DRIVING DIRECTIONS

You'll probably do some driving around the Bay in your search for sites. Just consult your outfitter, or one of the supply shops listed below, for directions to the site you choose or to the place they're conducting their lessons.

OUTFITTERS

BOARDSPORTS
(Store locations in San Rafael,
San Francisco, and Berkeley—
teaching facility in Alameda)
Lessons held beginning in April
Crown Beach Memorial Park
Alameda, CA
(510) 843–9283
www.boardsports.com

CALIFORNIA WINDSURFING
Foster City, CA
(650) 594–0335
www.californiawindsurfing.com

**SHORELINE AQUATIC CENTER
(SHORELINE REGIONAL PARK)**
Mountain View, CA
(650) 965–7474
www.shorelinelake.com

**SURFACE 2 AIR SPORTS/ASD
(ADVANCED SURF DESIGNS)**
Burlingame, CA
(650) 348–8485
www.asdwindsurfing.com

FOR MORE INFORMATION

**SAN FRANCISCO BOARDSAILING
ASSOCIATION**
www.sfba.org

RECOMMENDED READING

Baker, Nik and Daida Ruano Moreno. *The Ultimate Guide to Windsurfing.* Guilford, Conn.: Lyons Press, 2001.

Nadel, Laurie. *Dancing With the Wind: A True Story of Zen in the Art of Windsurfing.* New York: Paraview Press, 2001.

Oakley, Ben. *Windsurfing: The Skills of the Game.* Wiltshire, UK: Crowood Press, 1994.

Winner, Ken. *Windsurfing.* Champaign, Ill.: Human Kinetics, 1995.

SLEEP CHEAP

Mount Diablo State Park is a beautiful, and convenient, camping option right there in the San Francisco Bay Area. In addition, you'll find great hiking trails, incredible wildflower blooms, and horseback trails into the more remote parts of the park. The park is located on Highway 680; take the Diablo Road exit, then 3 miles east to Mount Diablo Scenic Boulevard. Visit www.reserveamerica .com, then search for "Mt. Diablo" for reservations.

Winter

Cruising Wine Country

Who Needs the Caribbean?

If you've ever taken a cruise, you know they generally involve travel before the travel; that is, you have to reach your departure destination before you even see any open water. Whether you're flying to Alaska or jetting down to Florida to pick up a ship bound for points south, you're paying to travel before you really get anywhere you want to go—namely, the delightful destinations your cruise ship has in store.

Throw in the length of most cruise adventures—a week, sometimes more—and you've got a trip not everybody can handle. Sure, these types of vacations are great and well worth taking, but what can you do if you're just not in that comfortable time-rich position, and you want to cruise away nonetheless? Wouldn't it be great if there were a cruise you could take that didn't involve all that extra travel, expense, and time away from your life?

Of course you must know, given the nature of this book, that there is. All you have to do is head to the San Francisco Bay area and embark on a luxurious, scenic jaunt into some of the state's most beautiful, activity-rich areas: the vineyards of the Napa Valley. You'll get all the benefits of cruising—beautiful ships, first-class treatment, cool shoreside activities—with few or none of the hassles described above. It's a holiday that, while not cheap, still lets you conserve quite a few of the resources you would find yourself expending with a full-fledged cruise in the faraway tropics. For wine, culture, and fantastic food, you won't be better served than you will be onboard one of the Napa Valley's first-rate cruising yachts.

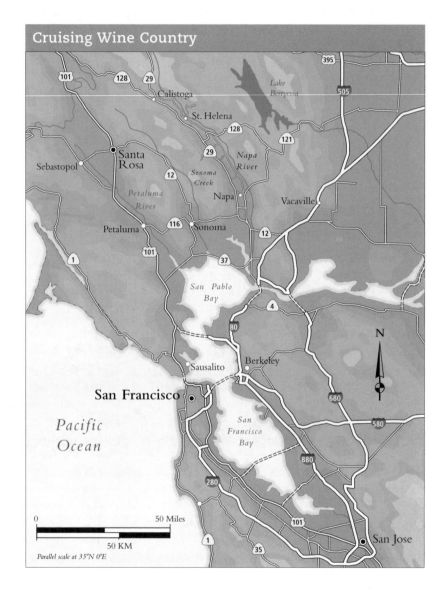

Cruising Wine Country

Compared to the massive ships you board for ocean voyages, the yachts that ply the Napa Valley are fairly small, as you might expect. There are, however, perks that come along with the smaller vessel. For one thing, you won't be lost in a sea of fellow travelers. (Cruise West's *Spirit of Endeavor* holds only 102 people, and American Safari Cruises only allow 21 passengers aboard its *Safari*

Quest.) You'll also be able to leave the evening gowns and dinner jackets at home—the dining atmosphere on these smaller ships is far more casual than you'll find on the luxury ocean liners, despite the fact that the food is just as good, if not better since the chefs don't have to feed a literal army. In all, the smaller craft make for a much more intimate relationship with the crew taking care of you and your fellow guests, a perfect atmosphere for making new friends over sips of crisp chardonnay. You'll have more desire to focus on your winery destinations, too, as the point of these trips is not necessarily to sit on the boat soaking up rays and sipping margaritas for a week.

One side note regarding funds: Napa Valley cruises are not cheap, though they are generally cheaper than cruises aboard big, full-amenity behemoths. Check with the companies listed below for their pricing, or visit their Web sites and gather the info for yourself. And when you're working out the dollars, keep in mind that cruises include a lot of what you'll pay for on any getaway, such as meals and guided tours, but any adventure combining these levels of luxury and intimacy is bound to get a little expensive. Just remember that on those big boats, you're still paying more, and nobody is going to know you from Adam.

As you might expect, the focus of any adventure into wine country is the *vino.* Your cruise will center on trips to the various wineries you encounter, as well as tastings with resident wine experts. (Given this focus, you'll definitely want to leave the kids with grandma for this escape.) Once you return to your ship, onboard wine specialists will school you in the finer points of the wonderful liquid. For beginners and connoisseurs alike, the education is a big part of the admission price; apply what you learn the next time you're shopping for a bottle and your selection will be that much better.

You'll get more than the wine to keep you occupied, though; the Napa Valley is rich in cultural and culinary resources, from fantastic private art collections to remarkable architecture straight from the green, rolling hills of France and Italy. Visits to Sonoma and Sausalito will get you into some nice shopping areas, and almost every trip either company offers makes a stop at Copia, the American Center for Wine, Food, and the Arts. The legendary vintner Robert Mondavi brought the center into being, and since the doors opened in late 2001, it has become a necessary stop for

Harvesting at the Jordan Vineyards in Alexander Valley. ROBERT HOLMES/CALTOUR

tourists in the Napa region. Here you'll find exhibits on America's special contributions to world cuisine, as well as interesting items worthy of the Smithsonian (Julia Child's copper pots, anyone?).

Keep in mind this little-known fact, too: Cruise ship vacations, while heavy on the perks, provide a lot of opportunity for outdoor adventuring. Take a Caribbean cruise and you might find yourself scuba diving, surfing, or engaging in other activities that rate fairly high on the extremity scale. Though the smaller ships don't offer quite as much in the way of amenities—these are destination-focused cruises, rather than trips relying on the boats themselves—the Napa and Petaluma Rivers still offer ample opportunity for activities that take you off your deck chair and get your heart pumping. American Safari Cruises in particular offers activities for more on-the-go cruisers, such as kayaking and biking. But even if you don't go the active route, remember to bring comfortable walking shoes—you'll be hiking around quite a bit as you take in the wineries and other sights.

For as long as vines have grown in the Napa Valley, people have been cruising its waterways. Joining this tradition is not exactly bargain basement, but it is well worth the expense when you factor in the wine you'll taste, the cuisine you'll sample, the knowledge you'll take away, and the friends you'll make. Throw in the ease of arranging such a cruise, the absence of long flights and long time away from work, and you've got a great way to pamper yourself without sitting through hours on a plane or using up all the year's vacation time. Save that time for the weeklong Alaskan cruise.

Price: Pretty high—more than $2,000 for four-day trips with American Safari (though that's the yacht with only twenty-one passengers). Three-day trips start at $1,700 or so. Cruise West's trips are a lot less, though still pricey: about $1,050 per person for a five-day, four-night escape, and "only" $700 for three nights.

Keep one thing in mind, though: This is lap-of-luxury stuff. You get what you pay for, and that means food, lots of wine, and pampering you won't soon forget.

(Winter, Easy)

DRIVING DIRECTIONS

Both American Safari and Cruise West depart from San Francisco and return there at the end. Call the company you decide to go with for exact directions to their departure points.

OUTFITTERS

AMERICAN SAFARI CRUISES
Lynnwood, WA
(888) 862–8881
www.amsafari.com

CRUISE WEST
Seattle, WA
(888) 851–8133
www.cruisewest.com

FOR MORE INFORMATION

WINECOUNTRY.COM
www.winecountry.com

COPIA: THE AMERICAN CENTER
FOR WINE, FOOD, AND THE ARTS
Napa, CA
(707) 259–1600
www.americancenter.com

RECOMMENDED READING

Allegra, Antonia and Richard Gillette. *Napa Valley: The Ultimate Winery Guide, Revised and Updated*. San Francisco: Chronicle Books, 2004.

Hill, Kathleen Thompson and Gerald Hill. *Napa Valley: Land of Golden Vines*. Guilford, Conn.: Globe Pequot Press, 2005.

Narlock, Lori Lyn, Thomas Keller, and Michael Carabetta. *The Food Lover's Companion to the Napa Valley: Where to Eat, Cook, and Shop in the Wine Country Plus 50 Irresistible Recipes*. San Francisco: Chronicle Books, 2003.

O'Rear, Charles. *Napa Valley: The Land, the Wine, the Country*. Berkeley, Calif.: Ten Speed Press, 2001.

Learning the Circus Arts

With the Greatest of Ease

Truly *original* adventures—you won't find too many, unfortunately.
Kiteboarding? It's crazy fun, but it's moving so fast into well-
known, accepted sporting territory that it's hardly new anymore.
Bungee jumping? Please—so ten years ago.

What you need is something truly original, something no one
you know has done yet, an experience you can hold up as something to separate you from the other adventurers you pal around
with. Something that gets your blood pumping but gives you a
good workout besides (so long, bungee cord). Something like—the
flying trapeze?

That's right—northern California offers more so-called circus
arts instruction per square mile than anyplace else in the world.
You'll find most of this education going on in the Bay area, though
a few notable exceptions conduct their programs way up in the
northern reaches of the state. Get ready for truly original adventuring as you take on the training required to swing on the trapeze,
balance yourself in all sorts of crazy positions, and otherwise learn
what it takes to run away and join the circus.

Perhaps the greatest thing about this escape is that you can start
off easy and progress to higher and higher levels of difficulty. Of
course, to do this you have to practice, and keep yourself in pretty
good physical shape; learning to swing on the trapeze isn't that
tough, but learning to be good at it is. This escape can blossom into

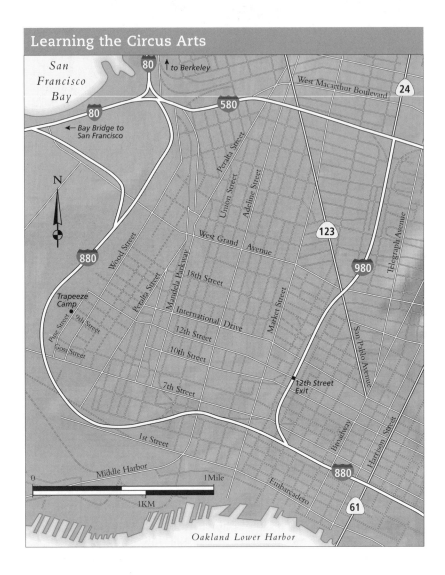

an ongoing pursuit if you want it to, but for that to happen, you should be ready for more strenuous activity.

Another great plus: This isn't the most expensive thing you'll ever do. Unlike more mechanized or equipment-dependent adventures, learning the circus ropes doesn't require much gear besides the muscles you're already carrying around. Intro trapeze lessons run around $30 to $40, and if you get into a run of lessons, you'll get a discount. Not bad, especially when you consider the fun you're having, the exercise you're getting, and the neat skills you're picking up.

Trapeze Arts out of Oakland has been teaching this stuff since 1994 and remains one of the few full-time facilities of its kind in the country. (The school offers seasonal classes in Lake Tahoe during the summertime, too.) Here you'll learn what it takes to get up in the air and start swinging; the goal isn't competition, but self-improvement and eventual self-sufficiency on the high ropes and bars. Of course, safety is job one—all students wear safety harnesses and perform over nets, as you would probably expect.

Despite the precautions, you'll be surprised at just how fast you feel comfortable up there, especially when you know what good hands you're in. The staff has more than forty years of combined teaching experience, along with extensive experience in circuses and performing organizations around the world. They teach actual professionals as well as amateurs like yourself, so they know what they're doing. After a few sessions with talented folks like these, so will you.

Trapeze isn't the only offering at the table, either. The class schedule includes trampoline instruction (fun and an *excellent* workout), tightwire and aerial arts classes, acrobatics instruction, and a whole slate of classes just for the little performers, from age 3 on up. The school offers classes nearly every day at a variety of times, so scheduling should just be a matter of figuring out when you can make it in. Just give them a call or visit the online schedule, and see what's going on when. And if your curiosity is really piqued, you might want to check into a lesson discount—remember, if you take a bunch of classes, you'll get a pretty hefty chunk taken off your bill.

Quick preparation note: Before you go, make sure you have the right clothing on hand. Jeans and shorts are no good; pick up some tights or similar gear. Long or short sleeves are okay, and recommended footwear consists of socks and/or athletic shoes, though bare feet work just fine, too. And keep in mind that although you don't need a high level of fitness to get up on the trapeze, some endurance and strength will maximize your enjoyment of the activity. Hit the gym a little bit before you go, and eat right—you won't regret the forethought.

The San Francisco School of Circus Arts offers a broad variety of classes, too, from juggling to clowning and all the acrobatics you can think of. It offers programs for children and adult beginners, as well as classes for more advanced performers. This is a great base to

Catching some air at Trapeze Arts. JILL SILVER/COURTESY OF TRAPEZE ARTS, INC.

touch if you're interested in all things circus, as the school provides contacts and resources for those of us who might be thinking about our circus dreams a bit more seriously. It sounds crazy, but after all, part-time party clowns make a pretty hefty dime on the side for only two or three days of work per week. Take a few classes and really learn a thing or two, and you might have a fun hobby that doesn't just pay off in good times and laughs.

If you think you might be ready for a longer, crazier getaway, check out Wavy Gravy's Camp Winnarainbow, located up in Mendocino County, for a weeklong escape into a world of circus-style fun and games. The main point here is to have a great time while you learn to juggle, swing on the trapeze, improvise comedy, or do any of the other great activities you have to choose from. The camp provides an opportunity for adults to feel like they're back at summer camp for one week out of the year; the rest of the time, the kids themselves get the chance, so if you have a little one who's ready to join Barnum & Bailey, check out the kids' camp schedule.

Don't give in to society's pressure—you really can run away and join the circus, at least for a little while. It's a feeling you'll quickly cotton to, one that you'll love repeating every time you suit up for the flying trapeze. Pay Trapeze Arts or the SF School of Circus Arts a visit, and you'll be pining away for the big top when you're back at your desk, performing for a different crowd.

Price: $40 or so for one trapeze lesson at Trapeze Arts, then up from there, depending on how much you want to do. SFSCA charges according to the class you take; check the schedule for available classes and prices. Camp Winnarainbow is $90 per day, or $700 for a weekend-to-weekend stay.

(Winter, Easy, though a fear of heights could make it tough)

DRIVING DIRECTIONS

Trapeze Arts is located in Oakland, between Highways 580, 880, and 980. From San Francisco, cross the Bay Bridge, then follow the signs for Highway 880. But before you get on the highway, take the West Grand Avenue–Maritime Street exit. Go through the first light, turn right at the second light, and take the frontage road until it ends at Seventh Street. Turn left there, then go 1 block to Wood; turn left on Wood, go another block, then turn left on Goss. Follow this street as it curves to the right onto Pine, then continue onto Ninth Street. (See the map for additional driving detail.) The West Oakland BART station is just down the road, too, so if you take public transportation, just call Trapeze Arts and they'll come pick you up. SFSCA is located at Circus Center in the Haight-Ashbury district; head to the corner of Frederick/Lincoln Way and Arguello and look for the white post with "755" painted on it.

OUTFITTERS

TRAPEZE ARTS
Oakland, CA
(510) 419–0700
www.trapezearts.com

SAN FRANCISCO SCHOOL
OF CIRCUS ARTS
San Francisco, CA
(415) 759–8123
www.circuscenter.org

CAMP WINNARAINBOW
Berkeley, CA (headquarters—
September through May)
Laytonville, CA (campsite–June
through August)
(510) 525–4304 (headquarters)
(707) 984–6507 (campsite)
www.campwinnarainbow.com

FOR MORE INFORMATION

CIRCUS FANS ASSOCIATION OF AMERICA
www.circusfans.org

RECOMMENDED READING

Davis, Janet M. *The Circus Age: Culture and Society under the American Big Top.* Chapel Hill, N.C.: University of North Carolina Press, 2002.

Keen, Sam. *Learning to Fly: Trapeze—Reflections on Fear, Trust, and the Joy of Letting Go.* New York: Broadway Books, 1999.

SLEEP CHEAP

Campsites are available at Portola Redwoods State Park, located south of Santa Cruz. Between September and November, the sites are first-come, first-served; in the summertime, however, you can reserve sites up to seven months (!) ahead of time. Call (800) 444–7275 for reservations—camping in the fall is only $13 per night, though you won't get any RV hookups at Portola's sites. You can also camp on the 18 miles of trail crisscrossing the park, where backpacking is a big draw. Call (650) 948–9098 for trail camping reservations, which are required.

Paintball

Splat Me with Your Best Shot

Your limbs are heavy after the sprint from the barricade to the edge
of battle. The enemy is hanging too tough, three buildings' worth of
barrier between them and yourself, except for a tiny crack of an
alley between two of the tall structures. The first scout you came
across didn't have a chance to take you out—you drew quicker and
aimed better. Then you took the chance and bounded out, catching
another sentry unaware with a slug between the shoulder blades.
Edwards, your mirror image on the other side of the field, is already
out of commission, mowed down during his run toward the fire
zone. You curse softly as you hit the ground and try to figure out
just how you're going to reach that alley. Afterward, you promise
yourself, Edwards is buying the beer—you'll see to that.

If you've never gone paintballing before, you're missing one of
the coolest and most gratifying adventures out there. Whatever your
feeling about guns, this activity is not just for erstwhile militia
members; just about anyone can play, from kids to their parents.
The game gets better the more people you bring along, too, so feel
free to gather together as many allies as you can and start up your
own private army.

Just in case you don't know, paintball works like this: Each
player is equipped with a pneumatic air gun that fires brightly col-
ored, biodegradable gelatin capsules. These capsules explode when
they strike hard surfaces, including you, and leave a spray of water-
washable paint wherever you're hit. Games are won when players
complete the "mission" they are given. These missions run the

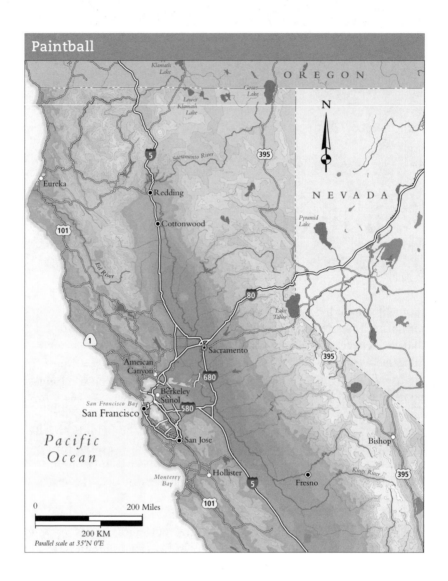

whole gamut; more basic, well-known games include capture the flag, straightforward team-on-team battlefield fighting, and storm-and-guard games, in which one team defends a site while the other attacks. Other more exotic variations include Bounty Hunter (every man for himself), Zombies (dead players rise to fight again), and Assassination (each team has a "President" to defend).

Games last about twenty minutes, though a long day of playing will probably involve some downtimes between your games—combat is pretty tiring, and you'll find yourself pleasantly tuckered out at the end of the day. Prices are also reasonable, though they do vary according to field and the day you're playing. You'll get different amounts of time for your cash, anywhere from four or five hours to the whole time you're there. Games do move quickly, so use your downtime to relax, replenish, and get the most out of the experience. It can get tough to stop when the adrenaline starts pumping, but too much play at once will crash you before you get in all the games you can.

First-timers playing on open weekends (the usual practice at paintball fields) should figure on seeing teams of ten to upward of forty people. These folks run the range, too, from little kids to near-professional paintball aficionados with their own guns and specialized gear. This variety is cool, but it also demonstrates why so many people choose to play in large groups—the fairness factor can get a little skewed when a few people are using fast-repeat, auto-fed weapons against stripped-down rental gear. To compensate, think about spending a few extra dollars to rent high-end weaponry rather than the standard setup. If you do decide to buy anything, go with quality face protection first; on many occasions, the rental masks are a little scratched up and fog somewhat easily, making battlefield vision a bit dicey.

As one would expect, safety is an important concern on the paintball field. Getting shot does sting, and at close range those balls can leave significant bruises; wear multiple light layers to minimize any physical damage, and keep in mind that you'll be lucky to feel anything with all the adrenaline moving through your veins. And I reiterate: The game is much more fun when you can see, as is life *after* the game. The rule "never take off your goggles" is as important to paintballers as "stay away from the fins" is to surfers. Never, ever take off your eye gear when the paint's flying.

Though most paintball facilities provide rental equipment (guns, fatigues, etc.), you've got to buy ammo. And when you run out, you have to buy more. As a result, players with a budget shoot sharp. Feel free to spray the place neon green if you've got the cash to buy more pellets—just bring enough to pay for what you want to shoot. Another piece of gear to think about beforehand is footwear—be sure to bring boots or sneakers that are comfortable, supportive, and okay for running through muck. Remember, too, that white tennis shoes show up very nicely against a muddy brown-and-green background.

Military experience isn't necessary to play paintball—all you need is a killer instinct, a bit of stealth, and a sharp eye. JURGEN KONIG/ISTOCKPHOTO.COM

If paintball begins to take over your daydreams, there are enough people in the same boat to constitute a bona fide community, complete with professional tournaments, equipment reviews, magazines—you name it. They are a pretty jovial group of people, passionate about their sport and happy to welcome new enthusiasts, even as they blast you with their high-powered weapons. This community will patch you in with people who want to play as badly as you do, and also represents a great resource for getting good equipment used; some paintball guns cost upward of $600, but the cost is worth it if you intend to play with the big dogs.

Even if you're not a paramilitary wannabe, paintball is fun stuff. The whole family can get in on it (though most sites require kids to be 12 to 14 or older), and it's a great way to start experiencing California's wilderness. You'll have a blast playing indoors, but outside, where you get the chance to belly-crawl through the leaves and slog through soggy ditches, makes for a far better time. And remember: Even if you're not wearing camo, rolling around in the dirt enough will make you just as invisible.

And let's not forget about the team aspects of the game—after a certain age, most of us never experience the thrill of team competition again. We miss out on the friendships formed on teams and the pleasure of having buddies to play games with. Paintball makes a great excuse for tapping back into these long-gone delights. Just round up a couple of folks from the office and suit up—or, if you're on vacation, get the whole family in on it. You might just show your teenage daughter or son that you have their back after all, despite their beliefs to the contrary.

Price: $30–$100 (depending on how long you'd like to play, how much ammo you get, etc.)

(Winter, Easy)

DRIVING DIRECTIONS

Contact your outfitter for directions to their facilities or playing grounds.

OUTFITTERS

THE ADVENTURE GAME
(LOCATED NEAR THE BAY AREA, WITH
A NEW FIELD NOW OPEN IN
TUOLUMNE COUNTY)
(209) 965–4755 (Tuolumne),
or (800) 824–5150
www.adventuregame.com

SUNOL PAINTBALL
Sunol, CA
(510) 489–9499
www.sunolpaintball.com

AMERICAN CANYON PAINTBALL
JUNGLE
American Canyon, CA
(707) 552–2426
www.paintballjungle.com

DIAMOND'S EDGE PAINTBALL
Cottonwood, CA
(530) 347–5279
www.diamonds-edge-
paintball.com

RECOMMENDED READING

Adams, Terry. *Gun-fu: The Martial Art of Paintball.* Woodland Hills, Calif.: Armed Citizen Press, 2002.

Barnes, Bill. *Paintball! Strategies and Tactics.* Memphis, Tenn.: Mustang Publishing, 1993.

Malensek, Scott. *50+ Ways to Play with Your Paintballs.* Haverford, Pa.: Infinity Publishing, 2002.

SLEEP CHEAP

The Sunol Regional Wilderness, located just east of Oakland and Berkeley, features overnight tent camping for only $12 per night. It's within close range of three mentioned paintball outfitters (American Canyon, Sunol, The Adventure Game) and offers a lot of great outdoor activities to boot. From the Oakland/Berkeley area, drive east on Interstate 580 to the junction with Interstate 680 in Pleasanton; at the junction, go south on I-680 and exit at Calaveras Road/Highway 84, just south of Pleasanton. Turn left onto Calaveras Road and proceed to Geary Road, which leads directly into the park. For questions or reservations, call (510) 636–1684.

Railroading Northern California

Ridin' Cali on the Rails

Sarsaparilla, hitching posts, dusty saloon-lined streets, and covered wagons. Each of these symbols evokes the spirit of the West, that mythological American land where many of our most cherished legends were born. However, it's good to remember that, eventually, the American West, and California specifically, were indeed tamed; all it took was a few basic advances—namely, growing commerce and its necessary partner: a strong transportation system capable of bringing lots of stuff from point A to points B, C, and beyond.

If there is any mode of transportation that symbolizes this evolution from the wild to the wildly successful, it is the locomotive. A hundred years ago, railroad tracks crisscrossed the whole state's expanse, delivering people to and from the boomtowns there, and bringing the gold of the Gold Rush to the rest of the world. As more people realized California's amazing potential, the railroads began hauling other goods—mostly meats and crops, which soon made California the country's number one food exporter.

Of course, riding the rails as a passenger had its drawbacks back then. You had to have a few bucks in your pocket for one thing, as well as the time to do it; tickets (outside of the cattle cars) weren't cheap, and you had to pay for all the amenities you needed over the course of the long trip. When mass flight came along, it made passenger trains something of a novelty, though one with enough

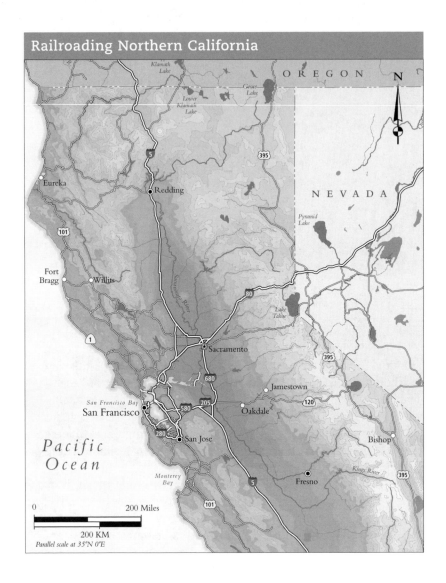

historical and leisure potential to attract those of us with an abiding interest in the good ol' days.

Luckily, northern California still boasts its share of railborne attractions, from Fort Bragg's resurging Skunk Train, a beautiful crawl through redwood country, to Sacramento's excellent California State Railroad Museum, widely known as one of the best in the United States. If you're the kind of person who still has a ton of Lionel trains steaming around the basement, or even sitting in boxes there, you'll love a three-day voyage through California's railroad history, reliving the steam-driven days that made today's world possible.

For a terrific first-day overview, visit the Railroad Museum, home to a fantastic and ever-changing host of trains and railroad memorabilia. Here you'll get the big-picture history—the development of steam technology, environmental and social impact—as well as original, quirky exhibits that show off train culture in all its glory. Take some recent and upcoming exhibits, for example: railroad posters, highlighting America's historic (and continuing) love of travel; toy trains, in all their obvious appeal to railroad aficionados; even an exhibit built around "drumheads," those illuminated round signs that used to grace the backs of passenger trains. Add all this to the nearly forty historic locomotives on display here, and you've got a great day's worth of education and imagination, one perfect for sharing with kids who may never have even seen a real locomotive before. (A good friend of mine who happens to be four thinks all trains look like Thomas, that little blue train with the face who stars in kids' books, TV shows, etc. No kidding!)

The locomotives displayed here run the gamut and provide great insight into the machine's various incarnations. Nineteen of them are steam-powered, while another nineteen are first- and second-generation internal combustion locomotives. You'll see big guns like the million-pound (that's 500 tons, pal) Southern Pacific No. 4294, as well as the comparatively tiny Gov. Sanford, built in 1862 and used until 1895, when it became a display piece in a number of collections before reaching its current place in the museum's environs. Each is meticulously restored, and even the little guys have a heaviness, a *bigness* to them that makes you wonder just how they moved in the first place.

On your second day, though, you'll get a chance to see those big horses move if you head over to Jamestown and check out the Railtown 1897 State Historical Park. You'll also find one of the nation's last operating railroad roundhouses, where locomotives were repaired and stored, as well as quite a few trains you didn't know you've seen before. Railtown's locomotives have starred in more than 200 motion pictures and TV shows *(Back to the Future 3* and *Little House on the Prairie,* to name just two), earning the park its nickname, the "Movie Railroad."

On weekends from April all the way through to October, you can ride behind these famous, old-school locomotives through the

Some denizens of the California State Railroad Museum in Sacramento.
ROBERT HOLMES/CALTOUR

beautiful Gold Country around Jamestown, either inside enclosed coaches or in unique, open-air observation cars once used for sightseeing in the Canadian Rockies. Longer, themed excursions run throughout the year as well, from wildflower trips in the spring to summer wine-and-cheese excursions and a special New Year's Eve train. Take a walking tour of the roundhouse after your ride, and you've got a pretty good insight into what day-to-day operations were like at the hundreds of roundhouses that dotted the countryside back in the day.

The Skunk Train, one of California's most venerable tracked institutions, has seen some pretty tough times recently. The 40-mile line, named for the malodorous air its early locomotives left behind, has carried passengers and freight between Fort Bragg and Willits since 1925. It declared bankruptcy in late 2002, though, and its last trip of the season, on Labor Day, 2003, could have been its swan song. Thankfully, a savior rode in to save the day—namely the Sierra Railroad Company, which operates dinner and excursion trains out of Oakdale and Sacramento. There's no telling what the new ownership will bring, but there's word that the company could increase the number of excursions between Fort Bragg and tiny Northspur, the redwood-ensconced midway station, and add vehicle transportation to the roster of services the line offers. The Skunk should be up and running soon, so stay tuned; just check with the Sierra Railroad periodically for updates, and you should be in the loop.

In the meantime, try the Sierra Railroad Dinner Train for excellent fare and scenery along with frequent special events like killer murder mysteries and Wild West shows. The train leaves from Oakdale and provides a packed weekend schedule all through the year, with weekday lunch and dinner excursions departing during the summer months. The Yolo Shortline Railroad, or "Wild Berry Express," takes you along the Sacramento River and through lush Yolo County, home to a ton of orchards and fresh local produce. Throw in open observation cars and a concession car for grubbin', and you've got a great afternoon's worth of steamin' around.

Want your weekend escape to satisfy a history fix you've been hankering for? Then take in a few of California's railroad-related attractions, and start reliving the old days—a little dash of Wild West with a big dollop of Industrial Revolution, all with an entirely American flavor. Take it with a tall sarsaparilla, if you get the chance.

Price: $100 to $300 (for the weekend, depending on accommodations and food)
(Winter, Easy)

DRIVING DIRECTIONS

To the museum (from San Francisco): Take Interstate 80 east to West Sacramento. At the I-80/Business 80 split, follow Business 80 to downtown Sacramento, then as the freeway climbs up over the Sacramento River, take the Interstate 5 North exit. Exit at J Street (a one-way, eastbound street) and go 2 blocks to Fifth Street. Turn left, then turn left again at I Street. Follow the large overhead signs to OLD SACRAMENTO/RAILROAD MUSEUM.

To Railtown 1897 (from S.F.): Take Interstate 205 east to Stockton/ Modesto. Follow the signs to Highway 120/108 east, then take it to the Yosemite turnoff. Continue following Highway 108 toward Sonora and Jamestown. Highway 49 merges with Highway 108 before Jamestown; once in town, continue on 49/108, passing the historic downtown district, for approximately half a mile to Fifth Street. Turn right onto Fifth Street (south), and follow the road for approximately 1 mile to the park.

OUTFITTERS

CALIFORNIA STATE RAILROAD MUSEUM
Sacramento, CA
(916) 445–6645 (24-hour information)
(916) 323–9280 (museum front desk)
www.csrmf.org

RAILTOWN 1897 STATE HISTORICAL PARK
Jamestown, CA
(209) 984–3953 (business office)
www.csrmf.org

SIERRA RAILROAD DINNER TRAIN
Oakdale, CA
(209) 848–2100
www.sierrarailroad.com
(also check here for Skunk Train info)

YOLO SHORTLINE RAILROAD (WILD BERRY EXPRESS)
Sacramento, CA
(800) 942–6387 (reservations)
www.yslrr.com

FOR MORE INFORMATION

The museums mentioned above should be able to answer any questions you might have about California's railroad history and heritage—after all, that's their job.

RECOMMENDED READING

Reinhardt, Richard. *Workin' on the Railroad: Reminiscences from the Age of Steam.* Norman, Okla.: University of Oklahoma Press, 2003.

Alexander, E.P., ed. *Iron Horses: American Locomotives, 1829–1900.* Mineola, N.Y.: Dover Press, 2003.

Porterfield, James D. *Dining by Rail: The History and Recipes of America's Golden Age of Railroad Cuisine.* Irvine, Calif.: Griffin Publishing, 1998.

SLEEP CHEAP

Jackson Demonstration State Forest, located near Fort Bragg, makes a great camp spot for folks spending the day on the Skunk Train. There are two main overnight camping areas with a number of campsites, including equestrian camps. Campsites have picnic tables, fire rings, and pit toilets, though there is no water at the campsites or day-use areas. Pets are allowed with a leash. The best part: It's free, provided you have a permit. Call (707) 964-5674 for directions and more information.

Elephant Seals at Año Nuevo

The Elephants of Winter

Everybody has their conception of what seals are supposed to look like. Most of us have been to Sea World, the aquarium, or the zoo, so we know that seals are cute and agile, whiskery little buggers who love to play when their trainers throw bright multicolored beach balls out into the water for them to fetch. They are somewhat on the small side, with dark fur and largely pleasant dispositions, by all accounts.

Of course, these aren't the only seals in the ocean. The popular concept of the seal is, in fact, largely made up and based on our domestication of them and their bigger relative, the California sea lion. The popular conception of seals as cute, zippy clowns crumbles, however, upon one look at the massive, unwieldy mountain that is the elephant seal, one of nature's greatest examples of gigantism and a valued resident of the northern California coastline.

Año Nuevo (New Year's *en español)* State Reserve plays host to one major herd of these huge creatures, and the winter months bring the most dramatic point at which to view them—the mating and birthing season. A day trip to Año Nuevo will put you right in the middle of this incredible natural display and leave you with a new perception of the word "big."

Elephant seals take their name from their faces—specifically the long, swinging snouts that hang down over their mouths. They spend the majority of their lives in the sea, for obvious reasons—

they're absolutely freakin' huge, with males weighing up to two and a half tons and measuring to 16 feet in length. (Just to put that in perspective—a big elephant seal is about as big and as heavy as a Toyota.) They come ashore only when they have to for molting (shedding skin and hair), mating, or birthing, and it shows—elephant seals crawl around fairly slowly and awkwardly, as dragging all that mass around is no picnic. They prefer the ocean, where their formidable bulk is an asset rather than a disadvantage.

And what an asset it is—elephant seals dive up to 2,000 feet when they're searching for food, mostly rays, squid, and small sharks. The deepest recorded dive for an elephant seal is 5,000 feet, demonstrating that these big fellas roll in territory normally reserved for the biggest of the big ocean predators: sperm whales and even the mighty, never-spotted giant squid. However, despite their size and mastery near the top of the food chain, the elephant seal still has its share of anxiety over being eaten, as killer whales and bigger sharks—like the great whites off the California coast—can make a nice big meal out of a hapless elephant seal.

Of course, the big seals do have another enemy, one that nearly drove them to extinction: us. Like most sea mammals, they have had a tumultuous history that almost ended long ago thanks to human greed. These giants have loads of blubber on them, just like whales do—blubber that insulates them on those deep dives and produces a high-grade oil when treated properly. In the 1800s hunters slew a few hundred thousand of them, so many that by the end of the century, there were only fifty or one hundred left in the whole world—the members of one last colony, located on Guadalupe Island off the Baja California coast. In 1922 the Mexican government placed this last colony under protection, and the United States followed suit a few years later. Luckily, the story ends happily; today there are about 160,000 elephant seals swimming the seas, having made their first appearance on Año Nuevo in 1955. The first pup was born there in 1961, and the number of pups born has increased every season since, to the point that about 2,000 were born each year in the mid-1990s.

You can take in these mighty creatures as they birth and raise their families every winter, from about mid-December up through March. The first part of December is off-limits, as the pregnant females and adult males are just arriving at that point, and the males are establishing their "harems." After this arrival comes the breeding season—the time during which you'll want to visit and the time during which the most stuff is happening. Giant bull males are

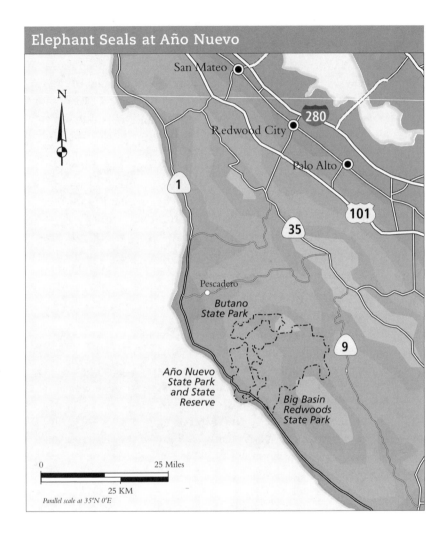

Elephant Seals at Año Nuevo

San Mateo

N

280

Redwood City

Palo Alto

1

101

35

Pescadero

Butano
State Park

9

Año Nuevo
State Park
and State
Reserve

Big Basin
Redwoods
State Park

0   25 Miles

25 KM
Parallel scale at 35°N 0°E

fighting each other for breeding access, leaving scars and bloodshed in their wake; the pregnant females (all of which have been carrying their babies since the previous year) are coming ashore to give birth and nurse their pups; the pups themselves are getting their first crack at the water, learning to swim in shallow offshore areas or in rainwater ponds on the beach. The little ones (not so little—some of these kids approach 600 pounds) don't take to the water too well at first, but once they get the hang of it, they're hooked; during the last three weeks of April, they will go to sea and stay there, dispersing northwest to feed off northern Washington and Vancouver. They won't come ashore again until the next year, when the breeding cycle begins again and they're back at Año Nuevo one year wiser.

Año Nuevo offers naturalist-guided tours of the seal rookery, the only permissible access during the fragile breeding period. You have to make reservations thanks to the popularity of the 3-mile excursion over sand dunes to good seal observation points. Though this tour is two and a half to three hours long, you'll learn a lot about these massive creatures, along with a whole bunch about the area in general. Birds, for example, nearly steal the show from those big seals—in the fall you'll see plovers, sanderlings, turnstones, and a plethora of other seabirds. Brown pelicans move north each spring and hang out through most of the year. Your guide will also explain the area's unique geography, among other things.

Searching for an original wildlife viewing adventure in northern Cali? Look no further than the big, blubbery elephant seals of Año Nuevo—just make sure you bring your camera to capture their capering (or the elephant seal approximation of capering).

Price: $10–$20, depending on how many people go on the tour.
(Winter, Easy)

DRIVING DIRECTIONS

Año Nuevo is located just off Highway 1, about midway between Half Moon Bay and Santa Cruz.

OUTFITTERS

AÑO NUEVO STATE RESERVE
Pescadero, CA
(650) 879–0227 (recorded information)
(800) 444–4445 (guided walk reservations)
www.parks.ca.gov/default.asp?page_id=523

AÑO NUEVO STATE PARK
Pescadero, CA
www.parks.ca.gov/default.asp?page_id=22264

FOR MORE INFORMATION

FRIENDS OF THE ELEPHANT SEAL
www.elephantseal.org

Female elephant seals aren't quite as massive as the males—but they are a whole lot cuter. COURTESY OF U.S. FISH AND WILDLIFE

RECOMMENDED READING

Cousteau, Jacques-Yves. *Diving Companions: Sea Lion, Elephant Seal, Walrus (The Undersea Discoveries of Jacques-Yves Cousteau)*. New York: Bantam Dell Publishing Group, 1974.

Emory, Jerry. *The Monterey Bay Shoreline Guide*. Berkeley, Calif.: University of California Press, 1999.

Spitz, Tullan and John A. Vlahides. *Lonely Planet Coastal California*. Oakland, Calif.: Lonely Planet Publications, 2004.

SLEEP CHEAP

Big Basin Redwoods State Park, established in 1902, is California's oldest state park and features more than 80 miles of hiking trails as well as camping facilities. You'll find showers, a visitor center, and a store for last-minute purchases as well. Call (831) 338–8860 for more information on the park.

Eagle Watching at Tule Lake

America's Nature

Each November, they start rolling in. From summer grounds in
Canada and Alaska, they journey south, over the Pacific Northwest's
palatial forests, until they reach their wintering grounds on the
Klamath Basin, namely Tule Lake National Wildlife Refuge. Just by
their presence, they evoke images of freedom, patriotism, and inde-
pendence; they are the physical incarnation of everything that stirs
us about America and its heritage, the symbol of more than 200
years of history. And for a few weeks every November, you've got
the chance to take in these spectacular creatures en masse, in
groups that rival in majesty the herds of elephants and prides of
lions that roam African savannas. Behold, the incredible bald eagles
of Tule Lake, the largest concentration of these magnificent birds
anywhere in the world, a wildlife adventure of monumental proportions. Come to Tule at the right time, and you'll see once and for all
that birding is about more than waiting for wrens and titmice.

Tule Lake is part of the much larger Klamath Basin National
Wildlife Refuges Complex, which includes five other refuges and
spans more than 200,000 total acres in Oregon and northern
California. Tule Lake itself covers about 39,116 acres of open water
and cropland, with more than 17,000 acres leased by farmers growing cereal grains and alfalfa. These crops provide a major food source
for migrating and wintering waterfowl, and there's no shortage of

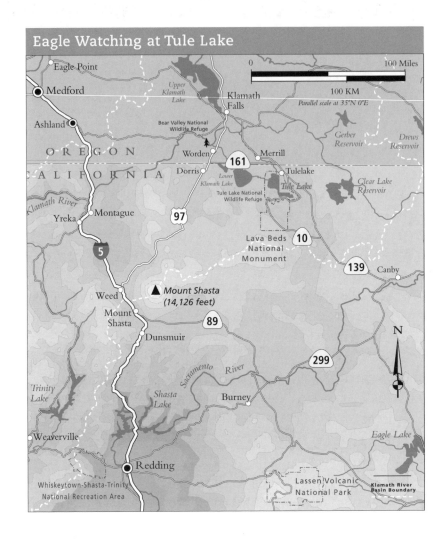

birds passing through—433 species have been spotted around the Klamath Basin, everything from blackbirds to peregrine falcons.

The eagles fly down in the winter mainly to take advantage of the basin's huge population of other birds, namely the waterfowl. When there are this many animals together in one place, a few are sure to pass on; when it's winter and the pickings are slim, their odds get even longer. This is where the eagles come in—they scavenge the dead ducks and geese, showing once again that as far as nature is concerned, one duck's tragedy is another eagle's dinner.

A 10-mile touring route winds through Tule Lake, allowing for year-round observation. The birds you'll see depend on the season you visit: in the spring and fall, giant flocks of snow geese and mallards decorate the sky; in the summer, white pelicans and western grebes are the prime attractions. The eagles, however, show up in November and quickly settle into a daily routine grabbing up waterfowl carrion during the day and finding suitable roosts at night. January and February represent peak viewing time—the birds have all settled in by then, and the eagle population can reach more than 500 strong.

The sheer number of white-headed avians you'll see is a huge part of the appeal here. As any birder knows, spying a top-notch specimen often requires a whole lot of patience, as well as plenty of time in the bush. But keep your eyes open at Tule Lake, and you should spot dozens of these splendid creatures, even from the auto tour route. However, if you really want to capture your national symbol in action, get up nice and early and head to one of the refuge's photography blinds. From these close-up vantage points, you'll snap photos that will arouse jealousy at the birding club or even around the coffee table. "How did you get so close?" they'll ask. Feel free to make up a story if you wish.

Like most outdoor adventures, though, eagle watching at Tule requires a plan and some foresight. Most of the blinds are small— one-person small—so make sure everyone else tagging along has something to do if you're going to snap some shots. You're going to want to get there very early, too, as park regulations require that most of the good eagle blinds be reached by 7:00 A.M. during the winter season. Blinds require a small fee to occupy and are available for reservation two months out, so be sure and reserve your day long before you get up there. Keep in mind, too, that some of the blinds are in relatively difficult-to-reach locations; you may have to do some strenuous driving and/or hiking to get to the blind you're seeking.

Folks outside the blind shouldn't have much trouble finding other things to do. Even if the spectacle of the eagles gets old, there's hiking all around the preserve, as well as a visitor center and "Discovery Marsh," where they can learn all about wetlands and their denizens. Lava Beds National Monument is also very close by; swing by to get a whole different landscape experience. In fact, Lava Beds is so close that the two parks are practically related, so you may even want to combine your eagle watching with a visit to

Watching the flocks fly at Tule Lake. CHRIS BECKER

Captain Jack's Stronghold for a three- or four-day escape (see Escape 5 for the lowdown on Captain Jack). Hunters will be happy to know that multiple seasons overlap between October and early January; waterfowl present the best opportunity, though pheasant hunting is also permitted. If you have a hunting dog, bring it along if you plan to go for pheasant.

Most eagles vacate the feeding grounds by late afternoon after consuming as much waterfowl as they can handle. They then make their way to their night roosts, generally within huge, open-crowned conifers that allow for easy entry and exit. The trees provide protection from the slicing winter winds, as well as shelter from precipitation. The most important of these roosts, Bear Valley National Wildlife Refuge, is just over the Oregon border, near Worden, and though it's closed to visitors, you can gather outside the preserve to witness the breathtaking morning "fly out"—one hundred or more eagles all leaving their roosts at once to jump in line at the Tule chuck wagon. Bring some warm clothing and that ever-present camera, and you'll once again be treated to a sight that you'll never forget.

If you want to experience nature under its own conditions, viewing wildlife stands out as one of the best ways to do it.

Observing Tule Lake's eagles, however, is much more than looking at pretty birds—it's absorbing the heritage of a nation and taking time to consider that at its best, the good ol' USA has a lot in common with these majestic raptors. *Inspirational* is not too strong a word.
Price: $10–$30
(Winter, Medium)

DRIVING DIRECTIONS

Head north on Interstate 5 to Weed, California, then northeast 45 miles on Highway 97 to the Oregon border. Take Stateline Road (Highway 161) east toward Tulelake, to Hill Road. Turn south on Hill Road, drive 4 miles, and you're there. Bear Valley is just a little farther up Highway 97, just across the Oregon border.

OUTFITTERS

TULE LAKE NATIONAL
WILDLIFE REFUGE
(Klamath Basin National
Wildlife Refuges)
Tulelake, CA
(530) 667–2231
http://klamathbasinrefuges.fws
.gov/tulelake/tulelake.html

BEAR VALLEY NATIONAL
WILDLIFE REFUGE
(Klamath Basin National
Wildlife Refuges)
Tulelake, CA
http://klamathbasinrefuges.fws
.gov/bearvalley/bearvalley.html

FOR MORE INFORMATION

BALD EAGLE CONFERENCE
Hosted by the Klamath Basin
Audubon Society
(800) 445–6728
www.eaglecon.org

KLAMATH BASIN AUDUBON SOCIETY
Klamath Falls, OR
(541) 882–8488
www.eaglecon.org/kbas.html

RECOMMENDED READING

Gordon, David G. and The Audubon Society. *The Audubon Society Field Guide to the Bald Eagle.* Seattle: Sasquatch Books, 1991. (reproduction edition)

Summers, Steven. *A Birder's Guide to the Klamath Basin.* California: Klamath Basin Audubon Society, 1997.

Takei, Barbara and Judy Tachibana. *Tule Lake Revisited.* Edinburgh: T & T Press, 2001.

SLEEP CHEAP

Camping is available here at the south end of Lava Beds National Park, about 18 miles south of Tule Lake. The site has forty campsites suitable for tents and small- to medium-size RVs. Fees are $10 per night, per site, and it's first come, first served. Call (530) 667–2282, ext. 232 for details, or visit www.nps.gov/labe.

Motorcycle Touring the Pacific Coast Highway

Born to Be Wild

Take a fly on Highway 66 if you want to drive through America's classic, classy heart. For a ride through the nation's glorious soul, though, its most wonderful expressions of beauty, nothing fits the bill better than Highway 1, the Pacific Coast Highway. Though it goes officially by a few names throughout its journey up the coast— the Cabrillo Highway, for example—for all practical purposes "Pacific Coast Highway" is the only name you need to know. The PCH wends its way from Seattle to Los Angeles like a hazy, beach-side mirage, opening up into amazing horizon views beyond pictur-esque beaches and cliffs. As you make your way up or down the highway, the constants that follow you—the sun, the sky, the ocean, the landscape—remain so gorgeous that even long drives, otherwise tedious to the extreme, stay easy even miles and miles later as the road rolls out behind you.

As you might expect, a nice scenic drive is probably the best way to see this most eminent of American roadways. Each and every year, thousands of motorists from the United States and abroad show up in Cali to take their turn behind the wheel on the PCH, mostly as they get from point A to point B. Unfortunately, they generally enjoy the highway only as a sidebar, as a place that only serves the purpose of getting them from one place to another— too few actually take the time to explore the road itself the way you might explore woodland trails or ski runs on a mountain.

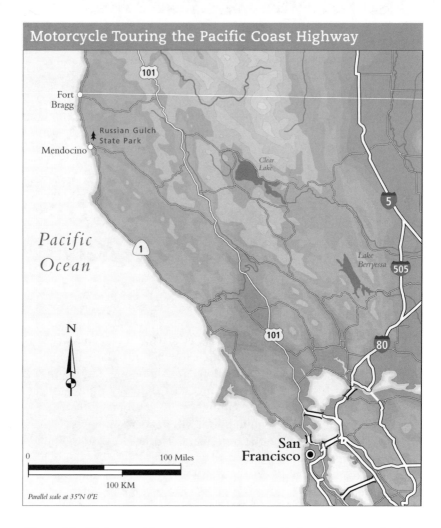

Fort
Bragg

Russian Gulch
State Park

Mendocino

Pacific
Ocean

Clear
Lake

Lake
Berryessa

N

San
Francisco

0   100 Miles

100 KM

Parallel scale at 35°N 0°E

Venerable Highway 1 has enough going for it along the way that you don't even need a plan when you set out; you can light out and just drive, stopping along the way when you feel like it and taking in the sights between impromptu breaks.

And the best way to take in the highway, the best way to take in *any* highway really, is to catch the wind behind you as you tool down the road on two roarin' wheels. Motorcyclists enjoy the PCH on a lighter level than those of us who are stuck behind the wheel, and seeing the road from a motorcycle is an utterly different experience than seeing it out your windshield. Motorcycle touring obviously requires knowing how to ride, but past this qualification it's incredibly relaxing and simple, especially on a spectacular ribbon of highway. And the PCH, particularly its northern portion, is certainly built for motorcycles; it boasts all that great ocean to gaze upon, dozens of towns featuring hundreds of diversions, and dozens of soft, sweet curves.

California, more than any other state or nation, has a legitimate claim to the title "Capital of Motorcycle Culture." After World War II, soldiers fresh from the terrifying thrill of combat came home, ostensibly to settle down and start new lives. A few, however, weren't satisfied with the vagaries of everyday life. They craved the adrenaline they had experienced on the battlefields of Europe and the Pacific, and searched for activities stateside that would give them what they needed. Motorcycles became their stand-ins for bombers and tanks, and the biker rebel was born. By the late '40s, the state crawled with Indians and Harleys, and motorcycle gangs like the Hell's Angels came to represent the most extreme wing of this thrill-seeking group. Today, though, thanks to all those guys who just didn't want to fit in, motorcycles have become a huge factor in California's unique culture and an accepted part of our collective identity as Americans.

Of course, Harley-Davidson makes the most popular bikes in America. If you've got any interest in motorcycling at all, you've probably owned, or pined away for, a Harley of your very own. BMW, Yamaha, and Kawasaki all make great bikes, too, but for a classic ride down the Pacific Coast Highway, you've just got to know that the Harley is the way to go.

Unfortunately, if you're traveling to California from out of state—or to the PCH from inland somewhere—you may not have your bike with you. Or you may not have a bike at all; maybe you had to sell, or your brother decided to borrow your bike and move to Kentucky. But have no fear: You won't have any trouble finding a sweet ride for rent, especially if you're in the Bay area. Many of these companies offer itineraries, too, so you'll have some idea about what you want to hit before you set out. If you really want to be taken care of, sign up for a guided tour—you'll be able to enjoy the highway in the company of like-minded adventurers and have an inside track on all the best things to check out along the way.

Of course, you don't have to take someone else's word about what to see out there on the highway. San Francisco Bay Area Motorcycle Rentals, for example, caters to more self-sufficient riders, folks who want to rent their bikes and get going on their own.

Roarin' down the Pacific Coast Highway. CHRIS BECKER

Dubbelju, another San Fran–area company, will give you itinerary help if you want it, though they will simply rent you your bike, too. Eaglerider Rentals will get you riding with a specific goal in mind; these guys deal exclusively in Harleys, and they're damn proud of it. The company offers a ton of touring options, from guided long tours starting by the Bay and jetting out for 1,600 miles, to self-guided tours to take along with you on your ride, containing attractions, hotels, and other points of biker interest. Before you set out, just call the listed companies and determine which one you want to go with. They all have their charms, and it's up to you to decide which one jives most with your vacation goals. For example: Do you need to rent riding clothes? Helmets? Boots? Know everything going in, and you'll be just fine.

Renting a bike isn't exactly cheap, but it's not nearly as expensive as a lot of other weekend escapes you can take, especially if you rough it a bit and camp your way down the road. Of course, as when you rent any large expensive piece of equipment, you can expect to put down a hefty deposit, but have no fear—if you don't ride like an idiot and respect the bike, you'll get every cent back.

Feel like you're trapped in a rut? Like you can't get away from the confines you live with every day? Then take a ride on the PCH and get a dose of true freedom, at least for a little while. Then, when you're back at your desk or feeding the kids, you'll have those wind-in-the-hair memories to escape to at a moment's notice, no matter what familiar territory the road takes you back to.

Price: For a three-day trip you're looking at $300 to $500 for the rental, a little more if you go for a real high-end bike.

(Winter, Medium)

DRIVING DIRECTIONS

The PCH is real easy to find—just head west until you hit the last piece of pavement before the ocean. But seriously—your outfitter will give you detailed directions to where you need to pick up your bike.

OUTFITTERS

DUBBELJU
San Francisco, CA
(415) 495–2774
www.dubbelju.com

SAN FRANCISCO BAY AREA MOTORCYCLE RENTALS
San Rafael, CA
(415) 456–9910
www.harleymc.com

EAGLERIDER MOTORCYCLE RENTAL (MULTIPLE LOCATIONS)
www.eaglerider.com

San Francisco, CA
(888) 390–6400

San Jose, CA
(866) 433–7326

FOR MORE INFORMATION

HARLEY–DAVIDSON
www.harley-davidson.com

RECOMMENDED READING

Hough, David. *Street Strategies: A Survival Guide for Motorcyclists.* Mission Viejo, Calif.: Bowtie Press, 2001.

Salvadori, Clement. *Motorcycle Journeys Through California*. North Conway, N.H.: Whitehorse Press, 2000.

Thompson, Hunter S. *Hell's Angels: A Strange and Terrible Saga*. New York: Ballantine Books, 1966.

SLEEP CHEAP

Russian Gulch State Park lies just south of Mendocino and is one of the few parks along the California coast that includes portions of the forest to the east. Throw in a couple other cool things to do (hiking, fishing), and you've got a great place to relax after satisfying your inner road gypsy. The campground here boasts thirty sites, any of which you can reserve by calling (800) 444-7275, along with showers and a picnic area.

Skiing, Snowboarding, and More at Mammoth

You'll Be Flyin' down the Mountain When You Come...

The wind in your face, snow swirling through your hair and brushing you as you coast. The *fwish* of the powder under you as you wind your way down a white, pine-peppered mountain. The warm fire after the day's done, feet propped up and a hot beverage cupped in your gloves. You might have poles in your gloves, or simply a board strapped to your feet—it's up to you, but in either case you're in for all these good times and more.

In fact, whether you're a shredding snowboarder or a straight-up skier, Mammoth Mountain calls to you, beckoning with runs galore and some great perks besides. Answering that call makes for one heck of a wintertime escape if you're up to the challenge.

Mammoth boasts some of the best skiing in America, hands down. In 2002–03, for example, the mountain saw nearly 250 straight days of snow, lasting from early November all the way through July. In addition, you'll see about 300 days of sun a year, meaning that these fantastic snow conditions walk hand in hand with beautiful weather nearly devoid of the nasty, wet cold you'll get at East Coast ski areas. Such a season makes skiing and snowboarding year-round pursuits here, though (of course) you're most likely to see your best conditions in the wintertime. What's more, Mammoth boasts excellent snowmaking on twenty-two trails in

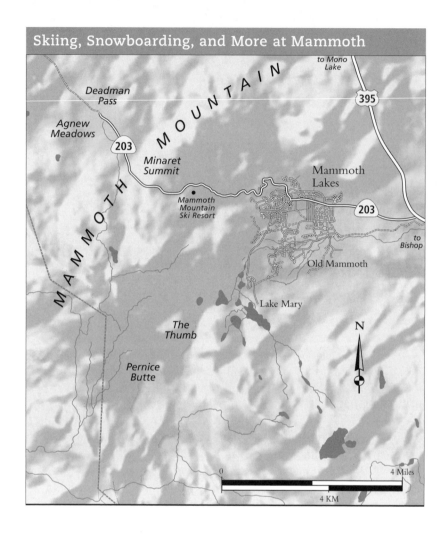

addition to heavy natural snowfall (more than 50 feet fell on the mountain in 2002–03), so even if you get there without recent storm activity, you should be well covered.

The place is big, too, as the name implies. Actually, it's not just big—it's *biiiig*. Try this on for size: 3,500 skiable acres, more than 3,100 feet in elevation, the highest ski peak in California at 11,053 feet (just a bit shy of Vail's 11,570 feet), and more than 150 trails to play on during your weekend escape. And try to take that whole weekend if you can—a winter playground like this doesn't stand for just one day of play, and you really need three days to get the whole picture. To truly enjoy this, you've got to see as much of it as you can, and it's well worth taking a few extra days to do so.

As you probably know, there are a variety of ways to go at the snow with long, flat boards strapped to your feet. And no matter which way you prefer, Mammoth Mountain and the surrounding environs have what it takes to bring you out. Cross-country skiers, for example, don't require the steep grades downhill skiers and snowboarders do; instead, they seek miles and miles of untouched backcountry through which they can slide and pole their way. Tamarack Cross Country Ski Center has about 28 miles of sweet, groomed woodland track for you to traverse, as well as lessons in a variety of cross-country styles for all skill levels, catering to most any group size. Besides all that, since Tamarack sits just down the road from Mammoth, the cross-country fans in the family will be able to get what they're looking for even if you're occupied skiing the black diamond bowls on top of the big mountain.

You snowboarders with a taste for the shred won't be disappointed, either. Mammoth's Unbound Terrain Parks provide every kind of diversion you can imagine; whatever your skill level, you'll have a whole slate to keep you busy. In the Family Fun Park, for example, you'll get a nice taste of what terrain riding is all about, thanks to the 10-foot half-pipe and the new Micro Jib-A-Luscious Zone, where a host of manageable obstacles await. Get a little experience behind you and you might want to head over to the South Park, where the obstacles get a little bigger and the boarding (or skiing, if you prefer) gets a little hairier. Take on Unbound Main when you've really got your stuff together—you'll face jumps of more than 60 feet—and attack the same terrain the pros on the U.S. snowboarding team train on. The Superpipe, a massive half-pipe worthy of its big-shot name, usually opens sometime in mid- to late November, placing it among the first big pipes in North America to do so. Of course, you'll want to be good and ready before you take on this particular park, but the level of challenge you'll find (as well as the adrenaline rush you'll get from conquering it) is well worth the practice required to get there. Of course, you skiers have just as much business in the parks as anybody else, so if you feel like getting your trick fix on beside your snowboarding buddies, by all means go for it.

If you're not so much into the trick riding, have no fear whatsoever—Mammoth will overwhelm you with trail options, no matter what your skill category or what kind of skiing/riding you're into.

A bird's eye view of Mammoth Mountain. ROBERT HOLMES/CALTOUR

Want to get up into some tough snow? Head to Lincoln Mountain and ride some of the most ridiculously nasty runs on the mountain (or in all of California, for that matter). Want to get a long, leisurely ride going that still pushes some buttons? Take the Face Lift Express chair up, then ride Center Bowl down to Stump Alley, where you can take it wide. Looking for a nice little place to get the kids acquainted with the art of the ski? Hit Sesame Street and let the fun begin. And if those tykes really like the feeling of snow gliding by under their feet, or even if your own technique could use some help in reaching the next level, visit one of Mammoth's excellent ski schools and get in on a group or individual lesson. Be aware, though—lessons sell out around the holidays, so plan in advance if you're getting to the mountain in full yuletide cheer mode or around one of winter's three-day weekends (Martin Luther King Jr. Day, Presidents' Day, etc.). Reserve your lessons at the same time you're getting your lift tickets, and you'll be set up when you reach the hill no matter what kind of crowd you're dealing with.

Looking for your snow fix in northern California? Look no further than Mammoth Mountain. The place never disappoints, and more often than not you'll find something new here even if it's your tenth trip to the mountain. Throw in excellent ski instruction and hard-core parks for every brand of boarder, and you've got something for all members of your clan. Just make sure you book that third day!

Price: $250–$500–plus (for three days)

(Winter, Medium)

DRIVING DIRECTIONS

From San Francisco and Sacramento: Take Interstate 80 to Highway 50, to the Kingsbury Grade cutoff, then on to Highway 395 south to Highway 203.

OUTFITTERS

MAMMOTH MOUNTAIN
Mammoth Lakes, CA
(800) 626–6684
www.mammothmountain.com

FOR MORE INFORMATION

GOMAMMOTH.COM
(866) 873–9275
www.gomammoth.com

MAMMOTH LAKES VISITORS BUREAU
Mammoth Lakes, CA
(888) GO–MAMMOTH
www.visitmammoth.com

RECOMMENDED READING

Deslauriers, Eric and Rob Deslauriers. *Ski the Whole Mountain: How to Ski Any Condition at Any Time*. Boulder, Colo.: Mountain Sports Press, 2002.

Forstenzer, Martin. *Mammoth: The Sierra Legend*. Boulder, Colo.: Mountain Sports Press, 2002.

Gordon, Herb. *Essential Skiing*. Guilford, Conn.: Lyons Press, 1996.

SLEEP CHEAP

Mammoth Mountain is a world-class ski resort, and although not exactly "cheap," it does offer some amazing accommodations. For example, check out the Mammoth Mountain Inn, located at the base of the main lodge; with its whirlpool spas and ski-up location, it's an experience not to miss. Contact them at (760) 934–2581 or (800) 626-6684, or book online at www.mammothmountain.com/plan/lodging/mmi.

San Francisco by Bicycle

Watch Out for Lombard Street!

In San Francisco, bicycles are not just something you jump on for a good time—people ride their bikes to work, to school, and just about everywhere else. You'll see little kids and grandmothers riding, along with office workers and hippie holdovers, and nearly everybody else, all taking advantage of the city's wide sidewalks and beautiful scenery. Sure, the public transportation system is fantastic, and if you need to get around, it's a great way to go; but if you want to get a terrific workout while seeing one of the world's prettiest cities, throw your bike on the back of the car and head toward the Bay. Or, if you're in the area and bike-less, go ahead and rent one—you won't be disappointed.

San Francisco is full of incredible sights, all of which are accessible via public transportation if you want to go that way. However, the point of this adventure is to turn the city itself into a bike trail network, a route over which you'll ride in order to discover all the great stuff along the way. This isn't about seeing the Big Stuff—anybody can tell you to go to Alcatraz, check out Fisherman's Wharf, and visit Haight-Ashbury. It isn't about biking the many parks in the Bay area, either; I'm talking about urban adventuring here, riding around the city itself rather than around the beautiful environs that surround it. It's about getting up close and personal with the city, riding and then getting off the bike to

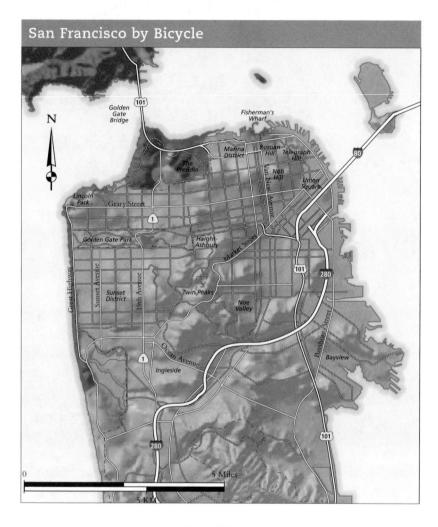

sample the pleasant hospitality of San Francisco's people and the little things that make this city not only a great place to visit but also a great place to live.

A number of factors will bring you out to the curbs and streets. First off, the weather in San Fran is gorgeous, even in the wintertime—you'll get a bit more cloud cover and precipitation, but the temperatures hover in the high 50s, making for wonderful sweater-and-slicker weather. Then there's the wonderful condition of the city's bike-friendly byways; you can literally get from one end of the Bay to the other on a bicycle. Projects like the Bay Trail, a continuous 400 miles of multipurpose trail connecting the area's many greenbelts and providing access to every nook and cranny of the Bay region, are fixing to make that route even easier. The bottom line: You won't find a more bike-friendly city in the United States than San Francisco. Look at the number of folks taking advantage of those wide bike byways and you'll see what I mean.

However, those of you who haven't done a lot of urban biking before might want to bone up a little with a class, provided by the League of American Bicyclists, in street skills for city bikers. The class gives simple, easy-to-implement advice on how to ride in urban areas, mostly in a lecture-and-discussion format. What's more, this class is usually offered free, and when there is a fee, it's very minimal ($5.00 to $20.00 or so). Road training is available, too, as the League also offers occasional "Day 2" classes in which students actually perform the tasks they were taught in the "Day 1" classroom session. Check the San Francisco Bicycle Coalition's Web site for information on these classes if you want an extra edge in touring the fair city on two wheels. Take a good look at the class schedule, too—these classes take place all over the Bay area, so those of you who might be in, say, Berkeley or Marin County will have a chance to get educated, too.

If you already know what you're doing out there on the road, though, it's best just to get down to it and start riding. Starting out in downtown San Francisco puts you within riding distance of multiple destinations, some of which even lie outside the city. Take the Golden Gate Bridge, for instance, over to Sausalito and Tiburon to sample the great shopping and food both of those places offer. Or simply stay within the friendly city confines and explore the more local, lesser-known sights. Of these, you'll find a multitude.

San Francisco is full of attractions that haven't yet made world-famous status and probably never will—but that doesn't make them any less fun. Take the famous Cow Palace, for instance, birthplace of the Grateful Dead's "Wall of Sound" public address system, consisting of 641 speakers and 72 overall tons of equipment, a system that (as you might imagine) only saw 37 shows before the band decided all the logistics and money just weren't worth it. Today, the Palace still hosts concerts, but it's the events that take place in between—the RV shows, boat shows, circuses, etc.—that make the place fun all the time. Check out the schedule and see what's going on while you're riding about town, then go over and check it out.

Looking for more kitschy fun? Head over to the Ripley's Believe Or Not!® Museum on Jefferson Street, where you'll find bizarre

Lombard Street could have been named the "#1 Calfburner in the Country," but "the Crookedest Street in the World" was a little catchier. ROBERT HOLMES/CALTOUR

sideshow-style exhibits like the Two-Headed Calf and the Shrunken Torso. You'll find the Wax Museum at Fisherman's Wharf on Jefferson, too, and though it's near one of those famous places I mentioned earlier—the kind of place anyone can tell you to head to— these two museums are weird enough to merit their own place on your itinerary. When you get down to Fisherman's Wharf (as I'm certain you will) on your two-wheeled journey, be sure to check out these monuments to the strange art of wax sculpture and the just plain strange.

Those of you wanting to burn your leg muscles to a crisp will have lots of opportunities to do so in San Francisco. The Russian Hill area, for example, boasts Lombard Street, the so-called Crookedest Street in America and a biker's uphill nightmare. Those of you not in the peak of physical condition might find yourself getting off the bike and hoofing it at some points, but don't be disappointed—even some truly hard-core bikers get the jitters in the face of such unapologetic steepness.

Of course, while you're riding from location to location, you'll be stopping along the way and seeing what you see. There's no way to lay all of that down here—pick up one of the excellent guidebooks below for a complete listing of things to do in the Bay area. The appeal here, the point of *this* adventure, is the bike. Riding will let you see more of the city than you otherwise would and let you have adventures and exercise you wouldn't get to have if you were just taking the train or, even worse, trying to navigate the city's prolific traffic. Bring the two-wheeled stallions or simply rent them when you get there, and your San Francisco adventure will benefit from a whole new layer of fun and exhilaration.

Price: Depends on whether you're renting a bike. Bring your own, and you're paying only for the food you eat, admission to the places you'd like to go, and souvenirs. Rent one, and you're looking at the above plus about $20 to $50 per day, depending on the bike you go for (i.e., high-end, tandem, kids, etc.).

(Winter, Medium)

FOR MORE INFORMATION

RIPLEY'S BELIEVE IT OR NOT!
MUSEUM
San Francisco, CA
(415) 771–6188
www.ripleysf.com

SAN FRANCISCO BAY TRAIL
San Francisco, CA
(510) 464–7900
www.baytrail.org

SAN FRANCISCO BICYCLE COALITION
San Francisco, CA
(415) 431–2453
www.sfbike.org

SAN FRANCISCO COW PALACE
San Francisco, CA
(415) 404–4111
www.cowpalace.com

THE WAX MUSEUM AT FISHERMAN'S
WHARF
San Francisco, CA
(800) 439–4305
www.waxmuseum.com

RECOMMENDED READING

Brown, Ann Marie. *Foghorn Outdoors Bay Area Biking: 60 of the Best Road and Trail Rides.* Emeryville, Calif.: Avalon Travel Publishing, 2004.

Hosler, Ray. *Bay Area Bike Rides.* San Francisco: Chronicle Books, 2002.

Kingman, Henry. *Short Bike Rides in and Around San Francisco.*
Guilford, Conn.: Globe Pequot Press, 1998.

Petrocelli, Michael. *San Francisco: Off the Beaten Path,* 2nd ed.
Guilford, Conn.: Globe Pequot Press, 2005.

SLEEP CHEAP

On an urban adventure like this one, you might be better off staying in the city rather than packing up your bike and leaving it. However, in keeping with the cheap sleeping spirit, check out one of San Francisco's many inexpensive hostels. Hostels attract people from all around the world looking for inexpensive accommodations and a social atmosphere; if you're looking for some of the same, visit www.hostels.com to find the best of what the city has to offer. There are a bunch of hostels in the area, each of which has its own set of offerings (e.g., kitchen facilities, Internet access, etc.). Just go to the site and check out the hostels there, write down the addresses, and pay them a visit.

Hiking and More in Big Sur

Paradise for the Prepared

Boogeying up the PCH, hugging the curves as it cuts up the coast like a silver wire, you'll quickly notice the differences between the northern and southern reaches of the state. Whereas southern California is cluttered, packed close with people, cities, and their attendant baggage, the northern coast is wide open; while the southern coast takes on shades of brown, gray, and tan, the northern coast exudes emerald and blue, as dark, bottle-green trees work their way from the ocean front to the high hills flanking the highway. Southern California's beaches are generally packed with hardbodies and other oceanside stereotypes; up north, however, you'll find deserted coastline long before you spy a *Baywatch* tower. Despite its charms, southern California can feel a bit dingy in spots, particularly when you approach the tentacles of Los Angeles, with its glitz and haze. The north just *feels* cleaner all around, and the air has a breezy, crystalline quality the smog down south must dissipate.

Under such conditions, choosing one piece of coastline to enjoy can get dicey. There are different things to enjoy no matter where you are, and many of these are so beautiful it'll break your heart. Eureka, San Simeon, Santa Cruz, Point Reyes—all of these places combine incredible coastal beauty with good times, both indoor and out. Only one, however, earned these words of praise from landscape

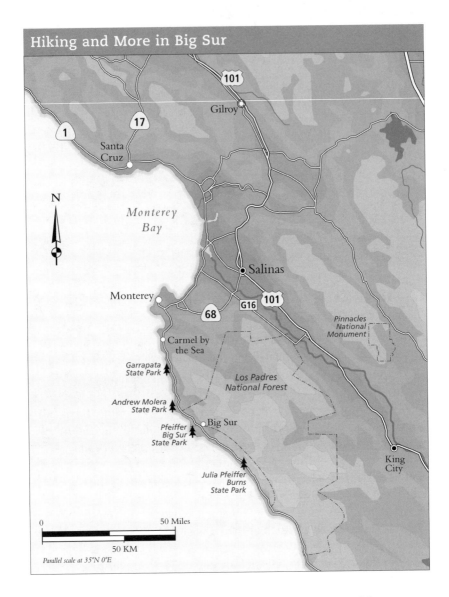

artist Francis McComa, who ought to know about natural beauty: "The greatest meeting of land and water in the world."

What hallowed location did Mr. McComa have in mind? None other than Big Sur, former hippie paradise and modern-day Garden of Eden.

Everyone knows Big Sur for its coastal beauty, and the winding route the PCH takes through it. What many overlook are the treasures on either side of that fabled coast—namely the miles of hiking trail that wind through the surrounding forests. You may be on your way to San Francisco or other points north, but these paths prove that you can't see everything Big Sur has to offer just by driving through it. Make some time to pull off and enjoy what you find just off the asphalt—you won't be disappointed.

Hang off the highway and head toward the interior, where the cool, comfy woods take advantage of the temperate climate the Pacific induces. Los Padres National Forest blankets Big Sur and extends inland for about 10 miles, presenting a lovely alternative to the ever-present sea. There are literally dozens of outdoor adventures waiting for you inland, everything from bird-watching to biking to swimming. However, you'll probably have the best time jumping on the ol' Shoe Leather Express and seeing the sights on foot—you can only bike on the pavement in some areas, and driving is something you could be doing back out on the PCH. The whole point is to get into the forest primeval, so pick up some park maps and go to.

I say "some" because you've got a ton of choices as to where you decide to stroll, based on difficulty, trail length, and landscape variety. Pfeiffer Big Sur State Park presents the best opportunities for inland hiking; it's got trails galore, as does adjacent Los Padres National Forest. One of the best known of these trails is the Pine Ridge, which runs deep into Los Padres and presents an excellent backpacking opportunity. The trailhead is right behind the Pfeiffer-Big Sur ranger station, so you can leave your car in that lot (for a small fee, of course) and be on your way. If the overnight trip just isn't in your cards but you still seek a challenge, make your way down to Big Sur River Gorge, located at the end of the short Gorge Trail. This area will test your resolve and your hiking skills, as it holds no developed trails and few signs of civilization. It's a tough jaunt, filled with loose rock, logs, and river features, so be careful—and don't dive into the river pools unless you'd like your head a little flatter than it is right now. Be sure to check out the trails at Big Sur's other parks, too—the hike to the beach at Andrew Molera State Park is a winner, as is Garrapata State Park's Peak Trail to Doud Peak, 1,977 feet high and a little over a mile inland.

After you get your fill of the inland, you might also want to check out the sights you can't see from dry land: those that lie under the Pacific surf. Many of the parks that lie on the coast have large protected areas offshore, which make for first-class scuba diving.

Lighting out on the Pine Ridge Trail. CHRIS BECKER

Warm and cold water currents meet right off Big Sur, presenting divers with the opportunity to see flora and fauna from both; if you have the time, skill, and inclination, it's well worth your attention. Various outfitters offer dive expeditions, but if you are already an accomplished diver, you can get special-use permits from the various coastal state parks and go exploring on your own.

A quick word on the Boy Scout motto: If you're not prepared to hit the backcountry before you get to Big Sur, you may be sorry. There are few places for buying provisions locally and almost nowhere to pick up any camp or backpack staples you may have forgotten. If you do have to pick up a few groceries, the price may floor you—I paid $2.69 for a can of Beef-a-Roni at a store that shall remain nameless, and that was one of their less egregious crimes. (Don't even ask about the can opener that was only good for two cans.) Bottom line: Driving on the PCH is awesome, when you want to be there. Backtracking because you forgot your sleeping bag is a royal pain, and it makes all those cool twists and turns seem like a big-time chore.

Just as desert or forest or open prairie will, oceanside scenery begins to blend into itself after a period of time. When this happens on a PCH journey, it's especially tragic, given the singular beauty of the place and its fame as the most picturesque highway around. Don't despair if you find yourself seeking a different view—after all, you're only human, and you can only soak up so much of the same scenery. Just turn inland at Big Sur, play in the woods for a while, and come back to the coast refreshed, with the ocean calling to you once again.

Price: $20–$50
(Winter, Medium)

DRIVING DIRECTIONS

All of the parks mentioned below are right off the Pacific Coast Highway in the Big Sur area. Take this route, and you get to enjoy the scenic ocean views on your way to the woods. This is truly one escape in which getting there is half the fun.

Most of the Big Sur trails start off in civilized surroundings before you reach the deep woods. Unfortunately, you don't have much chance to provision nearby without paying a fortune, so get what you need before you enter the Big Sur area. CHRIS BECKER

FOR MORE INFORMATION

ANDREW MOLERA STATE PARK
Big Sur, CA
(831) 667–2315
www.parks.ca.gov/default.asp
?page_id=582

GARRAPATA STATE PARK
Big Sur, CA
(831) 624–4909
www.parks.ca.gov/default.asp
?page_id=579

JULIA PFEIFFER BURNS STATE PARK
Big Sur, CA
(831) 667–2315
www.parks.ca.gov/default.asp
?page_id=578

LOS PADRES NATIONAL FOREST
Goleta, CA
(805) 968–6640
www.fs.fed.us/r5/lospadres

PFEIFFER BIG SUR STATE PARK
Big Sur, CA
(831) 667–2315
www.parks.ca.gov/default.asp
?page_id=570

VENTANA WILDERNESS SOCIETY
Salinas, CA
(831) 455–9514
www.ventanaws.org

RECOMMENDED READING

Henson, Paul, Valerie A. Kells, and Donald J. Usner. *The Natural History of Big Sur.* Berkeley, Calif.: University of California Press, 1996.

Kerouac, Jack. *Big Sur.* New York: Penguin, 1992. (paperback reprint ed.)

Schaffer, Jeffrey P. *Hiking the Big Sur Country: The Ventana Wilderness.* Berkeley, Calif.: Wilderness Press, 1988.

SLEEP CHEAP

Pfeiffer Big Sur State Park is a great place to set up camp—it's near a lot of great trails, beautifully wooded, and features the Big Sur Lodge, a sixty-one-room guest facility that also has a convenience store on-site (though again, it's expensive). Call (831) 667–2315 for camping information, or (800) 424–4787 for reservations at the Big Sur Lodge.

Ice Climbing at Lee Vining and June Lake

Scrambling the Slipperiest Slopes

You've climbed on rock all over California, and you've got it *down*. You know what you're doing out there, but you're looking for new challenges, too—more adventures to master, preferably while hanging from sheer walls of some kind. You've spent enough time on the rocks to want those hours to count for something; you don't want to start all over again at something else, picking up a whole new set of skills and working your way up to expert-level adventuring again. Instead, you'd like to branch out from where you've already been and simply expand the scope of the rock climbing you've been doing all along.

If that's the case, just sit tight and wait until the mercury starts to drop. Then, when white stuff covers the landscape outside, head out to the Sierra Nevadas and try your hand at ice climbing, rock climbing's wintertime counterpart.

Ice climbing is exactly what it sounds like—the act of climbing frozen water features (e.g., waterfalls) with short, modified pickaxes, crampons, and shovels. Each climbing route has a grade rating its difficulty, stretching from a 1 (short, not very steep, easy to access) up to 6 (very long, isolated climb, difficult to turn back once the climb's started) or even 7, though there are very few 7s out there.

This stuff is no joke—ice climbing is tough, and you have to be in pretty good shape to even think about taking it on. You'll be pulling yourself up that ice with a bunch of gear, along with heavy clothes that will limit your movements a bit too. Any climbing experience you already have will certainly come in handy, as conquering the ice draws upon many of the same skills traditional climbing does. At the very least, you have to know how to handle the ropes, tie the common knots, and belay your fellow climbers.

You won't find too many ice climbing sites in California, but options you will find are exceedingly fine. The eastern Sierra Nevada features the best of these destinations, namely Lee Vining Canyon and June Lake, both near Mammoth Lakes. June Lake is a great starter's location; the ice isn't terribly steep, but there are enough features to present a broad slate of practice possibilities.

While it is certainly possible to get out on the ice if you've never climbed it before, you should go with a guide to ensure a safer, worry-free trip. This isn't to say that you should just go with the first guide you find; in this country, professional mountain guides are pretty loosely organized, so just about anyone can hang out their shingle and claim to be one. I've said it at a couple points before, but I'll say it again for good measure: Do your homework before choosing your guide. Particularly with an adventure like this one, where danger comes with the territory, you want to make sure you're heading out with people who know what they're doing. (For some folks who know the ins and outs on the ice, contact the outfitters listed below.) One thing's for sure: You certainly don't want to wonder about the professionalism, skill, or competence of your guide when you're hanging 500 feet off the ground and the storm clouds come rolling in—wonder about those things beforehand.

One qualification to look for in your guide service is certification from the American Mountain Guides Association (AMGA), an organization dedicated to raising the standards of mountain guides around the country. AMGA-certified guides must demonstrate their skills to get certified, so you know you're dealing with a professional. Even better, find a guide who's certified by the International Federation of Mountain Guides Associations, an international organization that holds guides for rock, alpine, and ski mountaineering to the highest standards.

A few Sierra guides offer ice-climbing lessons at Lee Vining and June Lake. Sierra Mountain Center, for example, offers a two-day beginner's seminar that, more often than not, takes place entirely at June Lake. Here you'll learn how to pick out ice tools, the various

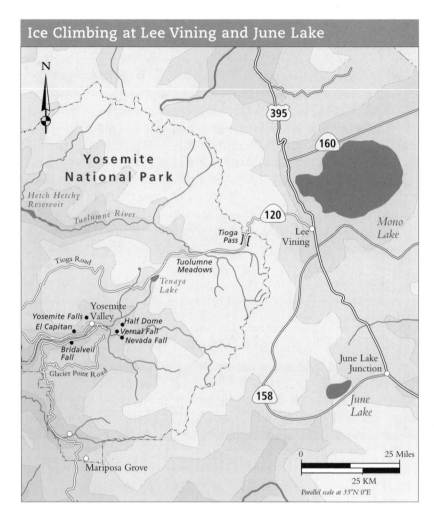

N

Yosemite
National Park

Hetch Hetchy
Reservoir

Tuolumne River

Tioga Road

Tioga
Pass

Tuolumne
Meadows

Tenaya
Lake

Yosemite
Valley

Yosemite Falls
El Capitan

Half Dome

Vernal Fall

Nevada Fall

Bridalveil
Fall

Glacier Point Road

Mariposa Grove

395

160

120

Lee
Vining

Mono
Lake

June Lake
Junction

158

June
Lake

0   25 Miles

25 KM

Parallel scale at 35°N 0°E

techniques for using them, and the ways in which you can join
these techniques together up on the ice. The Center will provide you
with tools if you don't have them, though you will have to rent your
harness and ice boots. This program covers all the bases, though,
which makes it a fairly good vacation deal; you'll get lodging along
with your lessons. Doug Nidever's Sierra Mountain Guides also
offers an array of classes, climbs, and seminars, most of them two
days or longer. You can talk to Doug about backcountry skiing, too,
if you want to get some powder under your jacket.

That's an adventure for another weekend, though—let's get back
to the climbing. You'll want to bring a couple things along with you

to ensure a good climb. First off, remember that the places you'll be climbing don't feature drive-up access—bring some snowshoes or even skis to avoid slogging through deep snow on the way to the climb. Be prepared for a bit of a crowd, too; as I said, there aren't a whole bunch of ice climbing sites in California, which makes places like Lee Vining and June Lake desirable destinations for climbers around the state and the country. This means more people to litter and disrespect the area, unfortunately—just make sure you don't fall into this category. Pack out any garbage you create, along with any you might see lying around. Respect is the name of the game, so come prepared to make a positive difference.

If you're looking for a wintertime activity similar to the climbing you get to do the rest of the year, then the ice is certainly nice. Get yourself an outfitter and set out for the frozen waterfalls of Lee Vining and June Lake, and you'll get a proper intro that will leave you in awe as you hang from the ice, beautiful landscape opening up all around you. You'll take away some valuable skills, too—the kind of skills you get to use the next time you're up on the rocks in the spring and summer. Give yourself an edge and a new way to spend your wintertime weekends.

Price: $200–$500–plus if you go with a guide, depending on the length of your trip.

(Winter, Difficult)

DRIVING DIRECTIONS

Lee Vining lies just outside Yosemite National Park, at the junction of Highways 120 and 395. June Lake lies just south on Highway 158.

OUTFITTERS

ALPINE SKILLS INTERNATIONAL
Truckee, CA
(530) 582–9170
www.alpineskills.com

COSLEY & HOUSTON ALPINE GUIDES
Bishop, CA
(760) 872–3811 (Bishop number)
www.cosleyhouston.com

SIERRA MOUNTAIN CENTER
Bishop, CA
(760) 873–8526
www.sierramountaincenter.com

SIERRA MOUNTAIN GUIDES INC.
June Lake, CA
(760) 648–1122
www.themountainguide.com

Reaching the summit. ANDREAS KARPERYD/ISTOCKPHOTO.COM

SIERRA WILDERNESS SEMINARS
Mt. Shasta, CA (runs trips in
Lee Vining and June Lake)
(888) 797–6867
www.swsmtns.com

FOR MORE INFORMATION

AMERICAN MOUNTAIN GUIDES
ASSOCIATION
www.amga.com

CALIFORNIA MOUNTAINEERING CLUB
www.californiamountaineer.com

RECOMMENDED READING

Chayer, Roger and Will Gadd. *Ice & Mixed Climbing: Modern Technique.*
Seattle: Mountaineers Books, 2003.

Lowe, Jeff. *Ice World: Techniques and Experiences of Modern Ice Climbing.* Seattle: Mountaineers Books, 1996.

Luebben, Craig. *How to Climb: How to Ice Climb!* Guilford, Conn.: Falcon, 1998.

SLEEP CHEAP

Since your ice climbing expedition will take place during some pretty chilly weather, sleeping in the ol' tent is pretty much out of the question. For a nice indoor alternative, visit the Yosemite Gateway Motel, located 14 miles from the east entrance to Yosemite and overlooking beautiful Mono Lake. The wintertime rates are excellent—only about $60 per night—and the accommodations are cozy. Give them a call at (800) 282–3929 to make your reservations.

Climbing Mount Shasta in Winter

The Peak of Adventure

You struggle a little in the thin air, trying to ignore the slight burning in your lungs, and reach just a little deeper. You know there's only one chance to make the summit, and you've been lucky so far—the weather's been great, the route breathtaking (literally), and now all that's left is the final 500 feet to the top. Your crampons dig into the snowpack, trying to gain the little bit of purchase that's going to carry you the next step forward, to your next step, and the step after that. *Think of the summit,* your brain repeats like a Hindu monk in the depths of *om. Think of the summit.*

If you're ready to hit the next level in your outdoor odysseys, mountaineering is one hell of a way to do it. There are few environments more challenging than sheer mountain faces and glaciers covered with year-round pack, nor are there many that are more worth your time—sweeping mountain vistas fill some of the best wilderness photographs ever taken, with good reason. And keep in mind that no matter which peak you scale, the number of human beings who have stood in that same place is incredibly small compared to the number of people walking around; take up mountaineering, and you're joining a very small club of dedicated, daring adventurers. And if you really want to shoot the lights out, hone your skills through the summer and fall, then visit Shasta when the snow is thickest—with the help of a trusty Shasta guide.

Of course, like anything really worth doing, mountaineering takes preparation and skill. There's also a lot of specialized equipment—crampons, ice axes, heavy clothing—that you may not have yet. You need to be in good shape, too; actually, the better shape you're in, the better. Mountaineering, especially if you're doing it on a "fourteener"—a peak more than 14,000 feet high—will take the breath out of you if you don't have well-developed lungs and some strength in your limbs. You don't want to go through all the trouble of getting to the mountain and learning to climb it only to peter out on your way to the top, so take this fitness requirement seriously before you make your climbing plans, rather than after, as you're sitting in the tent while everyone else is shooting for the summit.

In addition to the fitness work you can do on your own, you'll need to learn a couple new things about the mountain/glacier environment and how to negotiate it. Luckily, if you happen to be in northern California, this training is readily available on one of the state's tallest peaks: 14,162-foot Mount Shasta, the second-largest volcano in the lower forty-eight states. Even if you don't know the pick end of your ice axe from your adze, you can still enjoy mountaineering on Mount Shasta, thanks to the outfitters who have made it their business to mold Mount Shasta into one of the foremost training mountains in the country, no matter what the season.

About 15,000 climbers from all over the world reach Mount Shasta's summit annually. (If this sounds like a lot to you, consider that the climbing season runs from May to September, roughly 150 days—that's one hundred people on that massive mountain on any given day.) Many of them do it along the popular Avalanche Gulch route, a 6-mile trail that gains 7,000 feet of elevation on its way to the top. Though this trail is still considered backcountry (there are no official trails to the summit), traffic makes it visible late in the climbing season. It's not considered a technical route, but you still need crampons and an ice axe to climb this way; you ought to have some training, too, in order to learn how to use these items. Outside of Avalanche Gulch, there are sixteen other established routes, ranging in difficulty from beginning alpiner to hard-core ice scrambler. However, most of the people who climb Shasta do so during the warmer season, between May and October; if you make a climb in the wintertime, you'll find yourself on a pretty deserted mountain, accomplishing something that only a rarified few can.

All that romantic stuff aside, you still have to hold off that winter ascent until you're good and ready. First off, make your first

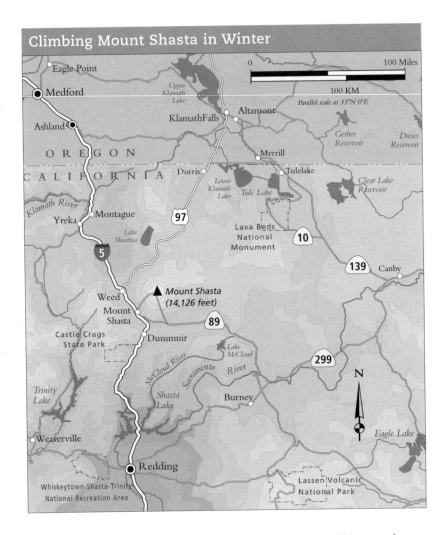

Climbing Mount Shasta in Winter

0   100 Miles

100 KM

Parallel scale at 35°N 0°E

Eagle Point

Medford

Upper Klamath Lake

Altamont

Ashland

KlamathFalls

Gerber Reservoir

Drews Reservoir

O R E G O N

Merrill

C A L I F O R N I A   Dorris   Tulelake

Clear Lake Reservoir

Lower Klamath Lake   *Tule Lake*

Klamath River   Montague

Yreka

Lake Shastina

97

Lava Beds National Monument

10

5

139   Canby

Weed   ▲ *Mount Shasta (14,126 feet)*

Mount Shasta

89

Castle Crags State Park   Dunsmuir

Lake McCloud

McCloud River   *Sacramento River*

299

Trinity Lake

Shasta Lake   Burney

N

Weaverville

Eagle Lake

Redding

Whiskeytown-Shasta-Trinity National Recreation Area

Lassen Volcanic National Park

climb in the summer if you haven't done it before. It'll be tough enough, and you'll get some idea as to what alpining entails. If you've already got some experience, however, and strong physical skills to boot, then you're already set to take on Shasta in the wintertime, when conditions are toughest and climbing with a guide is a must. Repeat, for the litigious: *In the wintertime, climbing with a guide is a must.* Safety is the number-one issue here—wintertime alpining is no joke, as you can probably imagine, and the dangers can get pretty extreme even if you're moderately skillful. Go with people who know Shasta like the backs of their hands, and you'll be far more secure for it.

There are more practical reasons to go with a guide, too, making it a year-round win for climbers like yourself. A guided ascent will lessen any logistical problems you'd face with tents and supplies, as the company you choose will take care of all that for you. You also won't get lost and potentially waste a bunch of your time wandering around looking for the best way up. On Shasta, where there are no defined routes, a guide will keep you coloring between the lines all the way up.

Three companies offer guided climbs on Mount Shasta, along with training classes in all manner of technical skills, and all of them offer wintertime expeditions as well as tours during the high summer season. These companies are all first-class operations, and they can all teach you what you need to know to reach the pinnacle. Most offer two- or three-day wintertime expeditions to the Shasta summit; Sierra Wilderness Seminars, for example presents advanced mountaineering and winter expedition courses at Shasta that culminate in summit attempts. For those of you with the time, SWS also offers a twelve-day winter skills seminar, which will teach you everything from technical climbing to winter shelter building.

Alpine Skills International offers a two-day climb up the Casaval Ridge route, as well as various two- to three-day seminars on alpining and winter survival. Outfitter Shasta Mountain Guides offers similar classes, as well as avalanche hazard training, a great skill to have if you're planning to find more mountains to scale in the coming years. They also offer quite a few chances to ski the mountain after your climb and strike your best Warren Miller pose. Just call all three outfitters, find out which one has the special something you're looking for, and go with them. As I said, they are all first-class, so you probably won't be disappointed no matter who you go with.

Mountaineering is serious business, but the rewards are as monumental as the peaks you get to climb. Mount Shasta offers you an opportunity to learn the alpine ropes, from easier summertime ascents to intense, snow-blown winter conquests. Just cut your chops during the warmer months, keep fit in the meantime, and return during the winter for the challenge that awaits you up among the white crags and cliffs. *Think of the summit....*

Price: $250–$500-plus for guided climbs

(Winter, Difficult)

Mount Shasta in all its snowy glory. PAUL SENYSZYN/ISTOCKPHOTO.COM

DRIVING DIRECTIONS

Mount Shasta is a big place, and the trailheads differ according to which route you'll be taking. Contact your outfitter for directions, and they will tell you where you need to go.

OUTFITTERS

ALPINE SKILLS INTERNATIONAL
Truckee, CA
(530) 582–9170
www.alpineskills.com

SHASTA MOUNTAIN GUIDES
Mount Shasta, CA
(530) 926–3117
www.shastaguides.com

SIERRA WILDERNESS SEMINARS
Mount Shasta, CA
(888) 797–6867
www.swsmtns.com

FOR MORE INFORMATION

MT. SHASTA CLIMBER'S GUIDE
www.climbingmtshasta.org

RECOMMENDED READING

Frank, Emilie A. *Mt. Shasta: California's Mystic Mountain.* Klamath River, Calif.: Living Gold Press, 1998.

Lewis, Steve. *Climbing Mt. Shasta: Route 1, Avalanche Gulch.* Hilt, Calif.: PhotograFix Publishing, 1996.

Selters, Andrew and Michael Zanger. *The Mt. Shasta Book: A Guide to Hiking, Climbing, Skiing, and Exploring the Mountain and Surrounding Area.* Berkeley, Calif.: Wilderness Press, 2001.

SLEEP CHEAP

Chances are you'll be sleeping at a base camp before you begin your ascent. If you need some nearby camping before your climb, however, visit Castle Crags State Park, located 6 miles south of Dunsmuir on Interstate 5. They've got year-round camping, as well as fishing, hiking, and all manner of good times in the Shasta-Trinity National Forest. The Pacific Crest Trail also passes through the park. In the wintertime, you won't need reservations; however, the summer months are a little busier, and reservations are recommended. Call (530) 235–2684 for more information.

Skydiving

Why Abandon a Perfectly Good Airplane?

People who are afraid of heights miss out on a lot of potential
adventures. In fact, this very book features no fewer than six
adventures that involve getting high up in the sky, along with a
whole bunch more—think rock climbing, alpining—that require dealing with a pretty significant distance between you and the ground.
If you can't handle putting too much air under your feet, you're
putting yourself in a box, one that limits the extent of your adventuring.

Now this isn't good, missing out on all that fun. Like smokers
who need to drop the habit, those of you who can't handle being
airborne must conquer that which holds you back. There's no better
way to do this than to take off in an airplane, fly up to a couple
thousand feet, and make your way back down to the ground via
parachute. It's penicillin for acrophobia, a way to conquer that mental bug preventing you from enjoying yourself under the loftiest of
circumstances. So get your courage up, and get ready to stretch
your adventuring possibilities as you push your fear out the airplane door and into the wild blue yonder.

Luckily, you won't have to take the plunge by yourself. If
you've never jumped out of an airplane before, you'll make your
first leap with an instructor in a tandem skydive. On this initial
jump, you'll be strapped to a professional skydiving instructor, who
will handle all the petty details (e.g., pulling the ripcord). As a
result, your only job will be to enjoy the flight and do exactly as
you're told, when you're told to do it. The point of this adventure

for acrophobes is to conquer their fear; for the rest of us, it's to learn a cool new skill and get to the point at which we can make that leap for ourselves.

Unfortunately, skydiving isn't available to just anyone. First off, you have to be 18 or older to get out of the plane. Second, you have to maintain a decent weight—generally under 220 or 230 pounds. Of course, if you're getting to the upper limits of this weight qualification, you're going to need a higher level of physical fitness; after all, 230 pounds of worked-out muscle hits the ground a lot better than 230 pounds of couch potato. Come prepared to jump with comfortable clothes and tennis shoes, and you're pretty much ready to go. One more note: Eat something light before you set out. Jumping on a full stomach is probably not a good idea, particularly if you've never jumped before, but jumping on an empty one isn't much better.

Skydiving outfitters are fairly uniform in their offerings. All the ones listed here offer tandem jumps, as well as additional instruction if you want to indulge your inner daredevil a bit further. When you jump tandem, you won't need a whole lot of preparation—usually the whole jump process takes an hour or two, from the bit of ground instruction you'll take, to the plane ride up, to the minute or two of freefall, down to ten minutes of floating down to the ground once the parachute deploys. If you aren't among those who feel queasy at the thought of flying through the air with the greatest of ease, each outfitter also offers an Accelerated Freefall (AFF) program, which couples a thorough training program with multiple jumps over the course of a few sessions. This is the quickest way to start pulling your own cord, as your very first jump will be solo (sort of—you'll still have instructors jumping with you to help out if you need a hand).

If you do choose to get additional certifications, there's no limit to how high you can fly. AFF is the quickest, best way to become a real skydiver capable of making your own jumps, but you'll have to set aside time to get the jumps and ground school that you need. Obviously, this is a bit more than a weekend escape, so take the tandem jump first, see how the air treats you, then decide if you want to go back for more, rather than setting yourself up for the big goal right away.

All that being said, there are some offerings individual companies make that distinguish them from other outfitters in northern California. Adventure Center Skydiving, for example, offers the highest tandem jumps in the state—3 miles' worth of altitude, resulting in

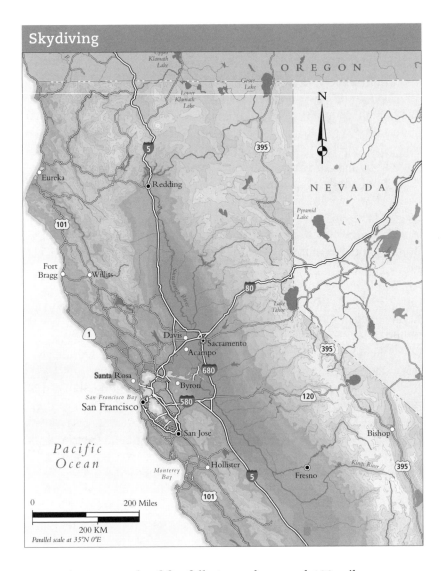

up to ninety seconds of freefall at speeds around 120 miles per hour. (Think about it—outside of a plane, have you ever traveled that fast in your entire life?) SkyDance Skydiving offers night jumps for more experienced 'chuters, though you have to have jumped with them during the previous month to ensure that you're already somewhat familiar with the drop zone.

Just remember: Northern California is thick with *accredited* (stress on accredited) skydiving outfitters. Call around before you choose one, but know also that anyone who is accredited will have a good idea what they're doing; you might just want to pick one based on where you'll be when you make your jump. Every one is going to be able to take you on a safe, fun jump and teach you more about the skydiving game if you want them to.

One of the best things about your first skydive is the price—you'll pay $150 to $250 for the adrenaline rush of your initial jump, with that high end coming for specialty jumps like Adventure Center's 3-mile dive. If you decide to pursue the sport, you'll obviously pay more for more jumps, but if you go AFF and pay up front, you're likely to get the best per-jump deals. And once you can jump on your own, each jump gets a whole lot cheaper, typically around $40 to $60 if you still have to rent your 'chute and other equipment.

Conquering fear is never easy. In fact, it's one of life's toughest—and most worthwhile—challenges. Overcoming your fears and leaving that airplane will leave you feeling like a million bucks when you finally reach the ground, ready to set out for the next step in your airborne adventure odyssey. Hang gliding, paragliding, soaring—all of these great escapes are available to you after you conquer that fear in your heart, the one thing that limits your ability to enjoy everything the outdoor world has to offer. So go ahead and get to it—life won't wait.

Price: $100–$250 (more if you want to go through the AFF program)
(Winter, Difficult)

DRIVING DIRECTIONS

Get in touch with the outfitter you go with, and they'll tell you how to get to them.

OUTFITTERS

ADRENALINE AIR SKYDIVING
Santa Rosa, CA
(707) 573–8116
www.skydivesantarosa.com

ADVENTURE CENTER SKYDIVING
Hollister, CA
(800) 386–5867
www.1800funjump.com

Another safe landing! TERRY HEALY/ISTOCKPHOTO.COM

BAY AREA SKYDIVING
Byron, CA
(925) 634–7575
www.bayareaskydiving.com

PARACHUTE CENTER
Acampo, CA
(209) 369–1128
www.parachutecenter.com

SKYDANCE SKYDIVING
Davis, CA
(800) 759–3483
www.skydance.net

FOR MORE INFORMATION

UNITED STATES PARACHUTE ASSOCIATION
(703) 836–3495
www.uspa.org

RECOMMENDED READING

Buchanan, Tom. *Jump!: Skydiving Made Fun & Easy.* New York: McGraw-Hill Professional, 2003.

Pyynter, Dan and Mike Turoff. *Parachuting: The Skydiver's Handbook.* Santa Barbara, Calif.: Para Publishing, 2003.

Derosalia, John. *Mental Training For Skydiving and Life.* West Hurley, N.Y.: Skymind, 2001.

SLEEP CHEAP

The Bay area is centrally located to all of the outfitters mentioned here; though some are a bit of a drive, you have to know it's worth the little jaunt to experience the beauty the land by the Bay has to offer. To get a nice dose, head to Mount Diablo State Park—the camping's great all year 'round, and if you do a little hiking, the view from the top of the mountain is unbelievable. You can even catch sight of Half Dome in Yosemite with a pair of binoculars and a clear day. Call (800) 444-7275 or visit the ReserveAmerica Web site (www.reserveamerica.com) to reserve your site.

About the Author

Chris Becker writes about travel, escape, and recreation. He lives with his wife Danielle and daughter Evelyn in a brick house in Phoenix, floating on an ocean of stucco. He plans to finish his first novel soon (provided *52 Great Weekend Escapes in Venice/Florence/Rome* can wait until afterward).

Help Us Keep This Guide Up to Date

Every effort has been made by the author and editors to make this guide as accurate and useful as possible. However, many things can change after a guide is published—establishments close, phone numbers change, facilities come under new management, etc.

We would love to hear from you concerning your experiences with this guide and how you feel it could be improved and kept up to date. While we may not be able to respond to all comments and suggestions, we'll take them to heart, and we'll also make certain to share them with the author. Please send your comments and suggestions to the following address:

> The Globe Pequot Press
> Reader Response/Editorial Department
> P.O. Box 480
> Guilford, CT 06437

Or you may e-mail us at:
> editorial@GlobePequot.com

Thanks for your input, and happy travels!